Why Men
Fall Out
of
LOVE

Michael French

Foreword by Herb Goldberg, Ph.D.

Ballantine Books
New York

Why Men
Fall Out
of
LOVE

What Every Woman

Needs to Understand

A Ballantine Books Trade Paperback Original

Copyright © 2005, 2007 by Michael French

Published in the United States by Ballantine Books,
an imprint of The Random House Publishing Group,
a division of Random House, Inc., New York.

BALLANTINE and colophon are registered
trademarks of Random House, Inc.

Originally published in different form in paperback by SelfHelpBooks.com,
a division of the Wellness Institute/Self-Help Books, LLC,
Pass Christian, Mississippi, in 2005.

Library of Congress Cataloging-in-Publication Data

French, Michael.
Why men fall out of love : what every woman needs to understand /
Michael French ; foreword by Herb Goldberg.
p.   cm.
Includes bibliographical references.
ISBN 978-0-345-49291-3
1. Man-woman relationships—United States—Case studies.   I. Title.
HQ801.F793 2007
306.70973—dc22
2006048436

Printed in the United States of America

www.ballantinebooks.com

4 6 8 9 7 5

Book design by Dana Leigh Blanchette

This book is for Patricia,

with love and

affection.

Foreword

Herb Goldberg, Ph.D.

Men today are clearly in the process of making significant changes. At the same time, deeper pressures created by centuries of toxic conditioning dehumanize them and severely damage their capacity for personal and intimate relating. In this remarkable and candid book, we listen to ten men of various ages and backgrounds delve into their most intimate relationships. How these men really feel about women, themselves, love, and commitment, how they deal with relationship crises, is both eye-opening and groundbreaking. All these men seek a different, expressive, and connected way of being. While traditional conditioning still tends to overpower the fragile beginnings of growth in men, these ten men—and I would guess millions more in this country—are clearly becoming aware of, and are on their way toward, a dramatically new way of being and defining themselves.

A primary part of recovering from past conditioning, and

moving towards a personally connected sense of oneself as a full person, is open and expressive exploration, analysis, and reflection of relationship histories. Most men define themselves by their most intimate relationships, yet perhaps a significant majority are far from happy, even if they're not always sure why. Many men feel to some extent damaged and self-hating, and these stories help us to see how this is every man's psychological heritage. For myself, as a psychologist and writer on the topic of gender and the male experience, a core dimension of a man's personal liberation is a willingness to disclose his inner life. Once men come out of hiding, they can address critical obstacles to their personal growth, and become better partners to the women in their lives.

The men whose stories are shared on these pages had the courage to unmask themselves, remove their façades, and share often painful, highly personal struggles, and the ways they went about trying to change themselves. Michael French's startlingly revealing book is a vehicle for both men's healing and transformation, and for women's illumination. Bringing the deeper realities of being a man out into the open is a noble gift that gives men who have not yet begun to acknowledge, explore, and change themselves a map with which to begin their journeys. It also gives women strategic insights into the male psyche, and specific strategies for preserving and improving their relationships. This book is not a polemic that takes sides in the gender war. Rather, it shines the same high-intensity light onto the often dimly understood reasons that both men and women fall out of love.

Why Men Fall Out of Love: What Every Woman Needs to Understand is a unique gift to anyone interested in the evolution of gender consciousness. The author has succeeded in doing something that few have been able to do: eliciting from a wonderful sampling of men their intimate relationship histories.

Considering how closed most men are about revealing their true selves to others, the personal stories in this book are told with amazing candor, revelation, and brutal honesty. It is a worthy accomplishment. For this excellent contribution, we owe the author our profound thanks.

Dr. Goldberg, a licensed psychologist, is the bestselling author of The Hazards of Being Male.

Acknowledgments

My special thanks to the men who were willing to share their lives and their most intimate relationships on these pages. I applaud them for their courage and candor. In the gender tribe, confessional men are not at the top of the popularity ladder.

I am indebted to Frank Baca for his encouragement throughout this project, and to John Webber and Bob Burbic for offering me lessons in coping. Also, a half dozen friends, men and women, read this manuscript in its various evolutions and made constructive suggestions, many of which were gratefully incorporated.

Harold Dawley, publisher of Wellness Institute/SelfHelp Books.com, provided me with editorial insights and was always supportive of this project, launching its first edition in 2005, based on forty interviews with men. At Random House/ Ballantine, my editor, Christina Duffy, helped make the book even more illuminating and accessible. As did Annie Lux with her multicolored pens. Thank you one and all.

My agent, Wendy Sherman, helped move this book from a small house to a large one, and my publicists, Jane Wesman and Lori Ames, gave it a diverse audience it might otherwise not have found.

Finally, my gratitude to my wife, Patricia, for the love and patience she's shown me over the decades, as well as the path out of some very dark nights. I hope I've been able to reciprocate. Openness and trust are the tensile strength of any enduring relationship.

Contents

Relationship Buster 3 The Perfection Impulse

Relationship Buster 4 The Fading of Attraction

The Thinking Heart A Rational Look at Love

Introduction

When Men Stop Loving

> The great tragedy in life is not that men perish,
> but that they cease to love.
> —W. Somerset Maugham

According to statistics from DivorceMagazine.com, one in two first marriages in the United States end in divorce, and almost two out of three second marriages meet the same fate. While at any given time 59 percent of the adult population is married, 10 percent divorced, and 7 percent widowed, another 24 percent have never taken wedding vows. What is unknown is how many relationships the average man or woman goes through before finding or not finding that special person. How many relationships simply implode, disintegrate, or fall by the wayside without anyone really understanding why?

About five years ago I was having a drink with a friend, a successful entrepreneur in his early thirties, when he suddenly volunteered, in a tone approaching despair, that he thought he had fallen out of love. It wasn't just that he had lost interest in his longtime girlfriend, he said. Something deeper was going on, something that made him sad. He and his partner weren't connecting for a *reason*—but he couldn't put his finger on it. Why couldn't he figure it out? Why was talking to his girlfriend about his emotions so difficult? What were his real feelings, anyway? And why did so few men open up to each other on this critical subject?

His frustration was brimming over, and he kept looking at me as if I held the answers. My friend knew I was neither a psychologist nor a relationship expert—I am currently president of an online sales company—but I was almost twenty-five years his senior. In addition to any wisdom he thought I had acquired from being "successfully married for many years," as he put it, he seemed to prefer my layman status, as if that made him feel safer in our discussions. As I would eventually find out, a lot of men, including myself, would rather confess to a crime they didn't commit than be caught in a therapist's office and admit that they can't solve their own problems. When I said I wasn't sure how to advise him, my friend was unfazed. He knew I would come through, he said, and he made me promise we would talk again.

Over the next few days I found myself pondering my friend's quandary, as well as the ups and downs of any intimate relationship, including my own marriage. On the domestic front I too was in rough waters, though I hadn't told anyone except a close friend at the gym. Now that our son and daughter had finished college and had their own lives, my wife and I were arguing more frequently, often over inconsequential things, and I intuited a deeper rift. Were we just empty nesters trying to adjust, was I stumbling through a garden-variety midlife crisis, or was this something more? Like my friend, I too wondered if I was still in love. Perhaps the spark of "being in love" had been replaced by habit and convenience. My friend, wanting help in solving his relationship issues, had unwittingly pushed me to explore my own emotions, including not a small amount of anger and frustration. I likened that anger to a low-grade fever that had been rising in me, slowly, over the years. Where had it come from, I suddenly wondered, and where was it taking me?

Within a week I found myself visiting my city's largest bookstore. After passing multiple aisles of self-help books by women, in one corner I found a clutch of books espousing a male view on relationships, masculinity, and emotions. I had skimmed Robert Bly's *Iron John* fifteen years ago, but the message had failed to resonate on any personal level. I had thought nothing more about that book, until now. Suddenly, I was reading everything I could in that forlorn corner, including the landmark *The Hazards of Being Male: Surviving the Myth of Masculine Privilege,* by Herb Goldberg; *Man Enough: Fathers, Sons, and the Search for Masculinity* by Frank Pittman; and Terrence Real's *I Don't Want to Talk About It: Overcoming the Secret Legacy of Male Depression.* I soaked up all the insights about men that I could, especially about their emotional growth and what they looked for in their relationships. As much as I learned, I was hungry for more.

When I revisited the section of books by women, I was impressed not only with the sheer quantity of titles but the depth of subject matter. In particular, the number of stories by women about leaving their significant others to pursue new passions and disciplines, or simply to take a sabbatical "to find themselves," so outnumbered chronicles of male pilgrimages that a couple of conclusions seemed inescapable. First, men were not "allowed" this same luxury of self-discovery. Whether it was their own prohibition or that of their culture, running off somewhere for a couple of months of soul-searching was frivolous and irresponsible. My second conclusion was that men were leery of confession. When they enter the adolescent world of competition, males grow cautious about showing their feelings or making themselves vulnerable. If you talk too much, or say the wrong thing, someone will take advantage of you, put you down, or quickly label you. Most men are conditioned to prefer, as I certainly was, hiding their emotions like a dog might his bones, digging them back up only when the occasion demands it. Emotions by rote felt safe, even if the process didn't feel genuine.

In the books I read, I saw that women shared their stories of courage and self-discovery like coin of the realm, and even if they were sworn enemies they still rallied to each other's side in times of crisis. They could talk about the most intimate subjects without a shred of self-consciousness. Openness seemed to be a fundamental definition of who they were. While a lot of women will admit to being catty, devious, jealous, gossipy, and vindictive—behaviors that start in adolescence and are the equivalent of physical aggression between boys or young men—they do so with apology, as if this isn't who they really are. They choose to define their gender more along the axis of solidarity, empathy, and sharing.

I found little evidence of an equivalent community of men. If women are empathizers, it has been written, men are systematizers, imposing a rational construct on, and attaching a goal to, virtually every facet of experience. Life must be quantifiable. If, for men, any action has to be of measurable benefit to someone, what is the motivation, beyond basic communication, for understanding where emotions come from and how they work? Is it too cynical to wonder if the emotional circuitry that men currently enjoy would largely atrophy like a useless appendage in the absence of women? Unless there is an obvious external danger, such as war or natural disaster, men generally do not band together to emote. Sports are the most prominent exception: the universal male outlet for fearless opinions, aggression, competition, bonding, affection, and hero worship. Religion and politics also invoke shared emotions. So do music, film, art, and books. These are all safe, institutionalized outlets, "approved for men," as it were.

Yet in general men keep their internal lives—and their more complex emotions—closely guarded, because either they don't understand them or they are afraid of being betrayed by them. That is the unwritten male code. Out of some weird male logic, men assume that the less they reveal of themselves, the more power they have and the less they have to be afraid of. Over the next few years, as I journeyed deeper into my own relationship and those of the men I interviewed, I would find that assumption to be not just wrong but the very opposite of the truth.

When I caught up with my friend a month later, his agitation had not diminished. He was no closer to a decision about his relationship, and he had not whispered a word to his girlfriend about what was bothering him. In typical male passive-aggressive fashion, he had put off any action that would bring confrontation. What *had* changed was his willingness to open up to me about his past relationships, as well as share stories about his successful but angry father, an overindulgent, fearful mother, and how his parents' marriage had shaped his attitude toward women and his own relationships. He also admitted he was afraid of leaving his girlfriend, even though he was no longer really attracted to her. When I asked what he was afraid of, he answered "I don't know what else is out there," and "Who knows, maybe down deep I still love her." There were multiple levels of frustration in his story, centered on an inability to put the pieces together. Opening up about my marriage, I told him I shared the feeling of being in the dark. We both talked up a storm, particularly about our childhoods.

"More guys should be candid about this stuff," my friend said as we parted, and we promised to meet again.

Yes, I thought, we should. The idea that other men who faced frustration, unhappiness, or confusion in their relationships might want to "come clean" had a certain appeal. If nothing else, it would let my friend and me know we weren't struggling alone. More important, I thought that a lot of men, and even more women, would want to know about the chemistry of emotions in men when they stopped loving, or called it quits on their relationships. If I could find men willing to be open and candid, I would encourage them to write down their stories.

What started as a simple and naïve launch turned into a rigorous sea crossing. Even with the promise of anonymity (all names and physical descriptions in this book have been changed, along with most professions and cities), asking men to write about their relationships made it crystal clear why there are so few books on the subject. There is no shortage of articles on men's views on sex (often written by women, even in so-called men's magazines), as well as on the qualities that a man looks for in a woman. But for men to be confessional about their darkest fears and most intimate emotions? This was top secret stuff.

Either in person, by phone, or e-mail, I approached more than fifty men—in the end, friends of friends of friends—between the ages of eighteen and sixty-eight. I asked each of them why one of his relationships, despite the most brilliant beginning, might have turned stormy in the end. What led to the collapse from *his* point of view? The interviewing experience was like trying to drag someone with stage fright, kicking and screaming, in front of a microphone. Despite a twelve-page questionnaire I had prepared to guide them, a lot of men complained that they felt lost before they put a single sentence on paper. A few insisted they had no relationship failures. Others were honest enough to admit they lacked the courage to revisit their painful pasts, or were concerned about hurting their partners, current or former, if they said too much. One man declined my offer because he thought "he would get in trouble." I asked if he meant with his girlfriend or wife. He blushed, perhaps ashamed of his lack of courage, then, like many others, dismissed me as an interloper. Even my entrepreneurial friend, who had helped start me on my quest (and who finally did break up with his girlfriend), couldn't be convinced to bare his soul on paper.

As I would learn over and over, a lot of men not only fear emotional pain, they are afraid to be transparent and vulnerable. To let an outsider even glimpse their confusion or suffering is a taboo that starts in adolescence and becomes more entrenched with adulthood. "Better to live in pain than to heal the wound" is a common if unspoken male mantra.

The fits-and-starts process of writing this book took three years before I garnered and edited nine good oral histories. I added my own because I thought it fit into the themes and insights of the book, and because I promised several men that if they committed to this project so would I. Many prospects were candid on the phone but insisted their stories never see the light of print. The metaphor of washing one's dirty linen in public came up more than once, as did the thought that relationships, particularly marriages, were "just too complicated" and should be shielded from scrutiny. I also interviewed seven or eight women about my project and asked for comments. All said they would be very interested in what men really thought about women, but a few hinted they didn't think men could be honest, either because they had so much to hide, were used to lying, or "didn't always know what really counted" in a relationship.

Perhaps those women had a point. The question of why men hide their emotional lives comes under scrutiny in virtually every story in this book. As does the question of what's important to a man and a woman in an intimate partnership—both differences and similarities. In the beginning, courage had to be stoked in almost everyone I interviewed. In the end, I got the honesty—or perhaps as close to honesty as men can come—I had hoped for. None of us looks particularly heroic. In these no-holds-barred self-portraits, we are not always the men that we—or women—would like us to be. But challenging the clichés of male behavior and attitudes produces the equivalent of what Picasso made from the standard images of women in his Cubist period: jarringly fresh, sometimes painful, but always revealing portraits. While ten stories and fifty interviews are not statistically significant, I suspect that the issues and problems that are raised—and the relationship lessons learned—are representative of a much broader population of men in the United States. Other countries and cultures might or might not be similar.

Much of what I learned caught me off guard. First, for a lot of men, the origin of the emotions of disengagement may start in childhood or early adolescence—perhaps at the same time young men first experience the emotions of falling *in* love. Falling in love is more than infatuation. It is the need to feel whole, to feel safe, to be healed, to join together with someone, heart and soul. In time, however, the need to be whole and feel safe can transform itself into the desire to tear apart, to reject, and to return to one's independence. The search for identity and happiness can mean a 180-degree turn on life's path, often turning back to childhood and a reconnection to select memories, issues, and unresolved conflicts. It is sometimes the desire to start all over, to try to undo the mistakes of the past, things either done to you or by you to others.

Second, while men are generally perceived as the uncommunicative gender, often stewing in their unhappiness, it is also the women on these pages who can be remote, angry, confused, or silent. More than one psychologist has weighed in on the phenomenon of metrosexuality, claiming that men in some ways are the new women, but it can also be argued that women are the new men, not just in terms of the workforce but in neuroses and self-destruction. Rage, guilt, self-hatred, and feelings of power-lessness can push anybody, man or woman, out of love with their partners or themselves.

Third, women are often accused of being disingenuous about their fears, doing everything to rationalize around them, but I came to believe that men are even more secretive. Even when they are being as honest as they can, there is something self-protecting, even self-censoring, about men. In addition to fear of judgment or ridicule, it's as if, having been impostors for so long, men can't always tell the difference between the masks they wear and their true identities. Or maybe they're not really impostors. Maybe there's no single authentic male self. Rather, men may have one identity for the woman they live with, an-other for business colleagues, another for old friends, and still another for their most private self—all of them real and legiti-mate. Where do all these personas come from? Do boys and young men adopt them in response to peer and societal pres-sures, as some psychologists suggest, or are they subtly imposed by a culture that wants men to assume multiple and contradic-tory roles that no single persona can encompass? According to other experts, some men, starting in adolescence, adopt multiple selves in order to fit in and be loved.

Fourth, no matter whose behavior is the principal cause of a couple's unhappiness, it is usually the woman who leaves the man. If married, according to statistics, women initiate the di-vorce two out of three times. Women are more likely to act to change their unhappiness while men tend to live with it. Accus-tomed to the social structure that a woman provides, a man usu-ally leaves his relationship only when conflicts with his partner become insurmountable, or he's found another woman.

Fifth, struggling to understand why their relationships im-ploded was not always a purely negative experience for the men

I talked to. If they found the courage to look deeply into the mirror, their journeys turned out to be a roller coaster of unimagined loops, twists, and G-force curves, but by the end they were emotionally stronger and wiser. With new insights into themselves and their partners, their attitudes and behaviors became more positive. For the purpose of this book, each of these stories has an ending, but in reality they all continue to evolve. When growth becomes a constant, it gains momentum.

Despite common belief, men don't necessarily fall out of love because a woman puts on thirty pounds and becomes physically unattractive, or because of fights about money, or because one partner's sexual needs are greater than the other's. These issues are just trip wires. Dig under the surface and you might discover in one partner (and sometimes both) feelings of abandonment, powerlessness, anger at one's caregivers, covert depression, a quest for validation, or a need to control. In addition, for some men any intimate bond is stressful—women make demands that men are unable or unwilling to meet—and except for their dependency on their partners, emotional and sexual, their relationships are inherently brittle. Whenever that dependency fades or vanishes, men are likely to fall out of love.

The ten men in this book—despite differences in how they were raised, their ages, professions, and socio-economic backgrounds—exhibit strong similarities in the way their emotions evolved. Not every reader will agree with what these men think, feel, and say about women and relationships, but perhaps the reading experience should be more about understanding than taking sides. One thing seems abundantly clear: conflicts that appear to come out of nowhere are often buried inside us, dormant from childhood, long before the first confrontation with our adult partners. What lives and breathes in secret is often not only more important than what we reveal on the surface, but ignoring it is perilous to our relationships. So many men and women are emotional time bombs and don't know it.

The reasons for falling out of love are layered and overlapping, but nevertheless there are four *relationship busters*—shoals on which relationships, like rudderless ships, tend to flounder and sink—that were recurring themes in the lives of the men I interviewed:

- The Loss of Intimacy
- The Quest for Validation
- The Perfection Impulse
- The Fading of Attraction

No doubt there are other danger zones for any couple, but these four relationship busters comprise the core of the book. At the end of every section is a box, "Tips for Avoiding This Relationship Buster," to help you sidestep each of these major pitfalls.

Equally important, the stories that illustrate each of the relationship busters reveal six key reasons why many men suffer, often silently, through long periods of unhappiness, fall out of love, or simply fail to maintain their relationships. These seeds of discontent can sprout unbidden in even the seemingly strongest and most secure of relationships:

- Childhood issues of anger and loss, and the need for reconnection
- Masculinity issues of identity, power, and fear
- Popular culture's emphasis on conformity, happiness, and overachieving
- Stereotypes that contradict who men really are and what they want

- Behaviors and attitudes of their female partners
- Processing and communication differences between men and women

In this book we meet ten men who explain in their own voices how their most intimate relationships ran into trouble; why they felt boxed in by one or more of the six key reasons; how communication with their partners broke down; and why sometimes their partners also fell out of love with them. Interspersed through each story are my own observations about these men as I got to know them and their struggles. At the end of the project I consulted with a licensed therapist to review and occasionally add to my observations.

For women who are baffled by the discrepancy between what men promise and what men do, who think men are hopelessly confused about what women want, and who are looking for a man who won't ultimately betray or disappoint them, here is some good news: most men are not as inscrutable, insensitive, or elusive as they sometimes appear. Behind all the clichés and stereotyping that men endure, they do have emotions, and there is a pattern to those emotions. They may be more repressed than a woman's, but there are ways to bring them to the surface, to build on those emotions as you build your relationship, and provide a safe environment where almost any couple can find happiness and growth.

If you're about to begin a relationship with a man, there are three questions to ask *before* you become emotionally involved. First, what is (or was) his relationship with his mother? Second, what is his definition of masculinity? Third, how does he deal with his failures and setbacks? When the moment feels right, ask him for thoughtful answers, not on-the-spot sound bites. If he won't or can't answer, or doesn't understand why you're asking, it might be wise to slow down your relationship. If he does take you seriously, the responses he gives—as the stories here demonstrate—may be the most reliable indicator of what kind of intimate partner he'll make. Will he be honest, trustworthy, and supportive? Or will he be emotionally insecure, uncommunicative, and have difficulty with trust and intimacy? If he is insecure and uncommunicative, what can you do to help him change?

Because men are often inadequate communicators, especially when their relationships sour, a lot of women make the assumption that men tend to be selfish, unfeeling, or cowardly. Sometimes men *are* selfish or unfeeling, but there are deeper reasons for their poor communication. More than one man told me it was easier just to "slip away" than to confront a failing relationship, because he felt inadequate to the task of explaining his feelings. Whatever he said, he knew he would be "outgunned and outmatched" by his partner. "When women dump men," he added, as proof of his theory, "they have no trouble citing multiple reasons why we disappoint them, or how we hurt them, or how superficial we are. They forget nothing. Those emotional reasons are all thought out and articulated in ways that no man can possibly match."

Few would dispute that women have a deeper understanding of, are more comfortable with, and are used to living within, their feelings. One man told me that his emotions felt like some kind of external attachment to his psyche, as if evidence that emotions had evolved later in men than in women. Others claimed they avoided confrontation with their partners because they didn't want to be judged or put down. A few admitted they didn't like confronting anybody, and wasn't it always easier just to move on without too much explanation and analysis?

It would be tempting to conclude that men are simply pragmatic and expedient and don't care about emotions, but these stories offer a deeper look into the male psyche. If you understand why a man often struggles with the whole notion of romantic love; why his emotions might be genuine but his behavior doesn't match what he feels; why his relationships often disappoint him; and how sometimes he falls out of love without even knowing it, you gain insight not only into men but how to make your own relationship stronger.

For men, reading these case histories is perhaps to look into a mirror, in private, and not be startled by what you see. These stories will offer insights, trigger memories, and put you on a path that makes you a more honest communicator, better lover, and caring partner. More than one man said to me that no couple knows what its relationship is all about until it threatens to fall apart. With self-awareness and a little work, one can identify that special core *before* things disintegrate.

The last two chapters of the book—*The Need for a Relationship Audit* and *Hope for Every Couple*—are for any couple willing to conduct an objective, open review of their relationship and act on it. As stressful as it may be having the IRS examine your tax return, scrutinizing your own relationship line by line is no easier. Another analogy might be looking forward to your annual physical—but this exam is about your emotional state. For men, the idea of an audit sounds like a masculine enterprise, but when its subject encompasses vulnerability and disclosing secrets, it might seem easier to attempt the summit of Everest. An audit, however, is in fact a way to be clear about your emotions and preserve the romance or special qualities that are the glue of your relationship. It also lends an element of realism and objectivity that can let you know if it's time to go your separate ways.

In assessing your relationship, to be whipsawed solely by emotions, either positive or negative, can be a form of denial for many couples. While emotions are critical to happiness, sometimes we need to dig deeper to understand where they come from and what they mean. Ultimately, every successful relationship, especially over time, is less about bliss and passion than trust, flexibility, growth, change, and the absence of fear. Hollywood and the media want us to feel differently, but underneath every bed of roses, behind the glow of every infatuation, is a complex tension between our idealization of ourselves (and our partners) and who we know we really are. Falling in love is about the former, but staying in love has everything to do with the latter.

Why Men
Fall Out
of
LOVE

1

The Hidden Lives of Men

For each man kills the thing he loves.
—Oscar Wilde

There are many stories by women about why they leave their husbands, partners, or lovers, but few by men who head for the exits. Are they not getting the attention they want? Are they simply tired of, bored with, or frustrated by their partners and want to trade them in—as if shopping for a car—for a newer, shinier model? Are they filled with so much anger, frustration, or confusion about their relationships, or other parts of their lives, that they don't know what else to do but leave? Maybe they're hoping to find a new woman to save them, or they're chasing a lost childhood. Many are clueless about where their emotions come from and how they work—they understand the effect but not the cause—and how important their childhood is to the man and intimate partner they ultimately become.

Their confusion also comes from mixed messages they receive from women. On the one hand, men are often chided for not being emotional or sensitive enough, but they also hear that emotions are a woman's domain and that men can't possibly understand their complexity or compete with women in this arena. So men think, with linear male logic, why bother becoming something, or attempt to master a skill, they can't possibly succeed at?

For men, falling *in* love seems relatively straightforward. It usually starts with physical attraction and/or infatuation, followed by an emotional connection, then attachment, openness, and trust and, as the relationship matures, companionship, a sense of responsibility, and dependency. Falling out of love is usually more gradual, complex, and unsettling, not just for its painful impact but because of the subtle, dimly understood reasons behind it. The thief who steals love away is sometimes another being who lives inside us. Often he is the child we once were and then abandoned prematurely. The thief is also the incessant voice of our masculinity, and our passive willingness to accept traditional male stereotypes. It is as well the "binge and purge" values of popular culture; the struggle to find healthy role models; the conscious and unconscious behavior of our female partners; and, not least, the difference between how men and women learn, think, and communicate.

The ten stories here offer different insights on why men struggle with love. One insight, hardly groundbreaking but still important, is that the nest and its boundaries send a mixed message to a man almost from the beginning. On the one hand, there is the idea of "growing up" and "settling down" and having a family—a primary definition of masculinity. On the other, most men, at some level, are inherently uncomfortable in a committed relationship. They think or fantasize about whether they chose the right partner, and isn't it too bad that they have to settle for just one woman because no one partner can satisfy a man on every level. Men tend to want it all, even if they're afraid to say so out loud, or admit that, practically speaking, the goal is impossible. The irony is that when their relationships run into trouble, men, rather than leave, often stay—out of convenience or habit, fear of the unknown, the sense that quitting means failure, or the belief that somehow they can fix the problem. The underlying assumption behind all four reasons—ubiquitous in male culture—is that a man must always feel in control of his own world.

In any relationship, as early infatuation gives way to the daily routine and compromises of living together, men dwell specifically on the limitations on their sexual freedom. What a woman may happily define as "security" and "comfort" often comes without the consent of a man's hormones. Perhaps he understood the theory of giving up his freedom before entering the relationship, but reality is another matter. For many, suppressing their attraction to other women comes at the price of finding fault with their partners or themselves, retreating into passive-aggressive behaviors, or wanting to escape from their relationships whenever possible. Men like this may simply not be emotionally ready for a serious commitment, but even when they are ready, their hormonal and psychological makeup means a need for exploration and a certain amount of freedom.

As hoary a stereotype as it may be, this is the basic definition of a hunter-gatherer. This does not imply a license to pursue other intimate relationships, but it does mean finding healthy outlets for independence, self-assertion, and emotional fulfillment: a world without women. Exclusive male enclaves can mean anything from car clubs, investment groups, sports, Rotary meetings, prayer groups, breakfast clubs, or just time alone for thinking or reading. In J. R. Moehringer's memoir, *The Tender Bar,* his adolescence and manhood are largely shaped by the company of men who gather in a bar to drink, to vent, and to be honest about their feelings, whether or not they are politically correct. The theme is men respecting and caring for other men.

It is also about being unintimidated, deflecting judgment, and burying your pain, including that caused by women, before it buries you.

Men who are work and responsibility obsessed often feel guilty if they have too much free time or hang out with other men. They think that they are "doing nothing," and that being unproductive is somehow unmasculine. In reality, "doing nothing" can be invaluable therapy. In the Manhasset bar where Moehringer centers his story, doing nothing but drinking means men running from their problems, looking for distractions, fantasizing about women, and being lost boys. Not all men are lost boys, but as Moehringer implies, many feel trapped or taken for granted. It's often assumed by our culture that boys will grow up on their own to become men because, after all, manhood, unlike being a woman, is just not that complicated. As Moehringer finds out, it takes not just a nurturing mother but lots of men—the bar is his metaphor for a much larger and more diverse male universe—to grow a boy into a man. If men are honest, most will admit they need a private world where they are not judged or stereotyped by women, and give themselves permission to explore whatever needs exploring. They need space. They need a place to feel safe.

In most cases, if your relationship is healthy, it's your partner who is your safe harbor, but even the best relationships don't satisfy all needs. Psychologists have written on the necessity for men and women to keep growing emotionally outside of their primary relationships. In the last generation or two, women have learned the value of growth through independence, but men appear to be far less confident and adventurous, as if they don't trust their instincts, have a fear of making a mistake, are afflicted with guilt, or think they will earn the disapproval of their partners if they become too independent. They rationalize that they don't have time for such self-indulgence. Whether men restrict their own growth and freedom or they allow their partners to intimidate them, if opportunities for self-assertion and exploration are cut off, falling out of love may be the result.

Where does this male vulnerability and lack of confidence come from? In the opening scene of Martin Scorsese's film, *The Aviator,* a preadolescent Howard Hughes is being given a bath by his beautiful Victorian mother. As she caresses his chest and arms with a bar of soap, we sense his vulnerability as well as their mutual adoration. His mother seems in total control of Hughes's emotions, and what she is telling him—to be afraid of people who have typhus and cholera—is reinforced when she asks him to spell the word "quarantine." After making sure he understands the danger of disease and germs, she adds, "you are not safe." This may be a mother who has only the best of intentions—she just wants to keep her son alive—but the unintended consequence of her message is that Hughes develops a lifelong fear of not just germs and disease, but of failure at almost every level.

On the surface, Hughes's adult life is a chronicle of one brazen accomplishment after another, as if to show the world and himself that he is a superhero. Ever the perfectionist, he is as hard on himself as on those around him. He also tries to be perfect in order to push away his fears. At his core, however, the dark message from his mother prevails. He *is* afraid—of germs, of losing his mind, of rejection by those he loves, of having his weaknesses exposed to the public—but he can't make himself tell anyone. He tries to be confessional with his principal love interest, Kate Hepburn, who reminds us in some ways of his mother. But Hughes is never totally candid with her. He thinks his problems will ultimately go away because, after all, he is the genius and superhero who can conquer anything.

In the end, as in a Greek tragedy, Hughes's fears destroy him. The bar of soap he carries in his pocket is more than evidence of an obsessive-compulsive disorder or germ phobia: it is an ironic message that his problems are internal. Like many men who are boxed in by their fears, Hughes feels alone in the universe. He can't love any of the women he so badly wants to connect with. He is afraid they will abandon him because he thinks he isn't worthy of their love. Overwhelmed by his fears, he retreats emotionally and physically from the world. In his heart he kills almost everything he has loved. Only the beautiful, shiny planes he designs and flies—objects that can never abandon him—seem safe for his affection.

The film's depiction of Hughes is not unlike the lives of many of the men I interviewed. Rather than admit their fears, they preferred to hide behind their relationships, their bravado, their achievements, or other definitions of masculinity. Any display of weakness, any admission of confusion or unworthiness—not just for Hughes, but for a lot of men—are camouflaged by acts of reckless courage, indifference, anger, or denial. Any emotion that reflects vulnerability is the enemy. Anger in particular is used by men as a wall to hide their vulnerability.

Hughes's life was not unlike the movies he made, which were essentially dramatizations of male fantasies. For a lot of men, day-to-day reality is an oppressive world—a place of stress, tedium, ambiguity, endless responsibility and accountability—a world of shadows more than light, and from which they long to escape, if only they knew how. Male fantasies, running the gamut from sexual to the urge to be a superhero, are fundamentally about needing to retreat from a male world that is tightly and unforgivingly restrictive—to a male world that is unfettered, without responsibility, and judgment-free.

The Hazards of Masculinity

Masculinity was described to me by one man as a drive down a dark and endless highway, without road signs, rest stops, or any warning when serious danger is approaching and it's time to turn around. Once you were on the highway, he thought, there was nothing you could do about it. That was your fate. You just kept driving until the car died, you were buried in a rock slide, or you were so lost there was no hope of reaching your destination, assuming you knew what that destination was in the first place. Men love fatalism—it's one of their romantic streaks—perhaps because it relieves them of responsibility for making crucial choices, which they will be blamed for if things go wrong. Masculinity is both a problem and a solution for men. A problem because no one is quite sure how to define the term—something about ambition, leadership, and responsibility—and a solution because, despite a lack of clarity, it is a familiar and acceptable concept, a refuge, a place to hide. In *The Tender Bar,* the author learns from his hard-drinking mentors that every man has a mountain and a cave in his life—the mountain he is supposed to climb, and a cave, such as the bar, to hide in when he betrays, or has been betrayed by, his ambition.

The blueprint of masculinity, according to many psychologists, is embedded more deeply in our culture and in their DNA than men want to acknowledge. One problem for men is that not only do they have difficulty defining the "M" word, so do women. One young woman told me that masculinity meant having rugged good looks, acting like a gentleman, exhibiting confidence and independence, being competitive and successful, possessing the skills of a great lover, having courage, and being emotionally strong. When I suggested that no man I knew could deliver that Prince Charming package, she said that didn't stop her from looking for her knight in shining armor. Somehow she expected more from men than she did of her own gender. But men may be even harder on themselves. Those I interviewed recited the following components of masculinity: having a beautiful woman who loves them; being athletic; being the breadwinner, problem solver, stoical leader, and fearless warrior; making (and keeping) lots of money; having power and authority, confidence, and a sense of humor; being rational and not overly emotional; being practical and expedient, independent, and self-sustaining; being competitive and successful and achieving on every level; being a sexual stud as well as an empathetic lover, a responsible and loving father, and a family's provider and protector. Most of these are noble or idealized roles, and while no one claimed to have all these qualities, quite a few men said they thought they were supposed to have as many as possible. This is what they believed their culture, and women, expected of them. To be as close to perfect as possible was the masculine ideal, or at least not reveal your weaknesses and deficiencies. That men fall short of this goal, often dramatically—and how they feel about their failures—is just one of the secrets they don't like to talk about.

Admitting that the various definitions of masculinity are often in conflict with one another is one way to start breaking through the silence of the male code. One man told me it was drummed into him as a boy that, when he grew up, he had to succeed in his profession. There was no other option, his father said, if he wanted to respect himself and win the respect of others. An attorney now, putting in sixty- to seventy-hour weeks, he's had difficulty finding time to be a responsible husband and father—another definition of masculinity. When finally confronted by his partner, who demanded more of his affection and attention *or else,* he reluctantly agreed to a divorce rather than give up his career path or even cut down on his hours. While some women might also choose their careers over meeting family needs, I would guess the percentage pales in comparison to men. Several women told me they thought that most men define themselves by their work, but the majority of women—no matter how many hours they put in at their job—define themselves by what they do outside of work.

Just as lemmings charge blindly into the sea, men follow their primal definitions of masculinity with often unconscious devotion. It's the dark side of the herd instinct: they're too afraid *not* to follow. If a man has thought about it, however, he will tell you that wanting to be "a man" leads him down the slippery path of repressed emotions, deceit, frustration, and making difficult if not impossible choices. It can also lead to a fear and distrust of women. Some men I spoke with thought that it was easier being miserable on one level or another than to figure out a face-saving exit from their relationships without blowing their masculine cover. They had put themselves in a box, voluntarily, and closed the lid as if to prevent escape—but why? If it's all right for women to be afraid or anxious, or to talk about their failures, or seek help from one another, and leave a relationship if necessary, why shouldn't men do the same with equal confidence and openness? What is it about masculinity that forces men into a posture of stoic denial, or the pretense that no matter what the problem is, they can always tough it out or fix it? Why don't men allow themselves to learn from women?

As Goldberg, Real, and Pittman all point out in their books, most men, until they reach a crisis—such as losing their jobs or marriages, becoming seriously ill, or being humiliated by scandal—will never seek outside help or even hint something is seriously amiss. If a critical mass of desperation *is* reached, however, the real problem begins. For some, experiencing a serious failure is a crisis because it means they've flunked some test of masculinity. Worse, they may be exposed to the world and don't know how to deal with gossip and slander. All they feel is pain and confusion. Because too many men have never fully developed or understood their emotions, too often they have no resources to draw on, no safety net, no knowledge of how to heal themselves. Women often turn to each other in a crisis while men stand alone because it is the "manly" or heroic thing to do. But behind their stoicism they feel backed into a corner. Cynicism, running away, shutting down emotionally, rage, depression, paranoia, drugs, alcohol, or even suicide become tempting escapes.

That women have at their disposal a deeper level of self-intimacy—something to fall back on when a relationship crashes or tragedy enters their lives—may be one reason their rates of suicide are significantly lower than men's. Statistically, a far higher number of women than men attempt suicide, but their efforts are nowhere near as successful. This might mean that women know how to "send a message" while still surviving. When men try to kill themselves, it's almost always by violent means and almost always successful. That violence and a sense of failed masculinity are inextricably linked should not be a surprise. When you fail as a man, and you don't know how to heal or forgive yourself, or ask for help, some act of self-destruction may be inevitable. One man told me why he thought his father had committed sucide: he was so filled with rage—not just at himself, but at his deceased stepfather, who had emotionally and physically abused him—that his suicide was revenge against a ghost.

Men have no shortage of ghosts and demons in their lives. Like Howard Hughes in *The Aviator,* many appear confident and in control to their families and the outside world, yet because of unresolved childhood or adolescent traumas they have substantial fear or abandonment issues. Some men admitted to me that they were so sensitive to rejection, they had a latent fear that the women they fell in love with might ultimately turn against them, or simply change and become a stranger. Sometimes this reflected their insecure relationships with their mothers. No matter its source, insecurity is bred in a popular culture where "weeding out" and "moving on" have become more acceptable choices than tolerance, forgiveness, and the hard task of working through problems.

Our fear of abandonment is nothing new. In the Bible, Job, a good man who was afflicted with one stroke of bad fortune after another, felt deserted by God. In *The Aviator*, because Hughes had a dysfunctional connection to his mother, his descent into madness was fed in part by repeated rejections from women. That men can go mad if they don't find love is not an exaggeration, but losing love may be even more painful. The adage that "it is better to have loved and lost than never to have loved at all" would be disputed by a lot of men.

While they rarely admit it, most men do not deal well with pain, emotional or physical. Neurologically, they are simply not equipped in the same way women are. In the film *Million Dollar Baby*, one of the themes is how the two main characters cope with the pain of isolation and abandonment. The trainer, Frankie, and his protégée boxer, Maggie, gravitate to each other from pasts filled with rejection. The love and respect they find for one another—he becomes her father figure and she becomes his surrogate daughter—are ultimately tested by a tragic accident in the ring. Physical suffering, especially for Maggie, is not easy, but the emotional pain for each of the characters is what is most devastating. "Girlie, tough ain't enough," Frankie says to Maggie at the start of the film, but by the end of the story we know that girlie tough is a lot more formidable than male tough. Maggie can handle her suffering. Her death is noble because she's found her redemption—she knows who she is, and she did what she wanted with her life—while Frankie remains passive and tormented. He may be a Catholic buried in the ritual of suffering, but first and foremost he is a man struggling with his emotions. Frankie blames himself for both causing Maggie's ring accident and not finding a way to save her afterward, a typical male response when life spins out of control: not only must a man be the problem solver, but should he fail, he has violated the male code and now must be saved himself. Seeking redemption, Frankie sends himself into exile, yet there is nothing in the film to suggest he'll ever find it.

When a man fails in his relationship, he too looks for redemption. Initially, out of anger, he may fault his partner for the breakup. But in the end he points a finger at himself. He wonders what he did wrong and what he can do about it. It can be argued that women are less likely to accuse themselves of making a mistake, but when they do, they are more forgiving of themselves, or they seek out friends to support and exonerate them. Otherwise, many women tend to blame men, and why not? It is not difficult to jump on the bandwagon of male-bashing if men are already in the driver's seat. Why are men so passive about accepting blame, and perceive themselves as screwups? Why do they find it so difficult to forgive themselves? Perhaps digging for the reasons is just too complicated. A common scene in movies and books is the repentant male bearing flowers, asking forgiveness of his partner for an argument that was surely his fault. Even if he doesn't believe he was in the wrong, this ritual of atonement is so expected and ingrained in popular culture that not to observe it would only bring more recriminations. Asking forgiveness is the quickest, easiest way to end the conflict and move on. If men are anything, they are practical and expedient.

There may, however, be a very fundamental reason why men

beat themselves up. If no one is going to offer support or forgive them (unlike women, men do not usually rally around another man in trouble; instead, they isolate him or, sometimes, like predators, join in the attack), they have to atone by themselves. The more mea culpas, the better. The fact that a man doesn't understand what went wrong in his relationship doesn't mitigate self-blame. If anything, his ignorance only makes him feel more guilty. For a lot of men, any kind of failure is their fault because they are taught from childhood to excel and succeed. Failure is just not part of the male code. When it happens, a man thinks he has somehow let himself down, or let down someone he loves, or believes he has disappointed his childhood caregivers.

Feelings of inferiority were not uncommon in even the most achievement-oriented men I interviewed. I often found that the more they relied on acquisition and displays of material success as proof of their happiness, the deeper were their feelings of inadequacy. Inadequacy, I was told more than once, is what turns achievers into overachievers. Of course, feelings of pain, deprivation, and inferiority also spawn magical creativity. One has only to survey any field of writers and artists to know that from deep internal conflict and a need to assert themselves can come works of inestimable beauty and new perspectives.

No matter the outcome, the need to prove oneself is an aspect of masculinity that usually starts in adolescence. Determined to "become a man," teenagers will often set impossibly high standards for themselves. As they experience the inevitable failures of trying to measure up, they devise intricate, ingenious schemes to be judged a success by their peers, and particularly by girls. Young males learn to be cover-up artists, even con artists, at this hypercompetitive, hypersensitive age. "Winning" a girl over by artifice and deceit is condoned because without a girlfriend many boys feel stigmatized. It's the kind of stigma that sometimes leads to isolation and depression, so lies, or stretching the truth, are easy to rationalize. More than being a sports star or having money or being blessed with good looks, having a girl on his arm can mean the ultimate peer approval for a young man.

Behind his "victory," however, an adolescent often has a nagging feeling that he doesn't really know what he's doing, that he's a fake, and that at any moment his doubts and duplicity will be exposed to the world. Many men carry this fear and self-doubt into their adult lives, their professions, and their relationships, no matter how successful they try to appear. In terms of nurturing, approval, and acceptance, what these men didn't get from their families as boys and adolescents, they often want from their adult partner, or from popular culture. If they can just lose a little more weight, get that promotion, buy that cool car, live in a great neighborhood . . . surely their insecurities will melt away. The irony is that our culture, instead of bestowing the unconditional acceptance and approval that men (and women) want, offers instead more judgment, insecurity, criticism, rejection, and false hopes than even the most dysfunctional family could possibly devise.

Emperors of Denial

Like my friend who thought he had fallen out of love, a man can feel woefully inadequate when things go wrong and he tries to repair his relationship. He often has no clue where to start, or what the healing process is all about. Healing presupposes an understanding of emotions. As almost every child psychologist recognizes, male children and adolescents are generally not encouraged to indulge their emotions. (This was less true in the seventies and eighties, when the women's movement was having a more positive impact on male culture by encouraging families to sensitize and nurture boys.) Today, young men, starting as early as grade school, are encouraged to win, succeed, and achieve. That attitude includes, eventually, a successful adult relationship, even if males aren't always taught what relationship success means, especially from a woman's point of view. Indeed, one reason men fail at keeping their relationships together is they were never taught by their mothers, aunts, sisters, or grandmothers to relate to a woman in a day-to-day intimate context. What do women like to talk about with men? What do they like to hear from men? What are their romantic expectations and where do they come from? How do women communicate their deepest needs and how can men pick up those cues and signals? In particular, how do women communicate and deal with conflict, because rarely is it a linear confrontation. The ability of women to process and communicate what they want is often taken for granted by them. What comes naturally to women has to be learned somewhere, somehow, by men.

If his relationship fails, no matter whose fault it is, a man's entire world can come to a grinding halt. Feeling dejected and isolated, he may, like some men in this book, finally see a therapist and be given a strategy to unravel the mysteries that overwhelm him. Left to his own devices, however, anger, guilt, and frustration usually take over. Most men, rather than seek help or even admit their pain and unhappiness, will joke about their "confinement" and doubts about having chosen the right partner. If they do find the courage to confront their partners, they prefer an instant, linear, and rational solution—a traditional masculine approach to problem solving. To struggle with nuance, introspection, and the multiple dimensions of "emotional reasoning"—the ability to integrate emotion into the reasoning process, and to be aware of the emotional consequences of any action—is perceived by most men as a waste of time. The truth is not that it's a waste of time, it's that men are simply not good at it. "Emotional reasoning," is a skill that women seem born with but men have to learn. Until they do, when they run into a relationship storm, they significantly lessen their chances of getting back to calm waters.

Without the flexibility, relating skills, and patience to solve problems, many men just give up when things get too tough. They would rather walk out the door or dive into their private ocean of anger and guilt than be scrutinized and judged by their partners. Women give up on their relationships too—more often than men, according to most psychologists—but with a lot more thoughtfulness and less emotion than men bring to this process. The irony is that women are the emotional gender but can be coolly rational under fire, while men are supposed to be objective and in control but easily collapse when their emotions take over. They have difficulty connecting head to heart in any efficient way. For women, "emotional reasoning" may be a skill honed from centuries of survival. In medieval times, when men from a village went off to war, only to be killed in combat, their widows knew that to survive, and for the survival of their children, they had to adapt to a new man. There was little time for grieving, only for clearheaded thinking. Perhaps this is why today when a woman abandons her relationship there is little stigma. She's seen as liberating herself, or doing what it takes to survive, or what's best for her children. On the other hand, when men flee they are often labeled as irresponsible and cowardly. Women, hurt and angry at being abandoned, often use a man's definition of his masculinity against him. If he was supposed to be the protector and provider, they say, he failed not just his partner but himself.

But are men really failures? Are they so irresponsible or negligent? Perhaps the deck has been stacked against them and they don't even know it, or they don't know what to do about it. The truth is that a man who does not understand or feel comfortable with himself, was never nurtured as a child, never learned to trust and value his emotions, or never acquired socialization skills, especially conflict resolution, will almost inevitably wilt under the responsibility of a relationship or a family. He may not necessarily run away, but neither will he find deep satisfaction or meaning in his most intimate relationship. Men, who tend to define their relationships more by their actions (for example, "making a living" or "being a responsible husband and father") than their emotions, will often live with their unhappiness and confusion, sometimes unaware there even is a problem until their partners tell them. Too many men are the emperors of ignorance and denial.

This is not to say that men don't have emotional triggers, or that they're clueless, or that they can't fall out of love because they never fell in love in the first place, as some women asserted. Men have a different point of view. Many feel they are often driven out of love by their partners' behaviors. Among the men I spoke with, living with a controlling women was love's principal assassin. Men might be equally guilty of trying to control, but their efforts are rarely as sophisticated, subtle, or pervasive; they are not as embedded in their gender "language" as they are for women. Possessing a wide range of emotions, women have the ability to turn their feelings on and off, and jump from one to another, in the blink of an eye. Their control might come through interference, judgment, inducing guilt or shame in a partner, setting and changing rules, or withholding affection— some of which can be conveyed in a tone of voice, a hand gesture, a hurt glance, or a pregnant silence. Few men have such range or abilities. They are simply not wired that way. Yet many women are unconscious of what they do and the effect they have on their partners. That they can be intimidating to men comes as a surprise to them. Their self-image is so positive, and they are so supportive of one another, they think, how can strong men possibly be intimidated by caring women?

But men *are* often intimidated, even if they don't like to admit it. Under the surface, are they just wimps? Are they afraid of being labeled "babies," "candy-asses," and "girlie men," as one friend told me? For many men, the territory of emotions is covered with No Trespassing signs. They believe that women appropriate emotions to make feelings *their* club, *their* territory, from which, intentionally or unintentionally, men are excluded. (Many women have another interpretation: in addition to their neurological and processing differences, their reliance on emotions is role-playing that is handed down from their mothers, generation after generation.) If men feel inadequate about accessing their emotions, perhaps it is because, generation after generation, they have consistently denied a primary truth: the first step on any journey of self-knowledge—not to mention the skill to communicate with women—is acknowledging the importance of their emotions. It also means not being afraid to be vulnerable, or admit mistakes, and accepting that uncertainty and ambiguity, by pushing men out of their comfort zones, sets the stage for learning some of life's most important lessons.

The male taboo against admitting one's weaknesses and mistakes, however—against confession in general—is a powerful one. Men expediently confess to their partners in order to patch up their relationships (after all other strategies have failed), get something in return, or be dramatic and win attention—not to reveal their weaknesses. The same goes for men relating to men. Male friends who trust one another will share their fears and anxieties, but most prefer the safer, neutral ground of "guy talk." Analyzing why Peyton Manning is a better passer than Tom Brady, or comparing the new Canon digital camera to the Sony, offers the comfort of familiarity and avoids conflict and the need for self-revelation. Most men, unless out to obtain specific information, prefer to listen than to talk for a similar reason—why expose yourself unnecessarily? One man told me that by asking other men the right questions and listening carefully to their answers, he learns their weaknesses; by talking too loosely about himself, someone will learn his.

The Feminist Galaxy

Most men view the women's movement that was launched forty years ago as an unprecedented vehicle for women, giving them power, confidence, and upward professional mobility. Like peering in the window of a party to which they weren't invited, men have observed this phenomenon with envy and consternation, while largely ignoring its lessons and benefits. Some values of feminism—caring, empathizing, and nurturing, for example—have influenced men as fathers. The so-called "softer male" who connects to his children is a huge advance over the emotionally absent or stern father figures of a few generations ago. Yet overall, feminism seems to most men like a new planet in the solar system, spinning on a unique axis, its esoteric laws of gravity known only to half the population. Even though male-bashing appears on the wane, and there is a kinder, gentler feminism in the air, men still cling to the sidelines, nursing their questions like a bruise on the jaw. Will feminism ever go away? What are "they" planning next? Why are there books like *Are Men Necessary?* and *He's Just Not That Into You?* Why does it feel like women are ceaselessly putting men under a microscope, or trying to take their power away? A lot of men are aware that they disappoint women, one man admitted to me, but he also said half of his friends didn't care, and the other half didn't know what to do about it. There is a general feeling among men that women make relationships a lot more complicated than they need to be. Or perhaps they are simply more complicated than a lot of men are willing to deal with.

But men usually think these thoughts and ponder these questions in silence. Not only do they not like confrontation with women, they have largely refused to learn the lessons of growth, change, and adaptability that women have accepted. Perhaps men fear ridicule if they speak up, or ask for help, or try to change their lives. All their questions, all that male inertia and passivity, may come from an unwillingness to deal with their fears.

Due to the same passivity, stereotypes of male behavior and attitudes have not been seriously challenged either. In most sitcoms and commercials, men are portrayed as they have been for decades: as adolescent skirt chasers, sports-obsessed beer drinkers, car fanatics, action-movie addicts, buffoons, gamblers, jealous competitors, or preening metrosexuals. Except for sex, supposedly nothing gets men more aroused than "March Madness" or the NFL or NBA playoffs, or how fast the new Porsche goes from zero to sixty. Popular culture would have us believe that men are predictable and easy to understand. In his bestseller, *Dave Barry's Complete Guide to Guys,* the humorist suggests men live close to the surface, in the land of external pleasures, subject to the rogue waves of their testosterone and other wacky male impulses. When they get in some kind of trouble, which is often, it is usually a woman who has to come to their rescue. Poor, dumb men can't seem to do anything right.

Humor is based on truth: a lot of men do like sports, cars, motorcycles, beautiful women, sex, guns, gambling, tinkering and fixing, and electronic gadgets. But when exaggerated or told too often, a joke becomes a stereotype. Barry's book, written more than a decade ago, seems today little more than a string of clichés. But does anyone notice or object? It doesn't help men that no matter how they are portrayed, too many shrug off the barbs and caricatures as if to prove how stoical, indifferent, or superior they are. These same men listen docilely when women claim they are still the underprivileged gender, fighting the un-ending battle for equality of one kind or another. Not to react or speak up is to not care, these men believe. In the end, their indif-ference and lack of awareness distance them from reality. Most men I spoke with felt that, except for in the workplace, women have already won the gender battle. Overwhelmingly, they felt that women possess control and leverage in most intimate rela-tionships.

Even in the workplace, male "supremacy" is an uncertain as-sumption. Excepting the power or money worlds of Wall Street, Hollywood, the military, government, sports, and institutional religion—male bastions to the bitter end, perhaps—the glass ceiling could one day be history. According to the U.S. Depart-ment of Education, for the last ten years colleges have bestowed more diplomas on women than on men, and the "diploma gap" only appears to be widening. In most graduate schools, includ-ing law and medicine, women are at parity with men.

But equal pay for equal work, as well as sharing positions of authority—starting with white-collar tiers and working down—depend to a great degree on women. How aggressively do women want to pursue a career path and, specifically, which ca-reers? According to a 2006 article in *The New York Times*, since the mid-nineties the rate of women joining the workforce has slowed dramatically. Are women simply electing to stay home and be mothers? Are they declining high-pressure or prestige professions because they want a private life? Are they electing to go to work largely for money, not ego? Many say they learned from men—and all the superwomen of the seventies and eighties—that you can't burn the candle at both ends without paying a huge price.

In the last forty years, as women have become more vocal about gender issues, there have been some efforts by men to speak up about who they are and what they want. Remember all those shirtless men beating drums in the woods decades ago, and the Million Man March in Washington in 1995? Herb Goldberg and Frank Pittman, among others, have advocated dismantling old stereotypes and building a more realistic, healthier, model of male needs. Today, more men than ever gather to talk about issues and problems relevant to men—yet no effort has been sustained that is remotely equivalent to the women's movement. To say that a full-fledged men's movement is impossible because men are too competitive, fearful, jealous, and distrustful of each other begs the question. Those emotions and behaviors are their prison, the very problems from which a movement or more self-awareness would liberate them. Perhaps it's time for men to step out of their cells, be more assertive about their feelings, and begin to help, not isolate, each other. That would be a formula for self-healing, the prerequisite of any large-scale change of consciousness, and the beginning of healthier relationships with women.

The Loss of Intimacy

For most young men, the desire for sex is driven by their testosterone, a fascination with the female anatomy, and a need to be accepted both by a woman and their own peer group. Being "normal" and a fear of being left out drive adolescent behavior and values, but ultimately have little to do with a young man's happiness and deeper self-esteem. In order to avoid the whole stressful enterprise of an intimate relationship, for which they might not be prepared, a lot of adolescents prefer hanging out in coed groups or just enjoying the opposite sex as friends. Boys may want sex for exploration and pleasure, but most shy away from the emotional attachments and implicit promises that women believe come with physical intimacy.

For men, even as adults, sex raises as many questions as it answers about what they, and women, really want. A lot of men feel it's their role to make women happy by being great lovers, and that technique rules—but women have a different point of view. Women, especially the under-thirty generation, want sex as much as, maybe more than, men. It's a statement of liberation, pleasure, and control. Ultimately, however, they don't want just performance or pleasure, or even control; they want intimacy. Being a great (and lasting) lover is about being open, giving, and vulnerable. It's about allowing a woman to fuse her identity with a man's for a sublime moment, and a man fusing his identity with hers.

The problem for many men is that they don't understand the emotional language of women, and often women, perhaps out of fear of being exploited, or believing that men can't really be that clueless, do little to translate that language. If you really love me, women think, you'll figure it out. But a lot of men I interviewed haven't figured it out. That's why they do a lot of guessing, and make assumptions about women that are often wrong. In terms of intimacy or its prelude, men may observe the rules of romance because they know it's what women expect, but forever the conquerors, what they really believe, especially younger men, is that penis size or superior technique or a seductive atmosphere is what translates into "success." Popular culture reinforces that idea. Yet other men I interviewed knew that awareness and concern for their partner's feelings, and finding an emotional connection through sex, were as important for them as they were for women.

Just as women can be difficult to read because they're not revealing, men can be hard to decode because they're not comfortable with their own emotional circuitry. They know what they *should* be feeling, but for a variety of reasons, as the stories in this book will show, can't quite express it because they're feeling something else. Men are usually drawn into relationships by personality and physical appearance, and while women deliberately cultivate that attraction, they like to believe that the man who falls in love with them is falling in love with more than their personality, beauty, or sex appeal. A man is right for her because he's uncovered her essence, and understands and loves her like no one else has. But not all men manage this transition from "attraction" to "falling in love" with sincerity and sensitivity. To bridge that gap, they become skillful at small deceptions. It's their way of getting what they want—sex—without giving a woman what she wants—sex *and* commitment.

Alexander Payne's dark comedy *Sideways* is about two old college friends, Miles and Jack, who take a trip through California wine country one week before Jack's wedding. Women and sex are never far from their thoughts. Miles and particularly Jack lie so often and in so many little ways, to themselves and to the women they meet, that the audience wonders if they're even aware of ethical issues. They presumably know lying is wrong, but it's just part of who they are, and often necessary, in their minds, to accomplish their objectives. They rationalize that life for a man can be pretty tough, so they're entitled to take some ethical shortcuts. Jack and Miles also lie for empowerment in the sense that they know they're "getting away with something." The egos of many men, and the strictures of masculinity, are based on the premise that a man must succeed at all costs, even if it means stretching the truth.

The two stories that follow illustrate not only how differently men and women view sex, but how sex and emotional intimacy can first bind (and blind) a relationship convincingly, creating the feeling that it will go on forever, then, seemingly for no reason, tear it apart with gale-force winds.

Other themes covered in this section include:

- Why intimacy is ultimately just as important to men as it is to women
- How sexual acceptance and rejection for men and

women are inevitably tied to self-love and childhood
issues, even when they're not aware of the emotional
triggers

- How sex becomes the inevitable battleground when other
forms of communication break down and, conversely,
when sex deteriorates or disappears, so do other forms of
communication
- How men, when their relationships crumble, escape into
sex with other partners to avoid pain and self-
examination, and to feel better about themselves
- Why men and women subconsciously seek out partners
with certain attributes, even negative ones, that reflect
characteristics of their caregivers

2

Steven's Story

Sex is one of the nine reasons for reincarnation.
The other eight aren't important.
—Henry Miller

It's a fall Saturday night in southern New Mexico, crisp and cool with a dusting of snow on the mountains. Steven, twenty-eight years old, facing yet another argument with his girlfriend, Renee, has just walked out of the house rather than continue arguing. A real-estate agent with a degree in history, Steven has well-defined shoulders, an olive complexion, and wavy black hair. His grin is infectious, as is his personality. He's normally happy and optimistic, but tonight he's ready to throw in the towel. Steven and Renee have been living together for several years, slowly building their relationship, but lately the issue of physical intimacy has become a battleground.

"I need sex not just because I'm horny," he told Renee tonight before leaving, "but because it makes me feel good about myself, as a man, as a lover, as someone who hopefully has the gift of bringing pleasure to a woman. When you won't have sex with me, how do you think that makes me feel? How am I supposed to stay in love with you if there's no intimacy?" Furious at his selfishness, Renee tells Steven all he thinks about is sex, not love.

In happier moments, Renee is a bubbly, go-with-the-flow brunette. She has pensive blue eyes, a beautiful smile, and a great figure. She talks often about getting married, an idea Steven first agreed to—indeed, he was the one to bring it up. Now Steven's not so sure. He feels there's been a major change in Renee over the last year. Her interest in sex has almost disappeared. In the early days neither one of them could wait to jump into bed. Now Steven has to beg Renee to take a shower together or to devote Saturday night to fun and games. When he asks what the problem is, Renee says the only problem is that Steven is too demanding—sometimes he even intimidates her. When they get into a really serious argument, like tonight, she makes the charge that he's oversexed, as if it's a disease, which makes him feel self-conscious, almost ashamed. He wonders if Renee, having gotten the promise of marriage, was only using sex as a lure and basically gets little pleasure from it. He also had an affair early in their relationship—during a period when he and Renee had broken up—but he told her the truth when they got back together.

Steven was born and grew up in a tiny, mostly Hispanic town in southern New Mexico. It's the kind of place where everyone you pass on the road raises his hand off the steering wheel to wave. The population has "swollen" to around five thousand, but the native culture remains virtually unchanged. Steven's family has lived in this small town for five generations. His mom is a housewife and his dad is an auto mechanic. Thirty years ago his dad was a dashing Hell's Angel on a Harley who swept Steven's eighteen-year-old mom off her feet. Their domestic life has had its ups and downs, Steven says. After graduating

from college, Steven moved to a larger city where he eventually
went into real-estate sales and now earns a six-figure income.
For a self-described "small-town boy," he is understandably
proud of his successes, including buying his first home while still
in his twenties. He makes friends easily, and women in particular find him intuitive and sympathetic. In his relationships, he has
always seen himself as willing to learn from his mistakes. However, he wonders what it will take for Renee to learn from hers.

Life in my hometown is slow, easygoing, and friendly, but
with a great suspicion of outsiders. Children are
encouraged not to leave when they grow up. Traditionally, your
parents will give you a small parcel of land, cutting off a piece
of their own, and you're expected to buy your own double-wide,
have babies, then repeat the whole cycle with your kids. In the
Hispanic culture, the past is more important than the future.
My parents still live in the same mobile home where I was
born. Working with your hands for a living, hunting elk and
deer in season, drinking with your buddies—that's what men
have always done around here. Women stay home, have babies,
and keep house.

I could say a lot about the values of "my people," good and
bad, but I've learned to accept their resistance to change, their
strong family ties, and their utter lack of ambition. I was the
first college graduate in my family in six generations. If you
think that was easy for my dad to accept, I like to tell the story
of a girl named Linda from a local family who was an academic
superstar, got almost perfect SATs, and was accepted at more
than one Ivy League school. Her parents and relatives viewed
her success with great discomfort. Instead of commending
Linda for her odds-defying accomplishments, the attitude was,
"What, Linda, going to a fancy college, you think you're better

than us? You want to shame your brothers and sisters? You want to leave us . . . why? What's wrong with you?" She didn't shame her family, obviously; they shamed her. To Linda's credit, she left for college and rarely came home again. Fundamentally, mine is a closed, jealous, and insecure culture. Like a bunch of crabs in a bucket. When one tries to crawl out, the others grab it and pull it back in.

My relationship with my dad was one more of intimidation than intimacy. He was definitely not someone "in touch with his emotions." I remember when I was around ten I accidentally shot the window of a passing truck with my BB gun. Dad witnessed the event and grew furious. He was sure I had done it on purpose. He broke the gun over his knee, hit me with it, and then threw the barrel at me as I was running away. "It was an accident," I screamed. But he didn't see it that way, or maybe his anger came from embarrassment. I could tell my mother was not happy with his reaction, but there was little she could do. My father had no patience for my mistakes and misbehavior, and believed that swift and certain punishment was the most effective way to teach a lesson and to make a boy into a man. At the time I feared and disliked him, especially when he drank and came home late at night. Then the pettiest thing could set off his temper. But I didn't know enough to judge him. I thought all fathers in my town—fathers everywhere—did this kind of thing.

When I went elk hunting with dad, sometimes he deliberately left me in a distant valley and expected me to find my way back to camp. That was his test of manhood for me. I had to prove I was self-sufficient. I remember breaking down in tears more than once, yet after a number of these episodes I learned it was pointless to wallow in self-pity, and I knew I had to be tough and help myself. That was the extent of my intimacy with my dad—him teaching me "life's lessons." He didn't do a lot of talking. Once in a while, spirits bolstered by a few beers, he would open up and tell me he loved me. Yet the next day he was back to his rigid, remote self.

My mom was just the opposite. She was open and honest and purposefully nurturing. She gave me dolls for gifts, put me to work in the kitchen, and because I was an asthmatic she would rub my chest with Vicks and make sure I always had a humidifier in my room. This drove Dad crazy. He didn't mind me learning to cook, but washing dishes was "women's work," and he accused Mom of babying me with my asthma. While my mom disciplined me when I misbehaved, it was more of a constructive punishment—consistent and in control—and she would give explanations about what was right and wrong. She didn't spoil me, but I definitely developed my feminine side from the honesty and tenderness she shared with me. To this day I'm much closer to her than my dad. I also learned compassion and respect for women, though that message would get buried under my father's narrow interpretation of male-female relationships, especially during my adolescence.

When I was around fourteen, my mom and I found out Dad was having an affair. Mom was hurt and shaken. When I asked why she didn't ask for a divorce, she said, 'Oh, I wouldn't do that, I love your father.' Maybe that was true, or maybe she was just afraid to leave Dad, or she didn't want a confrontation with him, or she was just too dependent on him. I'm still not sure. But what had the biggest impact on me was her reaction of acceptance. This gave me the impression that it was okay for men to be disloyal to women—including me with my girlfriends—because either you'd be forgiven by the girl, or your behavior just wasn't that important to them.

Around the same time, one night my dad, drunk, took me aside to tell me about "the birds and the bees." Being a hunter, he chose the metaphor "bucks and does." I don't know why he

suddenly felt this need to be my sex-education instructor—
Mom had already told me everything—but he went on and on
about how I needed to be "the big buck," and that way I could
"get all the does I wanted, and that would teach them respect."
This was Dad's attitude toward women. Just be the buck. Don't
worry about any subtle communications, or kindness, or
sharing emotions. Just dominate and you won't have any
problems.

The compassion and values I learned from my mom were
quickly challenged by my junior high school peer group. Most
of my friends were more like my dad. Women were objects put
on this earth for the pleasure of men. If you were a teenage
boy, this meant a lot of "grabbing" girls wherever you could
find temporary privacy. In general, I caved in to my friends and
followed their lead. Incredibly, I found, the girls didn't mind.
They seemed to expect and want this crude behavior, as if they
had been brought up with the same values and attitudes as my
father. I didn't wonder about it then, but now I think this was
the behavior they'd seen with their older sisters and
girlfriends, and their fathers simply condoned it while their
mothers stayed silent.

Growing up in a Hispanic culture, Steven at an early age
senses its insularity, intolerance, and suspicion of outsiders. He's
too young to rebel against these values, but observant enough to
wonder if he's going to be happy fitting in. The particular message of male sexual domination and conquest—the buck versus
the does—is tested as early as junior high school and becomes a
rite of passage that makes him uncomfortable. He accepts his
father's values for now, but his mother's voice and nurturing
qualities provide an early warning system that the buck and doe
metaphor may not sustain him. His mother may be powerless to
change her role in a male-dominated culture, but at least she

passes on to her son the unspoken message that she is not that happy. Seemingly oblivious to his wife's emotions, much less his son's, the father appears determined to teach Steven traditional definitions of macho masculinity—stoicism, gender and sexual dominance, physical prowess, and never calling attention to oneself or having too much ambition. Being the teacher is a father's sacred, archetypal duty, and no doubt Steven's father thinks he will be a failure unless his son accepts his culture's values. If he doesn't accept them, the table is set for Steven for conflict and confrontation.

In my high school, sports were the major rite of passage for boys, and could be either a salvation or a curse. Salvation because sports are a testosterone release, and also teach teamwork and strategy—skills you can definitely use as an adult. Also, in many ways sports are a validation of male values: skill, power, success, and the importance of winning. For a young man, these become the benchmarks of self-esteem. I was gifted athletically, so that's where my self-esteem came from. Displays or even consciousness of emotions—beyond the "high" you get from winning—play no useful role. This is the dark side of sports. First, it's all about judgment. Those who aren't good enough to make a team are often ostracized or labeled as losers; those who do make the team are continually under pressure to live up to expectations. Second, you can't show vulnerability or pain. Instead, you learn to suck it up and pretend that everything is fine. In sports you communicate through your level of performance, not by your feelings. Contrast this with "female values" and the perception that emotions are the fundamental way of communicating. Women let you know right away that emotions are their domain and men are simply not equipped to communicate on this level. Men get the message—so a lot of us don't even bother showing our emotions. I think this reticence has a lot to do with sports and competition. If a man knows he can't win in one area, he is conditioned not to complain (he'll be judged a weakling), but to try something else where he will be successful.

Because I was a major jock, I was popular with both guys and girls. I particularly enjoyed hanging with girls. By the time I reached high school I dropped my old male friends because I thought they were still behaving immaturely. I adopted a whole new image. Part of being popular in my school was to have as many girlfriends as possible; consecutively or simultaneously, it didn't seem to matter. Of course, the ultimate achievement was to take a girl to bed. Yet as much as I wanted to have sex, there was something in me that just wasn't ready. Maybe it was a lack of understanding of what a girl wanted; maybe it was a fear of my untested sexual abilities. There was another inhibition that plagued me as well. I would walk away from easy opportunities to sleep with a girl because I'd suddenly have this incredible guilt. Because of my mom, I wanted to do the honorable thing with a girl, and exploiting her for sex didn't meet that definition.

In the end, however, I lost my virginity to a girl who was crazy about me, and no doubt I exploited that devotion. After all, adoration is a kind of hedge against your own insecurities. We were both drunk and virgins so I didn't have to fear being ridiculed for being more inept than she was. While the sex seemed exciting at the moment, the next day there was regret on both our parts. We decided to try it again, sober, but this time the experience felt awkward and mechanical. We never dated again. Looking back, I know now that a lack of emotion can make sex seem almost like punishment.

Each of my parents had a voice in my head. The tension from listening to both of them at the same time could be paralyzing. By the time I graduated from high school, however, my dad's view of relationships—the great buck standing supreme—was winning the day. My pursuit of as many girls as I could attract was such a strong impulse that even then I saw I would have difficulty in the future with commitment to one partner. Part of this came from my enormous need for validation, which, I think now, stemmed from a fear that had unintentionally been instilled by my dad. I didn't have confidence that I could do anything in my life unless Dad had specifically taught me that skill, like fixing a car, or hunting, or building a shed. On the one hand, he had made me tough and independent, yet that world of "street smarts" was so circumscribed that I had little confidence to try anything new. Dad had never taught me, or I had never learned, the intangibles and subtleties of life: how and when to take risks, knowing the limits of ambition, and believing that the universe outside my small town was worth exploring. My dad's world was almost completely tactile; the emotional, the abstract, and the world of ideas were of no use to him.

Even though I was a basketball star, I didn't get enough validation from sports. You could be a god one moment, but if you screwed up there was always someone to replace you, and suddenly you were feeling bad about yourself. Girls were the ultimate source of approval, not just for me but for a lot of my friends. Maybe I wanted more of the nurturing emotions that my mother gave me. Most men I know are hungry for an emotional connection. It's really why they're attracted to women. They may think the attraction is to physical beauty— and at first it might be—but ultimately they want and need emotional support, and the more the better. If you ask me, that's the main reason men fall in love.

My relationships took on a pattern. Bursts of bliss followed by disappointment. I would bask in a girl's admiration, exploit that admiration, get her to make out passionately or take her to bed, then be clueless about what to do next. I didn't know how to communicate emotionally, though I was intuitive enough to understand that this is what it took to sustain a relationship. But rather than make that effort, I simply went on to another girl. Sex with a new girl became the easiest way to make you feel good about yourself. And with each "conquest," you gained a reputation among your male friends as a guy who really knew how to handle women.

From sports, Steven absorbs positive lessons about confidence, teamwork, and leadership, but is smart enough to understand the limitations of men who are always trying to prove themselves—and communicate—through achievement and performance. While excelling in sports can give a young man great self-esteem and visibility with his peers, Steven makes the point that ultimate peer approval may come from the pursuit of girls and, in particular, taking them to bed. Perhaps the all-consuming goal of sexual conquest is conveyed no better than in a novel like Tom Wolfe's *I am Charlotte Simmons*, where college men in narcissistic heat grant themselves the power to do and say almost anything to seduce a woman. To keep a relationship alive, they find clever ways to cover up their deceit. The means—deception and lies—sometimes becomes an end in itself. Later in his story, Steven gives the example of trying to take a girl to bed when she suddenly says, "I know you love me." How many young men have the courage to say they just want to try sex, and that love can wait? Hopefully, there is affection involved, but the truth is that a young man's hormones are on fire. Adolescent girls should know that their power and self-esteem in a relationship come from knowing the difference between honest intimacy and a boy's horniness. Young men, to grow emotionally, and to gain insight into women, first have to experience some painful lessons, as Steven is about to find out.

At the end of my senior year, I entered into a relationship with a girl named Trisha. By this time I was beginning to glimpse how emotions worked for girls. It was like a universal language for them. I couldn't explain the specifics of the language—what was the equivalent of an alphabet or rules of grammar—but just from intuition I could decode parts of it. Trisha was the first girl to pull me into her life with the message that she needed me. She never said it in so many words but I felt it every time I was with her. She didn't care that I'd been a big jock or that I had a sense of humor or that I was reasonably good-looking. What counted was that I was the one who understood her. She wanted me to provide comfort and reassurance to her whenever she needed it. Physically, she was frail, and her eyes always hinted at an unspecified pain. The mystery of that pain only made her more intriguing to me. She was choosing me, empowering me to help her, to be her protector and confidant. She was giving me a kind of power that didn't relate to my achievements or any other high school value. She was asking me to give her the same kind of emotions that I wanted from her. I didn't mind. The act of giving satisfied me on a very deep level. In the end it was more important to me than receiving emotion.

The real lesson for me in all this was that the more a woman needs you, the better you feel about yourself. Maybe I was susceptible to this kind of thinking because I had such large validation needs, but Trisha was also a master at showing her affection and appreciation at the right time and in the right way. The sex was incredible because it came from a deep emotional place, at least for me. Was this love or manipulation on Trisha's part? I don't know. I don't know if Trisha even knew. This pattern was just part of her nature. As we dated that summer, I began to think I was indispensable to her, that she would always be part of my life. And the more she needed me, the more I needed her. In short, she had created dependency. What I didn't understand then was how strong a hook that can be.

That fall, Trisha went off to college, and within a month she wrote me that she had met someone who was more mature, more exciting to her, and, I assumed, better served her needs. And she stopped communicating with me. Just like that. It was my first "Dear John" experience and I was totally caught off guard. I was devastated, in fact. I had taken for granted Trisha's devotion to me—taken for granted that there was something wonderful and special about me—but suddenly I questioned everything. Had Trisha just used me? Was I really so special? I began to wonder who I really was, how I should define myself. How could I trust any relationship unless I knew who I was?

One thing I learned for sure. I could no longer live off the fumes of high-school success. The second thing, even clearer, was that while I had an inkling of how powerful the language of emotions was for women, how well it served their needs, it seemed to me that men were at a disadvantage. We didn't know the language. Soon I had another insight: one reason women ended relationships was that they didn't get the emotional support they needed, or their emotional needs were met by someone new in a different way. What was less obvious was how and when their needs changed. Trisha didn't drop a clue that I was going to be out of her life. Did she know ahead of time, or did her needs just change one day, surprising even her? She never shared her emotional processing with me, so how was I supposed to figure it out? It seems to me that instead of explaining themselves to men, women prefer to complain about how unemotional and uncommunicative men are, and that becomes their excuse for jumping to another man.

It took almost a year to get over losing Trisha. One day I ran
into a former classmate, Melinda, who had always been a
friend. I asked her to lunch and we talked about our lives. Out
of high school now, I had my first full-time job. While I was
enjoying being independent, I was also lonely. Melinda
admitted the same. Over the next few months, as we started
dating, I began to develop deeper feelings for her. And I got the
same message as I had with Trisha—Melinda needed me. One
night, kissing her in the car, I thought I was falling in love. At
times she could be negative, and never once did she pay for
anything—that was the man's job, she said—but I didn't care.
The more Melinda said she needed me, the more secure I felt
and the more I wanted to be her hero. I also opened up about
my past, including plenty of details, such as the times I took
advantage of girls in high school. I wanted to be totally honest. I
thought that the act of confession was the only way to get rid of
my insecurities and fears, and create a bond between us. I was
hoping Melinda would be just as candid with me, but as the
months went on I noticed I was doing more talking and Melinda
was doing most of the listening. Something felt wrong.

Then Melinda gave me a not-so-subtle hint. I had been too
candid with her, she implied. I was giving her more information
than she wanted to hear. But it was too late. I couldn't take it
back. Melinda was judging me by my past, not by the fact that I
was changing from a misguided teenager into someone trying
to become a well-rounded human being. She was thinking,
Hey, is this the type of guy I can trust and rely on as my
permanent partner? She finally came out and admitted that my
volatile past was a turnoff, and she ended the relationship.

I was beside myself. I was in love with this woman, and here
was another rejection. I cried on and off for days. I even
thought of suicide. I couldn't talk to anyone about what had
happened without feeling monstrously betrayed by Melinda, or

just stupid. Both Trisha and Melinda had come on to me as vulnerable and fragile—yet in the end they seemed to have grown stronger, while I was the fragile one. How could that be? I was a man. Men weren't supposed to be weak.

Like most adolescent males, Steven is unprepared for dealing with the complex emotional circuitry of teenage girls, or women in general, and is especially unprepared for rejection and the feeling of being manipulated. Confronting his own limitations, he learns that a woman's rejection means more than a broken heart. It also brings a feeling of failed masculinity. Being the buck who is supposed to conquer all those does, and instead ends up being conquered, does little to help Steven's fragile ego. It's not just the metaphor that is inadequate; it's a young man's lack of awareness of how a woman's emotions work, and his own. Because most men don't know how to heal themselves when they're feeling vulnerable or in pain, or ask for support from male friends, many will quickly look for another woman to salve their wounds and get their minds off their pain. If that fails, they might turn, for example, to their jobs, school, or sports—anything to restore a feeling of worth. If that strategy fails, men easily become susceptible to extreme stress, illness, rage, self-hatred, and even thoughts of suicide. Men are more vulnerable than many women may realize.

Two failed relationships in a row made me look at myself more critically. I had the habit of blaming myself when things went wrong—whether it was a basketball game or a fight with my father. I think a lot of men are inclined to think this way because that's how they're brought up. You're told you're "the man of the house" and therefore responsible for almost everything, and you have to accept blame when things go wrong. At least that's the way it is in my culture. Somehow I had screwed up these opportunities with these women. Now I had to reexamine myself and my values. To try to change my life I decided to enroll in college. I wanted to lose myself in a whole new environment.

One afternoon I met a woman, Renee, at the college fitness center. She asked me to help design an exercise program for her. I was 23 and she was 27, but I didn't think of her as an "older woman." First, Renee looked younger than me, and second, she was beautiful, which seemed to transcend any age issue. In my typical pattern, I also intuited something vulnerable about Renee. As we got to know each other, I learned that she was recently divorced, had a four-year-old son, and was unhappy in her relationship with her current boyfriend. She had also lost her father the year before. The message I got was she was emotionally alone in the world— and here I was, ready to play the hero again. That made me nervous. I didn't want to set myself up for more disappointment and pain. But Renee was a great flirt, sweet, bubbly, kind. There were sparks between us right away. I began to wonder: was I a magnet for this kind of woman, or was it the other way around?

Here was a woman whose emotional "scent" was even stronger than Melinda's or Trisha's, and I got totally drawn in. She would sneak out on her boyfriend to meet me for dinner or a drink. Finally, she broke up with him. Soon we were having sex, and the next thing I knew, Renee told me that she was in love with me. This was only two months after we'd met. I wasn't sure if I was in love with Renee, but when a woman says she loves you and you don't want to lose her, you'll end up telling her that you love her too. I mean, you can't say "Hey, let me think about it." You could lose the girl in a second. So you hedge your bet. A lot of guys do that. It happened to me in high school when I was trying to get a girl into bed and she said, "I know you love me." You end up saying more or less what she wants to hear. Women don't always seem to understand a man's mentality. When it suits their purpose, women will take your words literally, even when they intuit that you might be lying. They'll take those four little words—"I love you too"—and infer a deep and complex system of commitment to them, way beyond what you're feeling.

As I got to know Renee, I found her more and more irresistible. I was always proud to have her on my arm in public. Other men were jealous of me, and that jealousy just validated my taste. I know I have a hang-up about approval, and I like adrenaline, and when that combination comes in the form of a beautiful, sweet, admiring woman who whispers in your ear and takes you to bed, you are, by definition, in a state of bliss. Everything about Renee seemed spontaneous and innocent. But looking back, I think she knew how she was presenting herself. It wasn't as spontaneous as it felt. She would tell me almost anything that she knew would hook me. Because of Trisha and Melinda, I'm sure I was conscious of Renee's manipulation on some level, but my doubts paled compared to the emotions that Renee aroused in me. I accepted her female aura. When a woman wants something, her ability to communicate that need, including through her sexuality, is an incredible gift. I sucked up all her love and adoration with delirious gratitude. I also liked her son, Joey, even though my male friends warned me about dating someone with a young child. If there's a fight between Renee and me over her boy, I was advised, don't expect Renee to take my side.

The more I became involved with Renee, the more I realized I couldn't live without her. I was falling in love again and, unlike Melinda, Renee was a positive person. She urged me to continue with school and supported my ambition to become a real-estate agent. She didn't care about my immature past. She seemed to love me for exactly who I was. She was a strong, confident, moral woman who I respected. I decided that it was Renee I wanted to marry. When I took her to meet my mother, I was pleased with the instant chemistry between them. They were a lot alike. They felt comfortable with each other.

One romantic evening, I suggested the idea of marriage to Renee. She just looked at me, gave me a kiss, and said no. I was stunned. Was this a repeat of Trisha and Melinda? She wasn't rejecting my proposal for any emotional reasons, I soon learned, but for practical ones. Renee was about to leave her job and go back to college full-time. She had little money, except what she borrowed from her mom. How was I going to support her? Where were we going to live? Did I really know and love her son, Joey? She had thought this all out. I was an impulsive romantic—anything to lock her in place, just like my dad had done with my mother—a sort of a "tie them up" mentality. But Renee wouldn't have it. Burned in her first marriage, I figured, she was a lot wiser and more cautious now.

While they rarely articulate it as well as women, many men, to be happy, like to feel needed by their partners. For Steven, as he learns from Trisha and Melinda and then Renee, being needed makes him feel important and helps define him in the traditional male role of provider and protector. He feels even heroic. But there is another reason why men covet this role. Like women who tend to feel secure with partners who remind them of their fathers, many men will subconsciously seek out women who have many of the qualities of their mothers. Men want to be not just needed, but loved, nurtured, forgiven, indulged, and appreciated—all without really verbalizing it. They don't want to seem like "babies"—such neediness conflicts with the ideal of stoical masculinity—yet the quest for female approval is irresistible. This is essentially a man's search for his deepest vulnerability, and a way to deal with that vulnerability by finding the right connection, the right safety net, even the elusive Holy Grail that we call unconditional love.

Nurturing, which implies not just caring for someone but a bond of total trust and openness, is no small issue for men. Freud observed that "no one who has seen a baby sinking back satiated from the breast and falling asleep with flushed cheeks and a blissful smile can escape the reflection that this picture persists as a prototype of the expression of sexual satisfaction in later life." Freud's explanation of sexual fulfillment illuminates a larger point about happiness. In the first months of life, happiness is synonymous with unconditional love, from infant to mother and mother to infant. Each needs the other to be fulfilled. As the demands of life intrude, love inevitably becomes conditional. For many men and women, what follows is a lifetime search for partners who will bring them back, as close as possible, to that idealized state of unconditional acceptance. Steven, who had a trusting and open relationship with his mother, seeks the same from Renee. That's why introducing Renee to his mother and being pleased that the two "were a lot alike" makes him happy.

deferred to Renee's reasons for not getting married. I wanted Renee, so I thought I would wait till I had my degree and a job. I wanted to make her happy. But with Renee in school full-time, we soon settled into a routine that I found frustrating. I had begun working in real estate and had no problem attracting clients. Suddenly I was making good money. It was time to get married, I told her proudly. But Renee kept adding qualifications. She wanted to finish school, wanted us to know each other inside out, and wanted Joey to get closer to me. Then she suggested a certain type of engagement ring. I told her I would love to give that ring to her but I couldn't afford it just yet. Renee insisted the ring was an important statement—it proved my commitment to her—so she would wait. Clearly, she didn't want to marry me. I wouldn't figure out why for another year.

Time passed. Every day I was growing more confident about my work and the prospects of a solid financial future. Renee seemed to be on cruise control. She graduated from college but she was no closer to tying the knot with me. If anything, she wanted to slow things down. I think, looking back, that she saw my growing confidence, my interaction with new clients, including single women, and felt threatened. She was beginning not to trust me. She was becoming defensive. She tried to make me jealous by talking about guys she had met in college, but after my experiences with Trisha and Melinda, I had built up immunity to jealousy. Renee would also find reasons not to have sex with me, as if she thought that would make me more dependent on her. But all it did was make me angry. Whenever I suggested that she had a problem with sex, and maybe it had something to do with trust, she would accuse me of insecurity and selfishness.

What Renee didn't realize was that the more defensive and distrusting she grew, the less attractive she was to me. But I had a hard time telling her. By nature, I don't like confrontation or delivering bad news. I think I got that quality from my mom. It's one of my major weaknesses: I have trouble getting my emotions out—especially my anger—in a constructive way. I don't want to get out of control like my father, get drunk, and blow up at somebody. At this time, Renee and I were also having serious discussions about Joey: how he should be raised, forms of discipline, activities to do together. I pointed out that while Renee was a great mother in many ways, she was spoiling Joey by not enforcing some system of chores,

often letting him get away with petulant behavior. That upset
Renee. She reminded me that Joey was her child. I suddenly
remembered what my friends had told me. She thought I was
attacking her for being a bad mother, but I was only trying to
give her another perspective.

Rather than argue with Renee, I would just leave the house.
That always made her furious. I didn't realize then how deep
Renee's fears of abandonment ran. The more I learned about
her ex-husband—he was the one who initiated the divorce—
and her previous boyfriends who had also split with her, I
began to see how fragile Renee was. However, instead of this
making me love her more, which was my usual response to a
woman who was in need, I was getting turned off. Perhaps I
was too conscious of my own needs. Renee was impressing me
now as someone who, because of her fears, was becoming so
self-protecting that she was giving nothing back to me. It got to
a point where I couldn't say anything that was even slightly
critical of her or Joey.

The issue about how to raise Joey came up repeatedly. I
began to see something in Renee that I hadn't noticed in the
beginning. Joey was Renee's security blanket. He was the one
male in her life who would never reject her, and she didn't
want anything to jeopardize that relationship. If Joey and I
spent a lot of time together, I think Renee was afraid I might do
something to pull him away from her. Little arguments began
to mushroom into bigger ones. My emphasis was on exposing
Joey to the real world; not harshly, like my father had done
with me, but with plenty of support. Renee, on the other hand,
wanted to protect Joey from anything that she was afraid of.
And Renee, it would turn out, had lots of fears.

At some point I began to withdraw emotionally. I wasn't
making any progress in the relationship. I felt I knew Renee as
well as I'd known any woman in my life. There was a lot to love

about her, but she hadn't made the same effort to get to understand me, or value what I had to say. I felt taken for granted. After four years together, I told Renee I was giving up too much of myself, too much of my freedom, in order to make her happy. She wasn't making me happy back. I was particularly frustrated in trying to help her with Joey. Renee was teary, and then in the blink of an eye she was furious. Hadn't I promised her that I loved her and wanted to marry her? she asked. This implied a deep level of commitment that, morally, I wasn't allowed to break. I was dumbfounded. I had tried to marry her but she kept putting me off. How long was I supposed to wait? It didn't matter what I argued back. Renee was convinced that by breaking up I was betraying her and her trust, just like all the other men in her life.

I know I made things worse when I started seeing another woman, but why would I hang around Renee if she was only making me feel bad about myself? And, intentionally or not, she was good at that. When Renee found out about this new woman in my life, she said I had broken my promise of commitment to her. I had taken advantage. I was letting Joey down. And hadn't she been the one to push me to get my college degree and go into real estate? Renee wouldn't stop. I began to feel terrible. The amazing thing about guilt is that it really works. If you're bombarded with it enough, you're inclined to surrender. And women can dish it out more effectively than men. Call it a method of control. It's such an effective weapon because a lot of men don't know how to deflect it.

Renee and I stayed apart for about three months before reconciling. A year later we bought a house together and most of the time now we get along well. But I sense a strong undercurrent that still threatens to pull us apart. Renee remains riddled with little fears. Driving too close to another car on the freeway makes her anxious. If someone doesn't pay her a compliment at a party she is anxious. When I don't give her credit for the housework that she's done she gets anxious. If Joey is a few minutes late coming home after school she is anxious. You could say we both have validation issues, but Renee's seem more extreme and complicated. Or maybe she just has an anxiety disorder. One thing is I always try to help her, talk her through her problems, but she doesn't always listen.

One of Renee's biggest fears seems to be sex. Despite our honeymoon period when we first met, it's become clear she doesn't enjoy physical intimacy as much as I do. This drives me crazy sometimes. One time I brought home a couple of soft-porn videos, hoping this might get her in the mood. I hid the videos in my desk, waiting for the right moment to bring them out. But Renee discovered them on her own and exploded at me. She said Joey might have found them instead of her, did I ever think of that? And why would she ever want to watch porn? All porn meant was the exploitation of women. She said she was totally turned off by what I'd done. I couldn't get past her fury. When Renee is mad at me and withholds sex, it serves a dual purpose: it punishes me, and gets her off the hook.

There is another reason for choosing partners who remind us of our caregivers, even when we recognize their imperfections. There is the hope we can change them, or they will change themselves, into an idealized version of our caregivers. For Steven, he would like Renee to be the nurturing, caring, understanding, and accepting person his mother was. Renee's explosion over his porno stash may reveal her fear of intimacy, but also Steven's discomfort at her judgment. Why can't she understand, like his mom would have, he thinks, that he's only trying to help her? Steven wants to deal with Renee's anxiety and fear issues—he wants to make her better—in order to also feel good about himself. But Renee is her own person and needs to deal with her issues in her own way. When the transformation inevitably doesn't happen, and his whole effort backfires, Steven feels like a failure.

Their breakdown in communication ultimately gets channeled into fights over sex. "When Renee is mad at me and withholds sex, it serves a dual purpose: it punishes me, and gets her off the hook," Steven says. Perhaps what he's really saying is that by depriving him of sex, Renee inflicts the ultimate wound on a man because her rejection touches on so many nerves: it renders him powerless, rekindles adolescent anger, denies him intimacy and validation, and mocks his definition of masculinity where the man wants to be not only a great lover but the problem solver. When one partner attacks the other on sexual grounds, he or she is expressing discontent and deep frustration that other forms of communication have broken down. But it can also work the other way. When two partners are not connecting sexually, it can lead to a communication breakdown on all levels, and ultimately falling out of love.

Steven expresses classic male/female differences when it comes to sex and intimacy. For most women, their sexual behavior reflects their feelings about the relationship; their desire for sex grows as the relationship grows. For most men, the need for sex comes first, before they will let the relationship grow. As psychologists have pointed out, for men, sex creates good relationship feelings. For women, good relationship feelings create their desire and interest in sex.

Steven and Renee are in a power struggle. Running out on a fight with Renee, as Steven often does, is not uncommon for men. This "cut and run" strategy is not just because men don't like confrontation or emotional pain. It's a male way of showing control. It's also a way men deny their dependency and vulnerability issues. While they secretly want dependency, and to be open and honest, men have to feel totally safe when these critical subjects come up.

Many men like Steven end up blindsided in a relationship because it almost always starts out on a high note. At first the woman comes across as sexy, sweet, understanding, giving, and caring, as Renee does. Based on first impressions, men would like to believe women as a gender are delighted to be givers and pleasers just because that's what women do. But women give and please in order to be accepted. Once accepted, they want to be listened to, and they want their own power. In addition, in Renee's case, behind her façade of sweetness and kindness, resentment may be building over feelings of loss of self and of being controlled by Steven, or by men in general. Women may suppress these feelings for years, but when they come flooding out, men are often surprised and wonder where those feelings came from. They wonder whatever happened to the woman they fell in love with, the one who was so giving and caring. The problem for men like Steven is they take too much for granted. If they stop paying attention to a woman's emotions after they fall in love, a relationship has no direction to go but south. Men may secretly want to be nurtured, but women do too.

Renee is a beautiful woman with a great personality, but once anyone lets fear rule his or her life, you can't sustain a successful relationship. I've told Renee several times I'd be happy to go to therapy with her. There has to be some reason she's leery of sex and has other anxieties. If I'm being the unreasonable one, if I'm bullying her, or I'm doing something else wrong—maybe that "buck and doe" metaphor is still subconsciously ruling my life—I'm open to finding out. But Renee refuses to get help. The problem is never her or us, she implies. It's me. I'm too pushy, too critical. I'm overwhelming her, she says, and that's why she retreats. But when I back off, she doesn't change or have any motive to change. She retreats, all right, into her fearful state. It's so frustrating to see this. Ultimately, I feel inadequate for not being able to do something to make her happy.

When I talk to Renee about having our own child, she balks. One is enough, she says. I would really like to have a child, but if not, at least I want to share responsibility for Joey. One role a man is supposed to assume in a relationship is that of the father. I want to be a good father. I certainly want to be a more sensitive and caring father than mine was to me. But Renee keeps pushing me back. It's as if Joey was a movie or a book that she alone created, and she retains all rights to him. How do you respect someone if she doesn't respect you enough to grant you equal parenting powers with "her" son? And if you don't respect her, how do you stay in love with her?

Renee's hang-up about sex is also troubling to me. Maybe it all ties in with her lack of trust of me with Joey. Intimacy is all about trust, isn't it? Renee always tries to work around our lack of sex by offering romantic solutions—we could just cuddle, or take a hike in the mountains, or go dancing. I like to do all those things—romance is fine—but they're not a substitute for sexual intimacy. Sex makes me feel good about myself. I want to be a great lover just like I want to be a great father. I want to be appreciated not only for my physical skills but for my ability to communicate on an emotional level. Sex is one way I can show my emotions without having to be the master code breaker. Without a commitment to physical intimacy from her, I don't think my relationship with Renee has "parity." Something will always be out of balance. I won't feel that she loves me the way I love her.

When Steven urges Renee to come to grips with her sexuality, that means digging into her painful past. According to Steven, Renee has put herself into a box that feels safe, but what she's keeping out are the fears she needs to deal with. She not only hurts herself, he says, but passes those fears on to her son by being overly protective of him. If they feel insecure, or put the role of mother ahead of everything else, women can easily hide behind their children. A child becomes a huge security blanket. As Steven points out, a son is the one male in a woman's life that, deep down, will never reject her. Men should be sympathetic to a partner seeking validation from her child, but when the child becomes her main source of approval and emotional satisfaction, it may be a red flag. Steven wonders why he should give all of himself to Renee if she is holding her emotions back from him. Perhaps Renee picks up on Steven's attitude and perceives it as a threat, which makes her even more cautious. She's never going to entrust Joey to Steven's care if she doesn't first trust Steven. If he could learn to be more assertive, calmly and honestly saying what's on his mind, and less inclined to "cut and run," he could fulfill his leadership role that he desires in his relationship with both her and Joey.

After Steven has his affair, then reconciles with Renee and tells her about it, he is acting on the male delusion that women will always appreciate and respect a man's honesty. Women have another way of viewing and communicating the truth. When Renee says Steven is "oversexed," or when she gets upset with his porn stash, this is her way of saying that she's still hurt over his affair. Renee feels, as many women might, that Steven wouldn't have found another woman if he really loved her. That's her truth. Men need to acknowledge not just the difference in how genders communicate but how different their realities are. Women cannot be talked out of their perceptions and experiences with male "logic."

Men and women can fall out of love when they lose respect for their partners. For Steven, when Renee doesn't trust him to help her raise Joey, or when she's no longer interested in sex and won't explore or explain the reasons, he loses respect for her. From Renee's point of view, she may lose respect for Steven for always trying to solve her problems and not giving her credit for her efforts.

Does Steven really know what women feel about sex? The behavior of a lot of women is influenced not just by their personal histories but popular culture. From MTV videos to movies to sitcoms to fashion ads—most women flaunt their sexuality. It's assumed by men that this is one of their power and pleasure centers, that in revealing their sexuality they know exactly what they're doing, and that sex is important to them. Yet, behind bedroom doors, there may be deep anxiety. A lot of women, like Renee, can be reluctant to share their fears because they think they'll be letting down their partners. They'll also be letting down themselves by not measuring up to what a woman is "supposed to be." The same goes for motherhood. Popular culture would have us believe there is no higher calling for a woman than to be a loving and devoted mother. Renee receives a heavy dose of validation by always being there for Joey. But in Steven's view, Renee is overprotective and overcontrolling of her son and, in the process, shutting Steven out of her life. If their relationship is to grow, Renee needs to address her fears as much as Steven needs to give Renee the time and space to do it.

What happens if the power struggle between Steven and Renee is resolved and Steven gets the sexual intimacy that he wants? In his relationships with Trisha and Melinda, they both initially seemed vulnerable and fragile, but in the end he found out he was the fragile one. The truth is that once a man becomes dependent on a woman emotionally and sexually, he tends to fill up his emotional vacuum with her. She becomes his port in every storm. In so doing he becomes vulnerable. If a man doesn't have his own world of empowerment, and something goes awry in his relationship, the pain of what will be perceived as betrayal becomes a significant problem. According to Frank Pittman in *Man Enough,* rejection by a woman can trigger such overwhelming anxiety and pain that a man becomes desperate to win her back. But the reverse can also be true. Being deprived of physical and emotional intimacy, as we'll see in the next story, is a reason some men withdraw their love completely and look for another woman.

3

Roddy's Story

Sex is hardly ever just about sex.
—Shirley MacLaine

Meet Roddy, thirty-three years old, divorced, a small busi-
nessman/entrepreneur who is not afraid to put in long
hours. The oldest of three brothers, he enjoys boyish good
looks, reddish brown hair, a slim build, and a contemplative
face that comes to life every so often with a knowing smile or a
self-deprecating laugh. While his personality is laid-back, he is
observant and intuitive about what goes on around him. He describes himself as thoughtful and soft-spoken as well as hardworking, and someone who always keeps his temper. He also
believes he's a good judge of character, but admits to having
blind spots about himself. Honesty and directness are what he
respects most in his friends. He was married for almost three
years to Laura, a pretty, petite woman with deep-set eyes and
long red hair, and then endured a traumatic divorce. Though
dating again and, in fact, thinking of living with his new girlfriend, he is still hurt by his divorce, still analyzing the chain of

events that unraveled his happiness. While he says he is no longer in love with Laura, they live in the same city and get together sometimes as friends.

In Roddy's case, one reason he fell out of love, he says, was that he felt deceived by Laura. Laura levels the same charge at Roddy, believing that it was his involvement with another woman that sabotaged their marriage and pushed her out of love. Roddy has a different take on his extramarital affair. Looking back today, he believes that neither he nor Laura looked deeply enough into their pasts to understand why deceit and abandonment were such deadly trip wires for each of them. At Laura's core, he says, was a mixture of fear and confusion about who she really was, and an inability to be honest and forthright about her past.

When he first met Laura, Roddy was in his late twenties and she was five years older. It was a tough time in his life. Only months before, his father had passed away unexpectedly, just two years after retiring from teaching at the local high school. He and his brothers did their best to console and take care of their mother, because that's what responsible sons always do. It's a definition of being a man, he thought. In retrospect, however, he wonders why he and his brothers had no one to console them. "It would have been nice to have support," he says. "I know men are supposed to be emotionally tougher than women, but while I can't speak for my brothers, I didn't feel tough at all." Roddy admits he was in pain for very clear reasons—unfinished conversations with his father, regret for their past misunderstandings, and empathy for a man who after years of hard work deserved something better than an early grave. He thinks of his father frequently.

Despite our ups and downs, and a lot of frustration in trying to communicate, I always felt close to my father. He was born into a prominent Latin American family and admittedly was spoiled as a boy. One of his problems was, because he was overindulged by his parents, he never learned to be truly independent. When he had a problem, it was too easy for him to go to someone else to solve it. He never fully learned how to set boundaries, or to deal with conflict, or use his own judgment. Ultimately, in his twenties, he rejected his parents' lifestyle and came to the United States, where he met my mom. One of the upsides of indulgent, coddling parents, however, is that you're surrounded by love and affection, and you keep that love inside you. My mom fell in love with Dad, she said, "because he was the most sensitive and gentle man" she had ever met, and she "could connect with the childlike innocence he never gave up." My mom was terrific—gentle, calm, and just as sweet as Dad in many ways—and to this day I feel very close to her. My brothers and I could relate to Dad's childlike innocence as well, and no doubt his ability to understand teenagers made him a great teacher both for us and his high-school students. He was bright and knowledgeable on so many subjects. We had terrific intellectual discussions as we grew up. We were definitely a family of talkers.

However, because he never learned to deflect stress or set boundaries for himself, there was another side to Dad. He could easily blow up and fill the house with his anger. All of us dreaded the moment when he came home from a long day of teaching. You could just see that expression of defeat or exhaustion in his eyes. As a child I was sometimes scared of him, but as an adult I felt very sorry for him—he was so bottled up—and to this day I make a conscious effort never to give in to my anger or to try to intimidate anyone with it. I simply put up a wall with people who are out of control or are abusive to me. I empathize with them just as I empathized with Dad, but when someone is out of control, I know to keep my cool and walk away.

For a month after Dad's death, I was in a stupor and kept to myself. In my mind I kept going over conversations that I wished I had had with him. I felt we had so much unfinished business. About two months later I began to casually date several interesting, fun women. The ability to laugh and relax and forget my pain was great therapy. One night I ran into a group of women at one of the downtown clubs, and made eye contact with Laura. I had no idea who she was, but something just clicked. No doubt for most people the initial attraction to someone is physical, and maybe you're inclined to fall in love with someone whose looks are roughly at the same level as yours. I'm not Robert Redford, but I think I'm better looking than most men, and likewise Laura stood out from her girlfriends. An hour later Laura and I met by coincidence at another club. I joked with her that this must be fate. We ended up sitting together for half the night, and she reminded me it was Valentine's Day and asked if it wasn't appropriate that I give her a kiss. The request was such a surprise that I instinctively complied, and the kiss lived up to all expectations. That one kiss began a journey of romance with all the typical cat-and-mouse play of any early relationship. At first Laura thought I was a "player" and wanted little to do with me, but after several lunches and dinners I convinced her otherwise: that I found her interesting and pretty and sophisticated, and that I wanted to pursue a relationship.

I am a great talker and listener because I need to communicate. All my life, receiving and giving information has been crucial to my happiness, or just my ability to function. One of my pet peeves in business is people who don't return voice mail or e-mail promptly. They just sit on your message, like it isn't important, having no sensitivity that it may be important to you. My parents had an open, candid relationship and it rubbed off on me. I want a woman to know exactly where I'm coming from, who I am, and what I want for my future. I don't blurt it out all at once, obviously, but I move in that direction in any relationship—it's part of the chase for me. If you can't be totally candid with someone, what's the ultimate point of the relationship?

Because of all the emotions and conflicts my father's death dredged up in me, I was perhaps overly talkative with Laura as I got to know her in the next month or two. She was a great listener—empathetic, curious, and absorbed by my insights, even if she disagreed with some of them. I began to fall in love. I told Laura about my previous two-year relationship with a woman named Becky, a very independent, self-reliant woman with whom I had gone into business. The relationship had started out strong, but working and living with the same person put too much stress on us. It was painful—both the end of the relationship and my helplessness to change it. I like to think that I can fix problems. It's one of my roles, my definition of responsibility and, I suppose, manhood. But it didn't work with Becky. I couldn't fix a relationship that had become drained of romance and intrigue.

Laura told me that her five-year relationship with her boyfriend had recently ended because he didn't give her the time and attention she needed. He would work at his job all day and get lost on his computer at night. She felt taken for granted. She tried to tell him how she felt but he blew her off. I empathized because this was how Becky ultimately treated me. Laura also told me that at her age it was time for her to be with someone who was real and serious and could make an honest, lasting commitment. She admitted she felt the pressure of being in her thirties and not wanting to be left behind. Not that she ever used the term "old maid," but I think for most women, not having a solid, permanent relationship makes them feel something is wrong with them, that they're a failure or an outcast. At least this is true where I live. Maybe in large urban centers where women are more assertive and independent it's different.

When Laura said she wanted a commitment from me, I took that to mean marriage, even children. At first she was evasive about it, but she finally admitted that yes, a stable, loving marriage was what she coveted. My point of view was slightly different. I thought marriage was a historical institution of dubious relevance, but out of respect for the woman I was in love with, I told Laura I would honor her wishes. As for children, I don't have the ego that demands I reproduce. Laura was also mixed on having children—one minute yes, the next, "What's the hurry?" The reasons for her hesitancy only became clear after we were married.

The way Roddy and Laura met is crucial in understanding a masculine blind spot about relationships. They ran into each other at a club, made eye contact, and, according to Roddy, things just clicked. She kissed him and that sealed it for him, thus beginning his "journey of romance." Because most men lack real relationship skills, they are predisposed to believing in magical events, particularly when those events are accompanied by instant gratification of their need for validation. Roddy, still grieving over his dad's death, and troubled by his worth as a dutiful son, had a strong need to feel good about himself.

The seeds for future problems were planted when Roddy agreed to marry Laura even though he intuited he wasn't ready for this commitment. He said, "I wanted to honor her wishes." At that point, he should have insisted they both first work through their issues, rather than trying to be honorable or make Laura happy. The man acting as the "rescuer" is a great male fantasy. Many men have the misconception that if they give women what they want, even when it doesn't feel good to them, that love will bloom. The opposite may be true. Women can interpret male generosity as a kind of control—"I did something for you, now you owe me something"—and feel either powerless or turned off. Also, by accommodating Laura's desire to get married, Roddy may have been suppressing his own fear and resistance to the idea of commitment. By following a purely romantic path, trusting in love, as a lot of men initially do, Roddy is setting himself up for problems down the road.

We dated for two years before moving in together. Laura was a beverage manager at a hotel, earned a good salary, and worked long hours. She had an incredible work ethic. I had my own business and my hours were equally long, but it was fun to meet at night and laugh and be silly over our crazy days. Being a small-business owner was often a struggle, handling unending expenses and worrying about cash flow. It meant lots of anxiety some months. My determination to succeed perhaps camouflaged an even deeper anxiety. Why I was so motivated to be a success? I think a lot of it was to impress my dead father.

In addition to my own determination, Laura gave me confidence that I would succeed. Besides moral support and our mutual physical attraction, Laura had this style and poise, this presence that I gravitated to. We also had stimulating conversations on lots of subjects. But I thought our deepest connection was a childlike bond, like the one my parents had— open, innocent, respectful, and candid. While growing up, even before puberty, I made friends with girls more easily than I did with boys. For me, establishing a friendship with a woman is a critical part of a growing relationship. My definition of friendship was to hold nothing back from the other person.

I let Laura know right away how important I thought communication was. I told her being in love with someone is not enough to sustain a long-term relationship, let alone a marriage. (I had fallen in love with three other women, and none of those relationships endured—either because I was immature, or the women had needs that I couldn't meet.) In addition to love, I suggested to Laura, there has to be the deepest respect for your partner, for his or her thought processes, moods, will, and opinions, no matter how different they are from yours. You love someone for who he or she is as an individual.

Laura and I got into an almost Socratic dialog about this. Respect, we both agreed, is the opposite of control. Control in relationships, I believe, actually stems from the feudal idea of property rights and ownership. It's just been romanticized by the media. Think of Hallmark cards, the "I am yours and you are mine" concept—as if you own each other. I have seen men and women find ways, large and small, unconscious and conscious, to control their partners. It's almost a priority with some people, maybe because our lives are so chaotic and we live in an age where nothing feels certain after 9/11. It just doesn't work in a relationship. No one likes being told what to do or how to feel. Laura asked if I would ever try to control her in any way. I told her no, never, and she promised the same to me.

I also told Laura that I thought respect should automatically be given to your partner, to everyone in your life, until the person betrays that respect. This holds particularly true for a parent to his or her child. That's where it all starts: if you don't respect your children, they'll grow up not respecting themselves or others. Trust, on the other hand, has to be earned. That may seem like a subtle distinction, but to me it's crucial that you don't give someone your trust until he or she earns it. Laura wanted to know what it would take to earn my trust. I told her just to be honest and open and uncontrolling with me, just as I would be with her.

Sometimes I wasn't sure if Laura just found me incredibly amusing and eccentric or, as she later said, I was the most "different" and "interesting" guy she had ever dated. It reminded me a little of why my mother was attracted to my father. Laura certainly knew my thoughts and emotions well. I didn't hold back. She also let me know what she liked about me. Besides my confidence and work ethic, there was something stable and solid about me. She liked that I was always there for her. I wasn't coy or into hiding; I didn't duck any issue. I could be counted on.

In turn, I was drawn to her independence and self-reliance and her strong sense of self. This, by the way, is almost always the type of woman that attracts me, and no doubt my mom is a model for this. I feel that choosing a partner with those qualities validates the same qualities in me. I also enjoy, to a point, nurturing my partner if she needs some guidance. Maybe that's the male side of me, the one that has to fix problems. But just to a point. I am not an enabler. I particularly don't care for women who are overly dependent on a man, too needy, or have too many problems. That's why I'd fallen out of love with previous women. For me, independence in each partner is critical for sustaining a relationship.

Roddy, by not having a chance to prove himself to his father before he died, may have a stronger need than most men for giving and receiving information. From his female partners (who, in terms of communication, become a surrogate for his father), he wants to know that he is important and that his feelings and thoughts count. If he's kept in the dark by somebody, he finds it difficult to trust them. He spells out that need to Laura quite early in their relationship. If she doesn't meet his expectations, however, his own fears and projections will probably take over. Perhaps his insistence that each partner in a relationship be strong and independent is Roddy's way of not getting hurt whenever his partners let him down. By embracing a defensive mind-set, however, and setting up so many relationship rules, Roddy might be increasing the odds for failure for him and Laura.

aura told me she had been pretty independent since childhood, but she didn't give me a lot of details unless I pressed her. She just wasn't as forthcoming as I was about my past. She did tell me that when she was about two years old her mother divorced her father, and Laura ended up living with her mom, a freewheeling hippie who eventually gave birth to two additional children by two different men. When she was old enough, it fell on Laura's shoulders to fix meals, give baths, and supervise homework for her younger half siblings. Frustrated by not having a life of her own, and fighting a lot with her mom, Laura moved out when she was around twelve. She stayed with her dad in Washington, D.C., until she was eighteen and then went to college. Life with Dad wasn't much easier than it was with her mom. He chased women, sometimes almost as young as Laura, just like her mother chased men. When I asked for more details, Laura would become evasive, and while I was more than curious, out of our mutual pledge of respect for one another's privacy, I backed off.

Even with the few facts of her past that she did provide, Laura's longing for a solid, stable relationship made all the sense in the world, and I wanted to give her that. Before we moved in together, and later, when we decided to get married, I told her I intended to be faithful and loyal to her, and hoped she would be to me. I went on to say that I hoped we could meet each other's needs. Even though I thought they were obvious, because they would be the same as Laura's, I listed mine: affection, companionship, emotional and physical intimacy, trust, openness, and having fun together. Laura agreed. But if somehow things didn't jibe for us for a period, I told her, if one or both of us, for example, ended up having an affair, I thought it wasn't the end of the world so long as we were open and honest with each other and fixed the problem. I certainly wasn't intending to have an affair when Laura and I talked. My dad, as far as I know, never had one. But I knew many men who did "stray," and the reasons could be quite complex.

The two years Laura and I dated before moving in together were sexually quite incredible. Fireworks sex, spontaneous sex, playful sex, postargument/healing sex. Sex in bed, sex in the shower, sex on the kitchen counter. Sex that means freedom and commitment and the ultimate trust builder for a couple. I couldn't imagine being any happier physically with a woman. Once we moved in together, however, there were some subtle changes. Our daily lives, occupied with work, were the same, but nights felt different. For one thing, the sex began to wane. Not from any lack of desire on my part, but Laura often complained of fatigue from work or said she wasn't in the mood. In addition, the stimulating conversations we'd had in our courtship were largely replaced with dull, repetitive exchanges about topical subjects. Was Laura somehow changing? Losing interest in me? Was there a problem I didn't know about? When I asked what was going on, she assured me that everything was fine and that she just needed her space. She reminded me that I'd promised to respect her boundaries. She was happy in her life and in love with me, she said, and everything was wonderful.

But I wasn't sure how wonderful things were. Something felt askew. Laura wasn't being open and honest with me, I thought, and I suddenly had some new insights. Except for the quite clear goal of a stable and lasting marriage—and the emotional satisfaction she didn't get from her previous boyfriend—Laura didn't seem to have any other dreams or goals. Whenever I asked her what she wanted out of life, she had no clear answer, except for vague references to starting a family sometime in the future, while I had definite financial, material, and emotional goals. Laura suddenly struck me as adrift. She seemed to live off her spontaneous emotions, moment by moment, day by day, reacting more than planning. I got this feeling she had gotten what she wanted from me—a pledge to marry and settle down—and she wasn't prepared to delve into her life any further than that.

I was disappointed because we'd talked a lot about the great adventure that life was, the importance of taking risks, self-discovery, growing, and changing together. When I pushed her about that promise, Laura reaffirmed that she wanted to grow as a human being, but her words felt hollow. Maybe she did want to grow, but it felt like she was putting that responsibility on me, to lead and guide her. Was she simply burned out from a childhood of too much responsibility? Was I supposed to be the mentor or father she never had? This whole possible redefining of roles made me nervous about getting married. What was I getting into?

In the end, I pushed my doubts away and remembered my pledge to Laura of total respect, including for our differences. The wedding day arrived, we were with our closest friends, and Laura came into her own. My fears vanished. I'd never seen Laura so happy, and I told her so. She blushed and agreed. We danced the night away. Going to our hotel room afterwards, we had decent but not great sex. I was a little surprised, but I thought Laura was just wiped out from the day. The sad reality was that we did not make love again for another month, and then maybe only five or six times that entire year. Nothing came close to the passion and openness we'd experienced in the first year of our courtship. Laura seemed to fall back into a niche of mysterious self-absorption and emotional disengagement. At first I ignored the pattern, thinking we would adjust to marriage together. Instead, the distance between us grew. I was increasingly upset, and kept pushing Laura for answers. Was there something I'd done to her, or hadn't done for her? Was there something in her past she hadn't told me? Had she been abused by one of her parents?

Laura denied there was any abuse, but agreed she would see a therapist. Just to please me, she said, not because she was convinced anything was "wrong" with her. In fact, she added, she was going to prove that everything was normal. After several visits with a therapist she announced that things were as she expected: maybe she was a wee bit tense, adjusting to a new work schedule at the hotel, but otherwise everything was fine. She was normal, just as she'd thought. Okay, great, I said, but why were we still not having sex? If it made me happy, Laura answered, she'd buy some sex toys for us, and maybe that would bring some sizzle back. She bought the toys but never used them. Our sex life remained on life support. On top of that, I was struggling with my business, and I told Laura how much pressure I felt. Instead of being sympathetic, as she was in the beginning of our relationship, she got defensive. Her business days were just as rough as mine, she said, and I should stop feeling sorry for myself. I had learned that it was not in Laura's character to admit that she did many things wrong, much less that something was her fault. But I wasn't blaming her for anything, I was just looking for some empathy.

It also became clear to me that introspection and delving for psychological answers were not Laura's strong suit. Searching for answers meant there had to be problems, and Laura didn't want to admit there were any problems. While she found it interesting for me to talk about my past, I wasn't allowed into hers beyond the fragments she'd shared before we were married.

The more I pressed her with my frustration and unhappiness, the more defensive she grew. She finally said she just didn't see why sex was so important to me or to men in general. Sex was way overrated, she insisted. She began to ape the attitude of popular culture, citing commercials and sitcoms where men are portrayed as klutzes and buffoons, or immature adolescents who are perpetually horny. Women, on the other hand, are almost always depicted as clever, resourceful, sophisticated, in control, and skilled problem solvers. That's how Laura saw herself.

From *The Honeymooners* and *I Love Lucy* to *Married with Children* and *Everybody Loves Raymond,* the stereotype persists that men may think they are the dominant partner in a relationship, including sexually, but in addition to being outsmarted by their women, they are more prone to get in trouble, and it's a woman who inevitably bails them out. Basically, this is what Laura believed. I was immature and overly demanding, even a troublemaker. She also thought most men, including me, were clueless about their more complex wives.

I couldn't believe I was hearing this from Laura. It was as if she'd turned on me. One thing was true. She was complex, and I'm the first to admit I didn't understand her completely. But that was because she didn't provide the information to allow me to understand. I told her that most men are not as they are portrayed on television. We are not all testosterone-spewing adolescents or selfish cads. We have mature emotions and honest needs, especially when it comes to intimacy. On television, the topic of intimacy seems to embarrass most men. They either joke about it or hide from it. Yet that wasn't me. My emotions were on my sleeve. I was deeply frustrated, feeling vulnerable, and I wanted answers from Laura.

For a while, Laura insisted that simple romance should satisfy me. What was wrong with just cuddling and holding hands, she asked. I like romancing a woman, but ultimately it's not true intimacy. I also explained to Laura that to reject a man sexually was a blow to his self-esteem, and if I'm struggling with my business and I'm worried about failure, sex takes on an even greater importance in terms of validation and support.

If she hid her past from Roddy, did Laura think he simply wouldn't care? Roddy interprets her behavior as manipulative and controlling, accusations that would never have arisen had Laura been more open, or just sensitive to Roddy's sexual needs. Are a lot of women naïve about what sex really means to men? The cliché of "getting his rocks off" or "pulling a control trip" masks the importance to a man of tenderness, acceptance, and trust. Being held in a woman's arms at the right moment can be a subconscious reconnection to childhood and the feeling of being safe with one's mother. Good sex is also a promise that one is holding nothing back from his or her partner. Men may have a hard time asking for it, but if they don't get enough intimacy, over time it's a reason to fall out of love. Laura suggests to Roddy that cuddling or holding hands or kissing is all the intimacy she needs, but she doesn't understand that for most men romance is only a prelude to the special and deeper intimacy that sex confers. (For older couples, often the reverse is true: sex becomes less important as other acts of physical intimacy are substituted.)

Roddy's anger at being rejected sexually may be tied to non-sexual rejection during other vulnerable periods in his life. Perhaps the death of his father became an abandonment issue that he projected onto Laura. Roddy did his best, as always, to suppress his anger and frustration at being rejected by Laura. Getting into any kind of argument is dicey for Roddy, as it is for a lot of men, because they simply don't know how they will react, and they fear losing control. For both men and women, a harangue from a partner is often absorbed and tolerated out of the habit of silence they first learned as children because they were warned "not to talk back." Down deep, however, in the basement of resentment and anger, dwells a child who needs to speak up.

I reminded Laura many times how much I craved information, that it was part of the foundation of our relationship. Reluctantly, she finally told me specific stories about her parents, particularly her mom. Laura would come home from elementary school with friends, only to find her mother walking around the house stark naked because she believed nudity was "a natural state." Her mother made no apologies to a badly humiliated Laura. There were numerous other incidents of exhibitionism, like bringing home strange men and making love to them while Laura was in the next room. It was the kind of behavior that eventually drove Laura out of the house and to D.C. Exposed to the libertine lifestyle of her dad, dating girls barely older than she was, couldn't have made Laura any more comfortable. And she didn't go into all the stories that were on the tip of her tongue. But it was obvious to me that Laura, down deep, had come to associate sex with shame, lies, and manipulation. She was afraid of sex, I think, because she believed someone who enjoyed it must be dirty or deceitful. Maybe that was already her self-image from our sexually intensive courtship days. I don't know for sure—she never shared with me the sessions with her therapist—but there was a palpable ball of fear in her when it came to intimacy.

When I asked Laura why she hadn't told me earlier about the darker part of her childhood and adolescence, she said she was afraid that I would reject her. But isn't it worse, I asked her, to keep a secret that you've never dealt with? And what about your pledge to be honest with me? Laura said she didn't want to talk about it. She slammed the door on the whole subject. No more discussions about sex, no more talk of seeing a therapist, no more hints of wanting children. All she talked about in the next few months was her work. It was a blanket denial of our intimacy, as if it had never existed.

I began to see that Laura really had issues not only with her parents' lifestyles, but with the fact that she had to be the primary caregiver at a young age for her half siblings. I think she internalized a lot of resentment for being denied the chance to be a carefree child and teenager. As much as she hated being put in that role of responsibility, however, it was the pattern she became comfortable with and carried with her into adulthood. Part of the allure of hard work for Laura was not that she was so confident of her talents or craved independence, I think, but that work offered her the opportunity to get lost emotionally, or to avoid her feelings altogether. In her heart, she may have despised the burden of responsibility, which is why she looked to me for leadership, taking over even little things, including running most of our domestic errands. She wanted a break, a reprieve. When I suggested to Laura the obvious, that she needed to make the connection between her childhood and her current behavior in order to be happy, she became even more defensive. I was trying to control her, she said. I was invading her space. Down deep, she said, I probably hated her.

At this point I didn't know what to think. I wanted to seek out friends for advice, but my friends were also Laura's and I didn't want to embarrass her or us. The sex we once had—the fireworks sex, the knock-over-the-furniture passion—had that just been an act to win me over? What else had Laura been dishonest about? How about her relationship with her former boyfriend? Were her reasons for leaving him—his lack of attention to her—really true? And what about her mixed feelings about having children? Despite a fairly strong maternal instinct, I think Laura was afraid of being challenged not just by the work that kids can be, but by the emotional connection she would have to give them. She would be reminded of her own childhood and playing the role of mother to her half siblings at the expense of her own happiness and freedom. Maybe she was afraid of any deep connection. Did that mean our own relationship was a sham? Despite all our earlier talks and promises to one another, trust did not come easily to Laura. Fear can take over anyone's life, and if you hide it from yourself, maybe you think your partner won't see it either. But the partner always sees it. The partner sees it first. My deepest frustration was that, on the one hand, I was trying to be there for Laura, to help her, to "fix" our problems, but on the other I was supposed to be respectful enough to give her space when she needed it and to accept her moods. The two turned out to be an irreconcilable contradiction.

This all happened within the first year of our marriage. The second year was the final act. I had by now two powerful, conflicting emotions. One was that I was beginning to feel guilty and blame myself for not being able to help Laura. The second was pure anger toward my wife. She was being overly helpless and dependent on me when she should have been solving her own problems. Increasingly, she asked me to run errands, buy stamps, put gas in the car, as if she wasn't capable of doing even the most simple chore. Maybe she was clinically depressed, but how would I know if she didn't get help? In addition, she was making me feel insecure about my sexuality. Had I lost all my physical and sexual attraction? Did she know how she made me feel? No matter how agitated I was, because of my dislike of giving in to my temper, I refused to blow up at her. But I had to do something. I began avoiding Laura by staying out late, lamely telling her I had office work, while in reality I was with friends at clubs. If Laura suspected the truth, she didn't say anything. Maybe she didn't care. Maybe she was already falling out of love with me, as I was with her. Neither of us talked about it.

I'll give you my thoughts on why men have affairs. Usually it's not for control or power, or payback, or that they just can't keep their flies zipped. The emotional connection with your partner just suddenly goes dead, like a phone that's been pulled out of the wall. At least it feels that way, though of course it's not that sudden. There's a buildup of disbelief and frustration as you gradually become strangers to one another. Suddenly you aren't having sex at all, and the intimacy, not to mention trust and respect, between the two of you disappears. There's so much talk about how women are the emotional gender, but when they hold back for whatever reason, when you feel you've been cut off from those emotions, there's nothing you can do about it. You're stranded. Suddenly something snaps inside you and pushes you over the line, and you make the decision to have a relationship with another woman. The first time you do it is a shock to your system. You're filled with guilt and anxiety, which is balanced by an adrenaline rush like no other. The rush of being loved and accepted by someone new, someone who says she understands you and is sympathetic to your problems—that's hard to match. Even if you think you might be making a huge mistake, emotionally you are so starved you will do anything to get your needs met.

Roddy and Laura struggle with the distinction between sex and intimacy. Ideally, sex is not just about validation, but provides one of the deepest emotional connections to another human being. Many men, because they are poor at expressing their emotions, don't follow an act of sex, no matter how passionate it may be, with *talking* about their feelings—and so deny themselves and their partners an even deeper bond. In movies from the forties and fifties, offscreen intercourse ended with the man and woman lying in bed silently dragging on a cigarette. Today, we're more likely to see each partner diplomatically scoring the other's performance. Or maybe they whisper a couple of "I love you's" and go back to watching television. The tyranny of popular culture—the pressure to conform—diminishes the incentive for many couples to think about what works best for them. For some couples, particularly as they age and restructure their relationship, an embrace or cuddling may be more intimate than any sexual act. In a happy, fulfilled relationship, each partner knows not only the right expression of intimacy but also the importance of timing.

When Laura has a minibreakdown and becomes emotionally and sexually estranged, Roddy takes it as a reflection on him, that somehow he's lost his attractiveness, but he also realizes that Laura is probably wrestling with the demons of her past. However, in focusing so much on Laura, Roddy neglects to deal with his own childhood. Though he was careful not to show it to Laura, a lot of pent-up anger spilled out of Roddy as an adult. It first surfaced in the form of criticism of Laura. He gave something to her by marrying her, he thinks, but where is the reciprocity in the form of sexual and emotional satisfaction? Feeling pressured by Roddy, Laura shut down even more, which only gave Roddy more reason to be critical of her and ultimately helped push him into his affair.

Popular culture would have us believe that when a woman

has an affair, it's because she's not getting the attention, affection, and passion she deserves from her partner. That's not to say there's no guilt, remorse, or confusion afterward, but offsetting those emotions is the ability to forgive herself, to seek sympathy and help from friends, or to blame her partner for not satisfying her. However, there is a double standard: when a man has extramarital sex, he's usually perceived as abusing his power, selfishly indulging his lust, betraying his partner's trust, or wreaking havoc on his family.

But as Roddy asserts, despite the double standard, and the shame and guilt many men end up feeling, men have affairs for the very same reason that women do—to obtain that core affection and attention missing from their primary relationships. They want to know they are still deserving of love and that they are not taken for granted. In Roddy's case, in addition to public judgment, he may feel shame when he eventually accepts how Laura's traumatic past inhibited her sexually and emotionally. And, as we'll see, the balancing act of having a secret affair and managing a marriage is like walking a tightrope of dental floss across the Grand Canyon.

On the other hand, I think a lot of men, including myself, are cowards for not telling their wives when they have an affair. But there's a reason, besides not wanting to break up your marriage until you're absolutely sure it's beyond saving. You don't come home and confess because you're afraid of your woman's anger. No doubt this goes back to your mother when she shamed you or punished you. Some women can turn themselves into helpless victims or rageaholics at the drop of a hat.

As I began to stay away at night and meet other women at clubs, I was as subtle as a neon sign. Both men and women can smell someone's marital unhappiness a mile away, and they can exploit it before you know what's happening. But I wanted to be exploited. I was desperate for a connection to someone who would understand me. A lot of women think that men's sexual needs are so simple. I've heard women say, "I just give my husband a blow job once a week and he's happy." I just can't believe that. I don't think those women really understand men and sex, or the men they're with have no grasp of who they are. It's not about sex, per se. It's about intimacy and trust. Men need that just as much as women do.

The woman with whom I became involved, Alice, was more than sympathetic to what I was enduring with Laura. I don't doubt Alice knew what she was doing—putting an even deeper wedge between Laura and me—but I was not into moral judgments. I was so hungry for a physical and emotional connection that I couldn't stop seeing her even if I never stopped feeling guilty about betraying Laura. Night after night I would drown myself in the healing comfort of sex. Sex was this incredible ocean of relief, pleasure, self-discovery, and rejuvenation. For every rush of adrenaline with a new partner, however, there is part of your heart that wants to work things out with your wife. But ultimately it's wishful thinking if she gives no indication of wanting to work things out with you. Laura left me in a vacuum. I didn't even like to refer to what I was doing as "having an affair" because of all the connotations of cheating and deceit. From Laura's point of view, no doubt, my betrayal could only be defined as deceit and cheating. But from my point of view, Laura had deceived and betrayed me first. And I came to have real feelings for Alice that I never had for Laura.

I stayed away from Laura more and more. Sometimes I wouldn't come home at all. Laura had to have known what I was doing but, already schooled in the art of denial, she buried her head further in the sand. Not wanting to provoke conflict

and anger, I fell into the same silence as Laura. Finally, my
relationship with Alice became so obvious that Laura couldn't
ignore it. One night she confronted me, and when I admitted I
was in another relationship, Laura went ballistic, screaming
and threatening me with more than divorce. In retrospect, I
think a lot of her rage was directed at her parents, her half
siblings, at anyone who had let her down in the past. Despite
all the people she might legitimately be disappointed with,
including herself, she laid the blame for my infidelity one
hundred percent on my shoulders. I certainly accepted part of
the blame, for not being more aware of her demons, and not
being more sympathetic, but I threw some of the blame back at
her for her lack of honesty and candor. Back and forth the
spears went, reducing us both to tears.

I don't know how many evenings we had like that before I
moved out. Laura really didn't want to see a therapist again.
She just wanted me out of her life, as if that would solve all her
problems. It was the same drama, the same dilemma we'd
always faced: Laura walling out my need for communication
and sex because it touched a deep nerve of pain from her past,
and me shutting out Laura because there's no hope of reaching
my emotions or intellect through anger and blame.

As we watched our relationship slip away, as much as I
thought I understood my own emotional landscape, I
questioned where my strong need for validation and approval
came from. Your childhood is your best opportunity for building
confidence and loving yourself. If that doesn't happen, I think
sex becomes the alternative for a lot of men, just to prove to
yourself you're not a loser. Were my demands on Laura for
sexual intimacy excessive and unfair because they reflected my
own feelings of inadequacy? I did have my share of anger and
fears while growing up, because I got rebuffed by people who I
thought loved me. My inclination to seek out independent,

strong-willed women like my mother was for a reason. If a woman was secure and confident about herself, I thought, she was less likely to hurt me.

The reality, however, was that while I was attracted to this type of woman, once I got to know her I often found her confidence and bravado were a façade, and just under the surface, as in Laura's case, were problems that had never been dealt with. I got thrust into a role of rescuer that I didn't really want. Ultimately, I got hurt because Laura's unresolved problems became mine, and perhaps my unresolved problems became hers. I am not unaware of the great irony of our relationship. For someone who craves giving and receiving information, I certainly dropped the ball with Laura.

One of Roddy's blind spots was the illusion that in keeping his temper at bay, he would not be "bottled up" like his father. In fact, he too has repressed his anger, despite his almost religious zeal in communicating what he thinks are all his feelings to Laura. As he eventually recognized, just as Laura didn't come clean about her past to him, Roddy wasn't completely honest about his.

Roddy didn't fall out of love with Laura so much as give up on his relationship out of deep frustration. As he looks back on his marriage, what puzzles him most is why Laura withheld her past from him. But perhaps he doesn't understand the power of fear because he hasn't dealt with some of his own childhood issues. Laura may also have felt intimidated when Roddy insisted that she tell him what was "wrong" with her. When Laura finally does talk about the trauma of her adolescence, perhaps it's too late to overcome the damage caused by their loss of intimacy. Much of the self-worth that marriage gave Roddy, making him feel like a winner, is taken away by its demise. Roddy mentions how men turn to women and sex to get away from the fear that they're not attractive or that something is wrong with them. But women and the validation of sex can only cover up so much pain and insecurity. Men need to look more deeply into themselves for real healing.

Laura thinks of Roddy as deceptive for both having his affair and for hiding it from her. What may not be obvious to her and a lot of women is that a man's "habit" of being less than honest, or stretching the truth—a behavior that usually starts in adolescence—is further encouraged by the struggle over control of a relationship. Because control is another (often misguided) definition of masculinity—the perceived male requirement of being in charge—boys, and then men, have a second motive to deceive. Men will often subconsciously exaggerate, deflect the truth, or make excuses in order to keep that feeling of control. What an adolescent male learns as a "survival skill"—self-permission to lie—is soon embedded in his consciousness as acceptable behavior, not just in his relationships, but in other aspects of his life.

When a man or woman cheats, perhaps the other partner needs to be more understanding and forgiving, and not immediately see himself or herself as a victim. The complexity of motives in the "offender" often needs time and therapy to sort out. While revenge may feel good, the Pavlovian rush to judgment and kicking him (or her) out of the house can obscure deeper issues in both partners.

Laura's dramatic and immediate shift from her premarital behavior leaves Roddy deeply frustrated. She owes him a full explanation rather than exploding in rage after depriving him of sex for so long. These are issues that will never be resolved if the cycle of revenge perpetuates itself. "The moment I found out about her affair, I fell out of love with her," is a statement I heard from more than one man. I wonder if what they really meant was that their trust was fragile to begin with, and they had no idea how to repair it, so it was just easier to kill all emotions and start fresh. But not all new relationships fare well. Men on the rebound, still wounded, can be angry and vindictive toward the new women in their lives, or extremely vulnerable and susceptible to falling in love—that's the risk a woman takes.

Unlike Roddy, some men cheat or womanize constantly. These are usually insecure Don Juans seeking to define their masculinity by bedding as many women as possible. One man in his late thirties told me that having sex with as many partners as possible was the only thing that made him feel good. When I suggested that he might see a therapist, he said, "Why look for pain when I have so much pleasure in front of me?" Men like this are usually afraid of intimacy with a woman—of intimacy of any kind. The macho act of "conquering" helps them mask that fear, and to cover up any pain from childhood. These same men can seem like terrific lovers, but they slip out of a relationship when anything more than superficial emotions come into play. That kind of man is easy to spot when he fails to open up about other areas of his life, such as his childhood, previous relationships, or personal crises or setbacks. As someone once said, women can fake an orgasm, but only men can fake a relationship.

The Loss of Intimacy
Conclusions

Rather than speak up about what they want from a woman, many men initially hide behind a façade of emotional self-sufficiency. Afraid of admitting their vulnerability, they expect their partners to dig under the surface and intuit their real needs. When this doesn't happen, a lot of men still don't speak up. Instead, they will fantasize about other women, including indulging in pornography, or have an affair, to achieve some semblance of security, acceptance, satisfaction, and power. This may be especially true for men who did not get the love and acceptance they wanted as a child, according to those I talked with. They want those emotions more than ever as an adult, yet they have a harder time asking their partners, perhaps out of feelings of unworthiness or fear of rejection. But not all men are so timid. Both Steven and Roddy spoke up about their needs.

For a lot of men, the need for nurturing—giving and receiving—is not just the search for a reconnection to childhood, as Steven's and Roddy's stories illustrate, but a search for the familiar. Familiarity is a buffer against what a man doesn't know about his partner, the surprises that inevitably appear down the road. The *unfamiliar* is a great male taboo. It is a threat to a man's leadership, authority, power, and security. Perhaps this is why most men do not like to venture very far from their emotional comfort zones or areas of expertise. They don't want anything to go wrong, especially if it's something they can't fix. The joke about why men never ask for directions has serious underpinnings. Besides not wanting to admit incompetence for getting lost, they have to deal with the unfamiliar once they are lost. Self-image is on the line. In the matter of relationships, women often put down men who are commitment-phobic. What they may not understand is that a lot of men, like Steven, are reluctant to commit—even if they have strong affection and love for a woman—not just because they are leery of losing their freedom, but also because they have a fear of the unknown. Most men need to find a zone of familiarity in order to feel trust and to make the transition to commitment.

Fear of the unknown is also one of the reasons men often stay in moderately unhappy relationships. Money is another. A divorce or breakup is painful and expensive, they reason, and they also don't know what's waiting on the other side. Men generally don't like risk unless the risk/reward ratio is heavily tilted toward reward. One male definition of reward is having another woman to turn to. When Steven gets impatient with Renee he leaves her and finds another woman. Perhaps he thought he had fallen out of love, or was so disappointed in Renee that he saw no future for them. What he failed to consider were the repercussions with Renee if his relationship with the new woman didn't work out. Men appear to be selfish and uncaring, or even acting with deliberate malice, but often what they're doing is acting on impulse and whim.

Tips for Avoiding This Relationship Buster

1. Be aware that having a strong sexual bond with someone in the beginning stages of a relationship is not always an indicator of compatibility. Early sexual bliss often masks, rather than illuminates, deeper needs and issues, and not just for those on the rebound.

2. Set your own rules and boundaries for sex early on in your relationship, and let your partner know why. While men want sex almost from the beginning, most women need a bond of safety and trust for the sex to lead to true intimacy. If either partner wants sex for fun, as a fling, or just to explore, it's best to be up-front about it.

3. Recognize that men sometimes confuse sexual intoxication with falling in love and other "eureka" moments, such as "I've found my soul mate." This is often a marker of naïveté and a lack of emotional self-knowledge.

4. Verbalize for your partner your sexual expectations and needs, with the understanding that they can and will change with time. Communicate when you feel disappointed with the sex you're having, but it must be expressed in a safe, constructive, and nonthreatening way, and always give a "why."

5. Put your and your partner's sexual expectations in context with the other priorities in your relationship, such as support, loyalty, trust, empathy, and sharing. Recognize that the definition of good sex varies from couple to couple, and ignore messages of popular culture that make most of us feel inadequate or incompetent.

V alidation" and "self-esteem" may be overwrought clichés of popular culture, yet their pivotal importance in successfully navigating a relationship can't be overestimated. In order to stay in love, men need to feel validated by their relationships, which means having a loving and loyal partner, and in turn being respected as a protector and provider. When things get rough, and that validation is threatened, the best chance for survival is having strong self-esteem, along with other sources of validation such as friends, work, or any pursuit that reflects your competence or passion. In the best of all worlds, for boys to develop self-esteem, a nurturing mother is complemented by a male figure who is a strong leader, kind, patient, and fair. For many men I spoke with, the main problem they had with their fathers was not their lack of leadership or responsibility, but their inconsistent behavior and untrustworthiness. They viewed their fathers as loving but prone to breaking promises, helping them one moment only to let them down the next. Many thought their fathers were overworked, and therefore over-promised in order to be considered good fathers. Perhaps they were men just hungry for validation for being a good parent. They were also men who probably weren't validated enough by their partners, or their own fathers or mothers.

Being a good parent does not imply spoiling, coddling, overindulging, or overprotecting. Those behaviors are often controlling in nature, and can produce children, adolescents, and adults who are filled with a sense of inflated entitlement. On the other hand, genuine nurturing means bestowing on a boy (or girl) a prudent amount of freedom, including permission to take risks; forgiveness of mistakes (this is not incompatible with discipline); appropriate physical comforting; encouragement to be themselves; the right to talk about feelings; and the under-standing that success should not be gender-based. "Success" should also have as many definitions as there are people on the planet.

In the three stories that follow, we see men on a quest for validation—in their careers, from their caregivers, from their peers, and from their lovers or wives. Generally, it seems, the more fragile their self-esteem, the more persistent their quest. The struggle to relate to the women in their lives, wanting to please them so they will return respect and affection, leads these men to uncover some crucial and often painful truths about themselves.

Other themes discussed in this section include:

■ Why the heroes a boy chooses—whether it's Spider-Man, Michael Jordan, or a favorite brother—are a necessary source of power, inspiration, instruction, and liberation. Most men never outgrow their need for some myth or hero to identify with in order to give them feelings of power and autonomy.

- Why most girls devote the majority of their playtime to activities that involve nurturing and taking care of others—such as brushing a doll's hair, playing nurse, or planning dinner for the family. As adults, nurturing and caring are often their way of being in charge and having power in a relationship.

- How male role models who lack communication skills, are too achievement-oriented, or are emotionally absent give a young man the message that emotions are of secondary importance to his "success" as a man.

- Why in an intimate relationship, power, control, and leverage are often distributed unconsciously, sometimes leading to an unhealthy pattern that causes an erosion of love and trust. It's far better to be aware of and articulate the direction you think your relationship is going, rather than to blindly trust that things will just right themselves because you're in love.

- How a man's struggle to be "real" and reveal his true self in a relationship is sometimes difficult because he doesn't always resolve the conflict between trying to be the man his partner wants him to be, and the man *he* wants to be (or thinks he is).

4

Bill's Story

A man is a god in ruins.

—Ralph Waldo Emerson

On the same chilly fall night that we met Steven and Renee in New Mexico, it is a pleasant, balmy evening in Southern California. We find Bill, a successful lighting designer and museum curator, in his penthouse studio overlooking the glittering lights of downtown Los Angeles. Middle-aged, built like the football player he was in high school, he still has broad shoulders and a trim waist. Of mixed race, his rugged features and deep brown eyes make him handsome. Bill has always liked the company of women, and women like him for his sensitivity, empathy, wit, and humor. He has fallen in love many times, and has had three marriages, each lasting about ten years. He was always the one to fall out of love and ask for a divorce. Why he fell out of love, he's not entirely sure, but he believes it had something to do with a breakdown of trust, a feeling that his wife was no longer on his side—or could it be the way women can be so judgmental?

His relationship with his current girlfriend, a forty-year-old, pretty, quiet blonde named Alexandra, is on the rocks. After a big blowup, she and Bill haven't been in touch for three weeks. This has happened before—and they always seem to make up—but each new fight makes Bill worry it means the end of the relationship. He is suddenly depressed as he gazes out on the city lights. He thinks of other couples having fun tonight, being in love, or just content with their lives. Why is he sitting up here alone, stewing? He wonders if he's ever been truly happy in his whole life. What's wrong with him? He knows women are his validation—women make him feel good about himself—but when something goes wrong, as it has with Alexandra, Bill falls into a black hole of loneliness and self-loathing. He just can't feel good about himself without a woman who loves him. Instead, he almost feels rejected by the whole world. It's an emotional pattern he's had since adolescence after a traumatic childhood. He's been to countless therapists but nobody has really helped him. Looking out the window again, he thinks almost obsessively about Alexandra: how, when they first got to know each other, he knew she was "the one," the true love of his life that he couldn't live without. The more they fight, and the more times they walk out on each other, the more desperate he becomes to win her back.

Right now she won't answer his phone calls or e-mails, of which he's left dozens. One of the problems, he thinks, is that they are opposites. He loves people, parties, open energy; she prefers intimate moments with Bill, or just being alone. Bill, the communicator, lets Alexandra know his every feeling and impulse. She is revealing only when she's in the mood. He's sensitive and his feelings are easily hurt. Alexandra rarely acknowledges his pain or her own. Opposites or not, though, Bill is utterly dependent on her to tell him how much she loves him. But he also knows he can just as easily fall out of love if she ignores him too long. Then he'll be filled with anger and resentment and a sense of betrayal that goes back to his childhood—feelings that he believes helped sabotage his three marriages.

When relationships turn bad, from the man's point of view, it's not always a case of falling out of love with the woman. Sometimes a man falls out of love with himself—if, in fact, he ever loved himself to begin with. Does this happen to women too? I'm sure, but I think it happens more often to men because they put more pressure on themselves to achieve and be perfect. It also seems to me women are not as tough on themselves as men are. In general, women are more forgiving of their mistakes. For men, the ability to love and forgive themselves starts with their mothers. A mother has to really support and love you if your emotions are ever to "connect" and "be whole." You may look to your father as your role model for career and general male behavior, but in general it's your relationship with your mother that is your lifeline to emotional happiness. How you get along with her and how much you trust each other are indicators of how you'll deal with women in your adult life.

In an episode of *Sex and the City*, Sarah Jessica Parker's character, Carrie, is flirting with this cute guy at a bar. When he says, as a compliment, "You know, you remind me of my mother," a look of horror crosses her face and she ducks away. The message is, Hey, girls, be careful of any guy who is crazy about his mother because you'll end up competing with her for his affection. But that's a myth. Most men I know who have great relationships with their mothers end up with healthy relationships with their adult partners. The reverse is also often true. Unhappy with Mom, unhappy with your partner.

Maybe my childhood story is extreme, but it raises the same issues that a lot of my male friends face but don't like to talk about. They have negative feelings about themselves, and almost all can be traced to their childhoods. In my house are two birth certificates hanging on a wall. The first, issued by the Texas county where I was born, identifies me as a boy, but no name is given. In the box marked "race," the word "white" is checked. The second birth certificate, issued two and a half years later by a special court decree when I was finally placed by an orphanage with my adoptive family, lists my name as "Bill Simms" and the race box is marked "colored." Though I didn't learn all of my personal history until I was in my early forties, I'm the product of an affair between a divorced East Indian mother and a man of Italian-Jewish descent. The day after my birth, my biological mother turned me over to a prestigious Houston orphanage, where I remained for thirty months. During this period I was "placed" with five different families and "returned" to the orphanage five times. The family with whom I was ultimately placed was a mixture of African-American (still called "colored" in those days) on my mother's side, and Hispanic-Indian on my father's. Quite the melting pot.

My new family had no children of its own because my adoptive mother, Esther, couldn't conceive. Esther would turn out to be from the Joan Crawford school of mothering, which is to say she was beautiful, narcissistic, controlling, emotionally needy, and quick to anger. She wanted to be the perfect mother. It was she who insisted on the second birth certificate just to make everything look "legitimate." While she would later tell me different versions of my origins, her most common story was that she was really my biological mother, but had been forced by financial circumstances to put me in the orphanage. Two and a half years later she had come back to do the right thing and reclaim me. I don't think she was trying to spare me from some bitter truth so much as make herself look heroic. Even when I saw through this lie, and eventually found and met my birth mother, I never bothered to challenge Esther because it would only have made her furious. Esther has never liked being caught in a lie, and I'm not one who loves conflict— even though I've created quite a bit of it in my lifetime.

One of my strongest memories was when I was around eight and overheard my mother use a certain phrase about me. She was on the phone to a friend, talking about my "bad behavior," when she said, "You know, Billy is adopted, and we don't have much information about where he came from or who his real parents were, and you just never know what you're going to get." That last line—"you never know what you're going to get"—I would hear from my parents more than once over the next few years. It was something I would never forget.

Until I was eight or nine, Esther always picked out my clothes and dressed me. She loved to show me off to her many women friends. Even if my skin was lighter than that of the kids next door, and I was often looked at strangely, Esther was determined that I fit in. Fitting in was critical for her. Our house was the sharpest in the neighborhood, and we all dressed fashionably. Every spare penny we had went into appearances. If this sounds like stereotypical white conformist fifties culture, the reality was we were living in an African-American middle-class suburb, one of the first postwar communities of black attorneys, doctors, and accountants in America. Make no mistake: this was no bastion of black brotherhood or pride. These were African-Americans who wanted to be mainstream upper-middle-class whites. Like most everyone else in our community, my mother gravitated toward material possessions and status symbols, a habit I picked up as an adult.

My adoptive father, Jorge, was half Hispanic, half Aztec Indian, and didn't blend into the neighborhood color register any more than I did, but Esther's sense of denial was strong. She fantasized that somehow Jorge was special, the man of her dreams, though to me there was nothing exceptional about him. Jorge was good-looking, and sometimes a charmer, but I think he looked down on me as an adopted child, as if this was all Esther's idea (and largely was). I don't recall many times that we played together. What I do recall are the fights behind closed doors with Esther. They were usually over money, and even at a young age I concluded that money must be the most important thing in the world, the thing that makes you happy if you have it, miserable if you don't. Money would impress girls, I also deduced, so in my teenage years I spent a lot on clothes and a flashy car. I had no role model for saving or investing. Jorge was often traveling here and there on business, chasing different pipe dreams, most of which were failures.

A mother can have inestimable influence over a son. Esther not only runs the family, but sets the tone for its discipline, social values, and material ambitions. Without any brothers or sisters, and his father emotionally absent, Bill feels the full impact of his mother's controlling nature. Esther's statement that "you never know what you get" undoubtedly affects Bill's sense of self-worth and his future relationships with women. That he can't or won't discuss his real feelings with his father because he's away so much is another harbinger of trouble for Bill. Without a male role model that he respects and learns from, his future behavior is likely to mirror the manipulative and narcissistic practices of his mother.

The need for boys to have a strong male role model is crucial to their development. Early self-worth is based partly on the power of the hero they choose—identifying with Spider-Man, Superman, the Hulk, or G.I. Joe will never go out of style. Besides comic book characters, the hero role is also often filled by fathers, uncles, or older brothers. If family members are abusive or absent, the search for a real-life hero can be haphazard. Politicians, celebrities, and sports stars often fill the void, or a man sometimes tries to be his own hero, usually with the disastrous results that accompany expectations set too high. Men are desperate to be heroes, and as we'll see, Bill is no exception. Being a hero on one level or another is the quickest route to redemption.

realize, looking back, that besides needing a child to complete her ideal family, Esther also coveted a male companion, someone to fill the void that her physically and emotionally distant husband didn't. That companion became me. By the time I was four or five, I had learned two clear lessons from Esther. One, it was never wise to disobey her. Punishment was usually a whipping with a rubber electrical cord. There was also a veiled threat that I could be sent back to the orphanage at any time, though she usually backed away from this because I don't think she could have survived without me. The male companion issue, even if I was just a kid, was part of her identity. The other lesson I learned was how to be cute, charming, polite, informed, and ingratiating with all of Esther's women friends. This got me attention, even adoration, and I grew up with an easy charm and comfort with women, at least on the surface, which is characteristic of my interaction with most women today.

While popular with her friends, I was often a disappointment to Esther and her lofty expectations. Especially when she kept uttering that line, "You never know what you're going to get." I wanted to prove her wrong. But if I got a B in math, she asked why it wasn't an A. If she made me clean the dishes every night, she expected me to vacuum the house as well. Esther was a lonely, vain, frustrated woman. Yet she was so good at making me feel guilty that from an early age I came away thinking that when something went wrong in our relationship, it had to be my fault. The message, essentially, was that something was wrong with me.

In grade school I enjoyed academics but my social environment was lacking. Esther took me out of our all-black suburb and placed me in a Catholic school because it was reputed to offer the best education. I was one of a handful of nonwhite students who bore the brunt of the nuns' displeasure (including the frequent rap on the hand with a ruler) as well as getting my ass kicked in the schoolyard for being colored. After a few years of putting up with this, Esther had had enough. She accused the nuns of racism, pulled me out of the school, and enrolled me in an all-colored school several miles away. There I proceeded to get my ass kicked for being the only white kid.

Athletics was one of the gifts that allowed me some peer acceptance in grade school (and later in high school and college). However, never underestimate the power of bigotry and racism. By junior high I had developed a strong affinity for any persons who are oppressed or discriminated against. My role models—among them John and Bobby Kennedy, Martin Luther King, Gloria Steinem, and Franklin Roosevelt—were all people willing to challenge the system and effect social or political justice.

In his search for a strong male role model, Bill settles on historical figures who "challenge the system" and focus on issues of social justice. This is how Bill sees himself, someone who has been done an injustice (both by Esther and Jorge) but can somehow overcome it, perhaps as a leader who is not afraid to assault the status quo. Bill also finds salvation in sports and the peer approval it brings. His need for validation from others, and his search for happiness and meaning in his life, are the implicit search for ways to repudiate Esther's message that something is inherently "wrong" with him.

Bill may be an extreme example of someone facing obstacles in finding his literal and figurative identity, but a lot of men never have the opportunity to understand who they are. Denied the nurturing that girls generally receive, preoccupied with meeting the expectations of society, caught up in the hypermasculine competition of the workplace, and trying to be responsible husbands and fathers, they don't have the energy or time to delve into the male matrix. In what limited time they do have, the urge to escape into sports, computer activities, or cars, for example, is understandable. Besides a lack of ambiguity, these pursuits are either solitary or done with other men. Rather than interpret these "male" activities as adolescent in nature, as some women do, they should be seen as a substitute for an emotionally fragmented childhood, and an escape from relationships that can be fraught with complex demands and messages, such as those that Esther gives Bill. As we'll see, in addition to pursuing sports, Bill seeks other ways to put a distance between himself and his mother. In gaining his independence, however, his insecurities hardly go away.

n the late Fifties, Esther and I moved to California while Jorge stayed in Texas to pursue yet another entrepreneurial idea. To Esther, California was the land of opportunity, and represented a new life. Starting over and erasing the past was one of my adoptive mother's life themes. (Eventually it became one of mine, at least with women.) I was now around twelve. This time

I was placed in a more racially integrated school, but I still managed to get my butt kicked regularly, just in a more democratic way. I was sensitive and high-strung and easily offended, particularly when I was ignored. All my life I've reacted negatively when I feel discounted or marginalized. My reaction is never violent; rather I turn my back on the offender, and I am very slow to forgive.

Once I was in high school and developed some independence from Esther, I had no trouble making and keeping friends, both male and female. This is about the time I learned that, despite what Esther would have me believe, I can be intuitive, sensitive, and empathetic—what a therapist might refer to as my "feminine side," a term I have trouble with because it implies that those emotions largely belong to women. Whether you're straight or gay, I believe that men, if they give themselves permission, are capable of being just as connected to their emotions as women are, and while lots of women complain about lack of emotions in men, they usually do little to help men bring out their feelings.

After I finished my secondary education, I enrolled at UCLA. I was a good student, and in my free time I continued to seek new friendships. I also developed a pattern of exploiting social opportunities. I had this "me-against-the-world" perspective that is typical of an only child, especially an adopted only child, which is really an attitude of secret entitlement. For example, using my charm, I would convince someone to help me with a difficult class, or set me up on a date. Why? Just because I thought I deserved it! But I could also flip the coin and do favors for others, little and big, such as lend friends money, cook them dinner, or give them unexpected gifts. I became quite conscious of my need to please people, to be liked, and to have as many friends as possible. I also like to have friends who are not connected to each other, only to me, so if one of the friendships sours the others won't be contaminated. Being excluded from any group is another deep fear. It doesn't take a therapist to tell me I'm a textbook case of abandonment issues, yet over the years I've gone to a variety of therapists to hear exactly that message, over and over, and to wallow in it.

On the positive side, I usually respond to anyone who is kind, sensitive, intelligent, or funny. I genuinely want to be his or her friend, almost instantly. I especially gravitate to women who exhibit those qualities. When a friendship or a relationship with a woman goes south, I'm in trouble emotionally. I love hard and I suffer hard. I look for a safety net in times of crisis: a friend to confide in, a challenging job assignment to keep me busy, or another woman to tell me that I'm okay. I like a friend to tell me that when something goes wrong it's not my fault. When the safety net is not there, I fall into despair. There is an engine of self-preservation in me that drives me relentlessly away from myself and loneliness. I always need other people to make me feel good. I can't stand being alone: that's when all the demons of your childhood come out to play.

I realize that my self-preservation skills could be construed as artful manipulation. To women with whom I've been in relationships, I come across as someone who listens to and acknowledges their struggles. I think most women look for this quality in a man. Empathy sometimes means as much to them as a man's confidence, power, or money—all that stuff you read in men's magazines and which, unfortunately, is basically true. But looking at myself critically, am I only performing? Am I suckering someone in without exposing that insecure, volatile, high-strung, unpredictable being who lives inside me? My pattern is to have a woman fall in love with me before I expose my other self to her. Perhaps I lure them in under false

pretenses, but I'm not sure. Aren't they responsible for their
own emotions and judgment? I have this debate with myself all
the time. What is my real self, anyway? The fact that I crave
love, sometimes desperately, and go crazy when I feel
abandoned? Yes, that's real. I am also an empathetic, caring,
funny, sensitive person. That's real too.

Bill's struggle with his identity is partly driven by his fear of
loneliness and abandonment. In chameleonic fashion, he pre-
sents different aspects of his personality to different friends, trying to please everyone, fit in, and be loved. As we'll see, this is
especially true in his relationships with women. His constant
struggle to find his "real" self results from the absence of a supportive childhood environment that allowed for exploration
and self-discovery. He was too busy surviving Esther and longing for a real father.

The person I'm closest to in the world is my daughter, Liza.
She's the product of my second marriage to a talented
artist who is Caucasian. Liza is my only child, and obviously I
empathize with that station in life. Liza is beautiful and smart,
doing well at a prestigious East Coast college, and while we
sometimes argue, it is rarely over money. I have not reenacted
the roles of Esther and Jorge. I have gone out of my way to
always be there for Liza. I admit to loving her unconditionally.
That bond may be the most critical in my life, if for no other
reason than it is so difficult for me to experience trust with
anyone else. I would make any sacrifice in the world for my
daughter. Coming up with forty thousand dollars a year in
tuition, for example, has sometimes meant, in a lean year,
selling some of my art collection as well as forgoing a lot
of comforts. But I would do it again in a heartbeat. Liza is

also lucky in that her mother is equally nurturing and supportive.

Speaking of mothers, I should add that I didn't make contact with my birth mother until I was in my forties. Her name was Linda and it wasn't easy tracking her down. When I spoke to this stranger for the first time, I said, "This may be very difficult for you to hear and most difficult for me to say, but does July 16, 1946, mean anything to you?" After a very long silence she said, "Well, not really." And then she said good-bye and hung up. Linda wasn't rude or dismissive. If I heard anything in her voice, it was shock. I sat down and wrote her a three-page letter, giving my life history and adding that I was only looking for biological and historical information I could share with my daughter. Of course I wanted much more. I wanted to know why I'd been given up for adoption. I wanted to know something wasn't wrong with me.

Linda called me after she received my letter and gave me the true story. I broke down and sobbed and so did she. She admitted to being my birth mother and said she had never wanted to give me away, but her father had insisted. My father, the Italian Jew with whom she'd had an affair, had disappeared from her life, and Linda already had another child to care for. To this day Linda and I are in contact by phone, and I've had many visits with her, my brother, and the three daughters she raised with her second husband. They are all kind, wonderful people. I often wonder what my life would have been like if I'd been raised with them.

The difficult road to self-forgiveness, as Bill experiences, turns a lot of men into unsatisfactory partners for the women in their lives. They can't stop beating themselves up, or they become passive-aggressive, or they're restless to explore other relationships, or just to escape in general. Men like Bill, because of the messages they received from their caregivers, simply feel they're never "good enough." They often count on women to help them.

The empathetic, caring, sacrificing side of Bill—the side that allows him to relate to his daughter or seek out his biological mother—shows he is capable of trust and forgiveness. This is the person he'd like to be all the time. But as we'll find out, Bill is often more comfortable with his insecure and sometimes destructive persona. For many of the men I interviewed, the demons they live with most of the time are what they trust the most, as if we inherently are drawn to that which repulses us. Getting himself in trouble puts Bill in the position of being saved by the next new woman in his life. It's a common male fantasy— the woman who will always forgive or save him, no matter what mistakes he makes or how badly he behaves. But for men who can't forgive themselves when they screw up, the fear of a woman's judgment can push them out of love and out of the relationship.

While I felt a great weight lift from my shoulders after talking to Linda, my abandonment issues didn't go away. I think maybe we all carry inside us an emotional fingerprint, formed in the first years of our life. Like any fingerprint, it is both unique and impossible to alter—not by self-realization, not by new facts, not by years of therapy. It's our emotional identity, like it or not. Speaking of therapy, I've been told by more than one therapist that I'm obsessive-compulsive because of my need for control, afraid of both failure (rejection) and success (I don't deserve it!), and subject to severe mood swings. I can't deny any of it. When I get down on myself I'm a mess for days at a time. When I'm feeling up, I produce my most creative work, and feel most connected to the woman I'm with. Because I'm a designer, I also have almost a fixation on beauty and style. How I dress, what kind of car I drive, how I furnish my office, the work I do for my clients—I need everything to be extremely tasteful. This sometimes leads to major overspending, a legacy from childhood assumptions that money is the root of all happiness.

No doubt playing Russian roulette with money is one more mode of self-destruction. Another is that in my relationships I tend to start quarrels needlessly, even though I normally don't like conflict. I pick fights just to test my partner, to see how much she'll put up with. Or maybe I want to push a woman away because I'm afraid of too much intimacy. Too much intimacy means I'm overinvested emotionally, and if something goes wrong, the rejection will be way too painful. I've always been looking to be saved from myself, preferably by a woman— no doubt by an idealized version of my mother, the one I desperately wanted but never got in Esther, or the imaginary "what if" of Linda.

I've been married three times, and never for more than ten years. All three women were different in background and personality; what they had in common, besides being sensitive, funny, athletic, and professionally talented, was that in the beginning of the relationship they had a much stronger interest in me than I had in them. That's my modus operandi with women. I have to feel secure before I get really interested in someone. Once I have my confidence, I assess how physically and emotionally attracted I am to that woman, and the compatibility of our interests. The passion of the chase, finding out what the woman is all about, both emotionally and intellectually, is extremely important to me. Whatever woman I'm after, I want her to think of me as the most interesting, romantic, charming man she has ever encountered. When I have sex with a woman it's never casual. For me, sex confirms intellectually and emotionally that this particular woman is the right one for me. Depending how connected we feel, it's sometimes further evidence of how much she loves me. I like to keep alive the discovery and learning process between myself and the woman as long as possible. A relationship without excitement is ultimately one reason I fall out of love.

There are other reasons I fall out of love, to be sure. One is that I get so down on myself that I think of that line, "I'm the piece of shit that the world revolves around," or Esther's famous quip "you never know what you're going to get." And when I give up on myself I give up on my partner too. How can she possibly fall for someone like me? What's wrong with her? Can't she see what a mess I am inside? She must want something from me, or something's wrong with her, or she's clueless. Why should I stay in this relationship? I know some women who have similar issues of self-doubt, even self-loathing, and they too tend to always be in a fight or in flight.

By the way, I know a lot of men who are prone to self-loathing. For whatever reason, they think they're not good enough. Was it their fathers that set their expectations so high? Or their mothers, who never gave them enough love? The irony for me is that I've been married to some wonderful, loving women. In each of my marriages, I gave up on the relationship around year eight, then it took me another two years to wind things down and formally leave. All three marriages fell apart for the same reason and in the same way. Our arguments started out around money, but the issue soon became control and, ultimately, trust. Because trust comes so hard for me, I would find myself slowly disengaging from each of my wives after every significant argument. I rarely verbalized my unhappiness—I didn't know how, not in those early years—but I would keep score, subconsciously, each time I lost a battle.

Bill talks about men who don't like themselves, and for that reason set themselves up for failure, and ultimately give up on their relationships. The idea of "keeping score" when his partner won an argument and made him feel marginalized might mean he doesn't have the self-esteem to sustain a relationship long-term. As Bill says, every argument sooner or later came down to control and trust issues. Low self-esteem often translates into the need to control.

Not a small number of men and women, like Bill, jump from partner to partner because they're constantly seeking validation or they fear rejection. Because of their childhoods, control is more familiar to them than love and trust. But this kind of "relationship jumping" ultimately leads to getting locked into unfulfilling partnerships. Always needing someone to make them feel good about themselves, many men never get over the fear of being alone. For a healthy adolescent male, having different girlfriends as he grows up is a form of self-exploration. But for others, relationship jumping is a way to avoid the "loser" label, and is often accompanied by a strong attraction to athletics, steroids, sex, clothes, cars—anything that resembles a flashy, beautifully wrapped package with a gorgeous ribbon: anything to attract a girl. What many men fail to ponder—long after they leave adolescence—is what happens *after* the attraction process. Do they even know what's inside the package? Do they think no one will ever want to open it up and take a look? Some men, fearful of intimacy, will just pile on the wrapping paper and ribbons, hoping that will be enough to attract and keep a woman. Bill, however, knows there is something deeper in him. He just wants to find it and express it on a consistent basis. He wants to find the right woman to recognize that depth and goodness in him.

f possible, I like to maintain friendships with my ex-wives and old girlfriends because I don't want to hurt anyone beyond the damage that's inevitable with any breakup. I also have that need to be connected and still loved. Our recent blowup notwithstanding, I'm now in the fourth serious relationship of my life. Alexandra is in her early forties, and recently divorced from an attorney. My hope with Alex, who I love more than any woman I've ever been with (and I hope this is not my addiction talking), is to change from my control mode to an open, trusting way of being. Alex understands and accepts my history, including my hang-ups with Esther, my definitions of success and failure, and why my validation needs are so strong. I know that being a conscientious and loving mom to her two young children is the most important thing in her life. How she succeeds or fails as a mother defines her as a person, at least in her eyes. I think she often tries too hard and spoils the kids, but if I ever say that—if I even hint at it—Alex puts up a wall.

One of our problems is that Alex is not as strong a communicator as I am. Maybe I should say not as needy. In the history of my relationships, I have gone from self-conscious reticence to almost compulsive confession. Words comfort me because they convey emotion. I have to be in touch with anyone I feel close to. So when Alex turns silent I go a little crazy, especially since I've told her how I crave communication. I can send her an e-mail, or leave her a phone message, then wait days for a response. The interlude fills me with doubts. Did I offend her somehow? Is she seeing someone else? Is there something she doesn't like about me? Maybe I've gotten too old, or I don't have enough money, or I'm losing my looks. In our yearlong relationship we've had three serious breakups. The second occurred for no clear reason (to me) other than that she said she needed some time alone. Okay, fine, take time off, but just tell me why. I always need a why.

In calmer moments, I count my blessings. I've survived a lot. I have good friends. And when I love, I love with a big heart.

Women like Alexandra grapple with the same burden to prove themselves as men do, whether it's a career, motherhood, looking beautiful, or being helpful and nurturing. Her periods of silence and noncommunication, which Bill finds upsetting, may be her way of processing and working through her issues, as well as her need for space and autonomy. Her silences might also reflect difficulties with conflict or intimacy—Bill doesn't offer an explanation. Perhaps he is in too much pain to be able to empathize with her.

For a couple it's sometimes hard—if each has his or her own definition of success and failure—to understand and empathize with the other. A husband may wonder, for example, why his wife is obsessed with the way she dresses every day, while she may question why her husband worries excessively about money. If Bill and Alexandra don't communicate about their childhood issues, there's little chance of understanding each other's hang-ups. Once they do communicate, each needs to re-assure the other that as long as they give their best effort, failure is not only okay, but it is a vehicle for self-discovery.

Bill said that he likes to be connected to his ex-girlfriends and wives. "Staying in touch" was common with a lot of men I spoke to. On the one hand it can be a positive—perhaps a sym-bolic apology from the man, or the ability to nurture one an-other even after damage has been done. But staying connected can also reflect certain male insecurities: the denial that they were ever truly abandoned; the need to fill their emotional tank with a reserve memory or two in case their current relationship runs aground; the fantasy that even though a relationship is dead and buried from the woman's point of view, a man, with his special powers (superhero identification), can revive that relationship if he really needs to. The extent to which a man fantasizes about his powers and abilities is often in direct proportion to secret fears of his own impotence.

Bill also talks about the process of emotionally disengaging from each of his wives, and falling out of love with them, when he feels they are no longer on his side. He's now in danger of doing the same thing with Alexandra. Perhaps he wouldn't feel so betrayed if he didn't have such high expectations of what women can do for him. He needs to find some of his happiness outside his relationships, hopefully in an all-male world as described in Chapter One. Otherwise, men—perhaps because they're so needy, or think they're so powerful—have a tendency to want to make over women to meet all their emotional needs. Such a strategy usually leads to judgment and disappointment, and a man (and woman) falling out of love.

5

Tom's Story

In the Second Polarity—Destruction/Creation—a man is aware as never before of the pain and affliction that other people have wrought on him and also the pain and affliction he has wrought on others, including his family. At this point, aware of his own mortality as never before, he also has a strong assertive desire to become more creative.

—Daniel J. Levinson

Say hello to Tom, a retired businessman in his late fifties with a thirty-plus-year marriage and two grown children. He looks youthful—his hair is still not gray—and has a quick smile and penetrating blue eyes. Mindful of his health, he has always popped vitamins and worked out religiously. Tom considers himself an empathetic and intuitive male rather than rigid and authoritarian. Until recently, he's always been driven to succeed at work—his admitted definition of masculinity—and compares his work ethic to that of his deceased father, a successful doctor. Tom prides himself on a close and loving relationship with his two grown children, a bond he never had with his father. The relationship with his wife, Sarah, a tall, striking brunette with emerald green eyes and a killer smile, is more complex. She, too, is driven to succeed. Tom first believed this was a strong link between them. Over the years, though, it became a significant wedge in their relationship. Looking at himself critically, Tom has identified a series of codependencies with Sarah, among them the pursuit of money and security, that also once moored their relationship, but ultimately came to shake it to its foundations.

Between love and money, Tom thinks, it's a toss-up which one people value more highly. In movies, books, and talk shows, kudos go to love, especially romantic love, but in private he's not sure how most people feel. Romantic love is wonderful, he says, but it mostly affects adolescents and begins to fade by the time we're in our mid- to late thirties, at least if we're with the same person. On the other hand, money lasts a lifetime. It buys a membership at the country club, a trip to Paris, a painting by the artist you love, not to mention comfort, opportunity, freedom, and peace of mind: a happiness that is safe from the violent swings of romantic love. Money is the security blanket that kept Tom's parents' marriage together, and to an extent, his too. Seeing himself as a romantic person as well, however, he is sometimes ashamed of his materialistic values. He knows he's not alone. Money is how a lot of men keep score, define their happiness, and slake their insecurities.

I grew up in the San Fernando Valley in Southern California in the fifties, in an upper-middle-class WASP family. My father was a medical doctor and my mother was a housewife. She was a cold, beautiful woman whose need for attention shadowed her, and overshadowed the rest of us, all her life. I have a brother who is three years older than me, and while our temperaments and values vary greatly, our impressions of our parents are pretty much the same.

My dad was a sweet, caring man with a subtle sense of humor. He had many male friends and was particularly loved by his obstetrics patients for his bedside manner. By blood he was a quarter Cherokee, however, so he also displayed that particular Indian penchant for quiet self-absorption. He was warm and aloof at the same time. He never said anything about how he felt. Except for the last day of his life, I never got to know him much beyond his intelligence, easy charm, and strict work ethic. He never once raised his voice. Anger just wasn't an emotion for him. My mother could yell at him on occasion, and certainly a lot at my brother and me, but Dad would walk away rather than confront her. He didn't confront anyone, ever. He grew up dirt poor before the Depression and put himself through Stanford and then medical school at USC. He was an officer in the Navy, and was nearly killed by a Japanese sniper on Okinawa. Just before the war, he met and married my mother while she was finishing nursing school.

I think my father had a remarkable life but, typical of his generation, he rarely talked about his past. From letters found after his death, I learned that his half-Cherokee father, a barber, died from alcoholism in his forties. His mother, it appears, was cold, demanding, and judgmental. She died when I was around three so I have no memory of her, but according to my brother, she and my mother never got along. Their temperaments were too much alike. Dad, a devoted enemy of conflict all his life, was either too smart or too fearful to take sides.

My father had an office in our house and always locked it when he was away. When home, he spent hours there logging into ledgers every check he deposited or paid out. It didn't matter that he had monthly bank statements; there was just something about money and scrupulously keeping track of it that came from his fear of poverty. Even after he was a successful doctor, he would return empty Coke bottles to the market in order to get the two-cent refund. But he wasn't necessarily frugal. He could spend whimsically and to excess. I remember him going to a men's store one day and coming home with a dozen dress shirts and six pairs of shoes. He also had a habit of running off to Las Vegas six times a year for long weekends, usually with his male friends. My guess is he sometimes lost significant amounts of money, because my mother's screaming fits often came after his return from Vegas.

Despite all of his easy and many friendships, Dad was a loner at heart. While we had numerous annual family vacations to one national park or another, the emotional dynamic was no different than it was at home—four people coexisting quietly without any real emotional connection. We were definitely not a physical family. Hugs and kisses were rare. No one ever said "I love you."

My mother's attitude about raising children was Victorian. Seen but not heard. Until we were six or seven, when my brother and I misbehaved we were spanked with a wire coat hanger, or our mouths were washed out with soap (for saying "dirty words"), or we were sent to our rooms without dinner. Where my father was warm but distant, my mother was intense and purposeful. She loved playing the role of the doctor's wife. That social status was the pinnacle of her rise out of Depression-era poverty. I never felt she was comfortable in her own skin, however. Introspection was not her strong suit, yet she was quick to judge others. As a kid I was, in her eyes, irresponsible and unfocused. A lot of that was true. I frequently got into trouble with neighbors, and I was the class clown throughout grade school. Her primary duty in life, my mother later told a friend, was to whip my brother and me into shape. I think this was her definition of love.

As I got older—eleven or twelve—my mother grew more impatient with me, and with her own life. I'm sure the two were related. Getting older and starting to lose her beauty, I think she took out some of her unhappiness on my brother and me. When I entered junior high she told me it was time I became "a proper young man" and that she wouldn't tolerate any more misbehavior. The problem was, I never knew the meaning of acceptable, let alone exemplary, behavior. My mother didn't give guidelines, or for that matter, compliments or praise. Maybe it was a legacy from her mother—the idea that children, or certainly boys, didn't need to be praised because if you coddled or indulged them in any way they became spoiled. Yet I longed for her approval. My dad had his impact on me—he was my role model for achievement—but it was love and emotions that I wanted from my mother.

When I was fourteen, my mother contracted tuberculosis and spent almost two years in bed. During the summers I was sent away so I wouldn't disturb her convalescence. I lived with a family with six kids, on a farm in Oregon—old friends of my mother. I enjoyed the rural life because it was so different from what I knew. But what I remember most were the letters I wrote to my mother, which I found after her death. She had saved them without ever telling me. My letters were all incredibly sweet, anxious, lonely, and full of concern for her. Looking back, I see them almost as love letters. I was afraid for all the pain she was in. I was afraid I would never see her again. Once in a while I got a letter back, reporting that she was doing as well as she could, but no one had any idea how much she was suffering. I didn't understand the source of my anxiety at the time, but it was the same mentality, almost obsession, that would follow me my whole life. I kept thinking that if I told my mother how much I loved her, or if I did well in school, or in my career—if I worked even harder and showed her how successful I could be—one day that compliment or big understanding hug would come my way.

In high school I didn't have a great social life. On the surface, I was funny and charming and appeared confident, but underneath I felt a kind of paralyzing self-consciousness. While I dated sporadically, I was very careful not to get emotionally involved with a girl or get into a long-term relationship. I didn't think I could pull it off—I think I was afraid of my emotions, or didn't understand them—and the fear of failure, of rejection, was also a cloud over my head. Part of the problem was that I didn't have a role model when it came to intimacy. Mostly I was consumed with the future—college, career, that kind of thing— and I soon became the classic overachiever: foreign-exchange student, student-body treasurer, honor society president. I was even afraid of getting sick, because I thought illness was a kind of failure. If I stayed healthy, or gutted it out when I did get sick, I reasoned that someone would praise me for never missing school. When I graduated, I was the only one in my class who never missed a single day for six years. Except for my brother, who shook my hand perfunctorily, no one seemed to notice.

In judging the attractiveness of a man, most women rank self-esteem and confidence as "must have" qualities. Like strutting peacocks, dazzling their audience with brilliant colors, men often make a show of their confidence because that's what women want and expect. This is certainly what Tom did in high school. That he knew he was pretending was no doubt a source of anxiety, but he felt he had no choice. This is not dissimilar to adolescent males using lies and deception to get a girl into bed. It's linear male logic: to get what you want, just tell them what they want to hear, show them what they want to see. Burdened with the mandate to succeed, it's sometimes difficult for men like Tom not to be an impostor to some degree. Even after a man has won over a woman, he may fear that without a continued display of confidence, his partner won't respect him or will even reject him. Worse, a lack of confidence in one area is the harbinger of failure in others.

Tom's relationship with his mother is not unlike those of many men with domineering, judgmental, and insecure mothers, and well-intentioned but uncommunicative fathers. Tom wants to be emotionally closer to his mother, yet leery of her judgment, he is afraid of her. In high school that fear translates to a distrust of girls and intimacy. He accepts his father's passivity and makes the assumption that this is how men behave, that as long as they are breadwinners there's nothing else they're obligated to do. Tom learns as a teenager to hide behind achievement, not unlike his father, trying to get approval and validation through his accomplishments. But it's never the same or as satisfying as honest emotion and love, for which Tom is starved. He just doesn't know what to do about it. A lot of men told me that even when you're sixteen or seventeen, while you may not know what the rest of the world is like, you do know your family's values and you trust them. You just assume that your family's behavior is the definition of normalcy.

Out of frustration with her own life, a mother like Tom's is sometimes determined to mold her son into the kind of man she'd like her partner to be. This may be subconscious behavior, but it is likely to turn the child into an adult who feels burdened by expectations. He may feel, as Tom does, that he can simply never be good enough. In the back of his mind is his mother's voice, telling him what he needs to do to be loved. To disguise his fear of inadequacy, he makes himself as charming and sympathetic as possible, and he overachieves in spades.

As I grew up, Dad spent most of his weekends away from the house, which meant golf with his friends, trips to Vegas, woodworking, and photography—activities that largely excluded Mom. On weekdays he seemed to stay in his office as long as possible before joining us for dinner, and when we finally sat down, our conversations were never about how anyone felt, except for my mother who, with menopause, began to complain about one physical ailment after another. I remember how upset she became whenever my father received phone calls from his obstetrics patients. Even if the call was legitimate—the woman wanted to know if it was time to go to the hospital and deliver—my mom could get furious about dinner being interrupted. If Dad actually left for the hospital, you could see the abandonment on her face. I felt sorry for her. You would think that a doctor and husband would notice, but if he did, Dad showed no special interest. Looking back, their universes were so separate that I'm sure they thought about divorce, only they never talked about it. Besides the social pressure to stay together, one of their bonds was money. Dad earned it and spent his share on all the material things he never had while growing up. Mom spent her portion on clothes, cosmetics, and parties.

After high school, I went to Stanford, just like my father (and brother), and graduated with a degree in English. Mostly I studied, got decent grades, had a few inconsequential dates, and drifted home every summer for the mandatory manual labor job. In my senior year I applied to graduate school near Chicago, in no small part to get far away from home. I chose an MBA program because I had no desire to go to law or medical school, yet I wanted the security of making a good living.

My most significant accomplishment in graduate school was that I lost my virginity. This was during the late sixties, the cradle of the sexual revolution, yet I was the poster child for late bloomers. Jo was a sweet, smart, cute girl from Missouri. Her sexual experiences were also limited, but definitely not zero, like mine. Once we became emotionally involved, and we began to make love, it was very awkward for me. I was afraid of being criticized by Jo. I had no idea about technique, or what gives a woman pleasure. Essentially I thought a guy just comes, and a woman does too. I didn't understand anything about correlating sex with intimacy and trust. But after a while I became more comfortable with myself, and more confident in my skills, if not my deeper emotions. The same went for Jo.

Ultimately sex meant liberation for us. On weekends we also closed down quite a few bars on Rush Street. For the first time in my life, or since grade school, I was really having fun. But after going together for a few months we broke up. Looking back now, I just didn't know how to relate to a woman. I didn't understand how a woman thinks, feels, or communicates. Also, my anxiety over just about everything, particularly Vietnam and the prospect of getting drafted, didn't help. But I never told Jo. To reveal doubts about myself was an internal taboo. I thought it was better just to get out of the relationship.

The strange thing about our breakup was that while I initiated it, I took it much harder than Jo. I realize now that if you have abandonment issues, it doesn't matter who does the rejecting—you still suffer. Sometimes you reject your partner before she rejects you, to avoid that pain, but you only end up feeling guilty and inadequate. Jo seemed to bounce back and find another boyfriend right away. I had feelings of loneliness for almost a year.

By the time I finished graduate school, my need to be successful—and my corresponding fear of disappointing people—were ingrained. My self-esteem fluctuated on a daily basis. I constantly looked for approval from almost everyone I ran into—the waitress in the coffee shop, the cabdriver, the dry cleaner—and would do so on and off for the next twenty-five years. Then, later, as the tension in my marriage began to grow, I started to understand where my fears and anxiety really came from.

I was drafted into the Army shortly after receiving my MBA, and ended up at Fort Ord in Monterey, California. While I had been dreading this for more than a year, the reality was something of a relief. I had been drafted, against my will, so whatever happened to me now wasn't my fault. I couldn't be judged. Because I'd been an English major, I ended up editor in chief of the Fort Ord newspaper. It kept me busy, and kept my thoughts away from the possibility of being sent to a combat zone.

When I went home on Christmas leave that year, Dad seemed more tired than usual. But he was still his sweet self and, incredibly, the night I had to go back to Fort Ord, he asked me about the Army in detail. He also talked about World War Two, all the death and destruction he saw, how afraid he'd been, and how guilty he'd felt to survive. For those few hours I think I got to know him better than in the previous two decades. I kissed him on the cheek, said good-bye, and flew back to Fort Ord. At 2:00 A.M. I got a phone call from a family friend. My father had died in his sleep, apparently of a heart attack.

I tried not to cry on the flight home, but at one point I broke down and sobbed. I kept telling myself to suck it up, that I was twenty-three years old and needed to be tough, but I had absolutely no self-control. I felt this incredible hole in me and didn't know how to plug it. When I got home, my mother, in spite of being sedated by a doctor, was beside herself. Besides missing my father, I think she never imagined this kind of thing happening to her, and now that it had happened, she didn't know what to do. She was never the same again. She didn't remarry, despite many suitors. She became isolated, and somewhat bitter about no longer being accorded the status of a doctor's wife. More than ever she needed to be the center of attention.

Every weekend she would insist that my brother, who lived nearby, do her grocery shopping or fix something around the house or take her to dinner. Clearly, he was taking the place of Dad. Mom must have felt he was an improvement because my brother was giving her the attention that my father never had. This went on for years. I didn't know why my brother, by then a successful attorney and married, put up with this. (Today I do know. He was looking for that approval and love from her, just like I was in my way.) Part of me also wanted to be the dutiful son, but in the back of my mind I was thinking of my own needs, and about all the anger that I was beginning to feel toward my mother. Why did everything have to revolve around her? Why didn't she ever ask about me or my life? But conditioned not to complain, I pushed my anger away. I wish now, looking back, I had had someone to talk to. But my brother was even more uncommunicative than me, and I didn't dare bring any of this up with my friends.

Tom's anger toward his mother is understandable. He feels his love for her was never appreciated or reciprocated, and he probably didn't know how to express that to her without exploding. No doubt he's also aware that mother-bashing is not what men do. As J. R. Moehringer writes in *The Tender Bar,* "real men take care of their mothers." While there are no official statistics, retailers report that Mother's Day cards outsell Father's Day cards by a significant margin, and the majority of buyers are men. Whether from guilt, duty, or genuine love, men are reluctant *not* to honor their mothers. However, it's when that sense of responsibility and love somehow get distorted into a relationship of domination, control, and ownership that men like Tom begin to feel resentment.

It's important to make the distinction between men who had healthy, nurturing, and supportive relationships with their mothers—and who usually make sensitive, empathetic lovers and partners—and those who were ignored, suffocated, or controlled, even in the name of love. A lot of parents, because they were neglected as children, try to compensate by being overly indulgent parents. As we'll see, this is what Tom ultimately does, and perhaps robs his children of a certain amount of self-confidence, independence, and emotional maturity. But at this moment in his life, all he can think about is abandonment by his mother, and his long-suppressed need to be loved.

By sheer luck, I was never levied to 'Nam, and less than a year later I was honorably discharged from the Army. In a speed record that I was barely conscious of at the time, three months later I was married. In graduate school, a year after my breakup with Jo, I had met a sorority girl and drama major. Sarah was a tall, svelte brunette with high cheekbones and dazzling eyes. Intellectually, we were extremely compatible, and our dates were mostly to museums and art films; we could talk for hours on almost any subject. For the first time, I felt genuinely comfortable around a woman. Sarah also had a big personality—she had more energy than anyone I'd known—that brought me out of my emotional shell. The eternal optimist, she was never down, never in a bad mood. She was also Jewish, from a prominent Connecticut family, and that too had an exotic appeal for me. I wanted to be involved with someone who was as different from me as possible.

We kept in contact after I was drafted, and got back together once I was out of the Army. As I tried to adjust to the world, to find a job and a place to live, Sarah was the only one

who seemed to embrace and accept me. She was my
sanctuary. I was terrified of losing her. I also had strong
feelings for her, stronger than I'd had for anyone else. So I
proposed marriage and she accepted. She said she knew it was
her fate to marry a blond, handsome man from the West Coast.
I know we both had deeper, more complex feelings, but neither
of us really talked about them. I think, looking back, neither
Sarah nor I considered ourselves especially emotional people.
It was clear from our dating that we had a lot of similar goals
and interests, and we both perceived those as our strongest
bonds.

I had only met Sarah's parents once, when they visited her
in L.A., but suddenly I was living in a spare bedroom in their
house and getting to know them well. Sarah's mother was
gorgeous—a former Ford model—and a talented Vassar
graduate who was full of personality, humor, and warmth. She
was the perfect mom. I had no idea at the time what impact
this had on Sarah. My fiancée was very pretty but she lacked
the poise and classic beauty of her mother. Sarah's dad was
from a wealthy family, a graduate of a prestigious college, and
a successful stockbroker in Manhattan. He was on the formal
side, a judgmental man whom I was always careful to step
lightly around. Sarah seemed close to both her parents. I
interpreted these as loving, caring relationships. Unlike in my
family, I saw no evidence of sullen anger, self-pity, lack of
communication, or hidden agendas. They were all interested in
me, and for once I could talk freely about almost anything,
including my feelings. This family had it all together. I thanked
God it was so different from mine.

About six months after Sarah and I were married, we got
into our first serious argument. I don't remember the subject,
but I started it. We were outside a restaurant, and people
overheard us. Sarah was shaken. Ironically, for someone who

had plenty of insecurities and who had a father who never fought, I could hold my own in a confrontation. Part of this was anger at my mother, I'm sure, getting misdirected at Sarah. It was also my misguided concept of masculinity: rather than surrender, a real man fights for what he wants or believes in. Where I picked up that attitude, I'm not sure, because it was just the opposite of my father. "Tom," Sarah finally said that night, "I can't stand to fight with you." She told me that her parents didn't even raise their voices, let alone get into arguments, and she didn't want to either.

I soon learned that Sarah liked keeping anything that was unpleasant, like our argument, a secret from the world. The rule was that you always "put on a face." If your dog had just died or you'd been in a major car accident, if someone asked how you were, you just said, "Wonderful, thank you, how about you?" Sarah admitted her mother had raised her this way. I was confused by this message. After escaping my repressed family, and being encouraged by Sarah's parents to talk about my feelings, my inclination was to be more truthful, more emotional, even if it meant occasionally blowing up. But Sarah had received a different message. At the end of the day, her persuasive gifts won me over. I promised I would try not to get into arguments with her. I wanted her to be happy. I didn't know it at the time, but this seemingly harmless capitulation marked the moment I went back to burying my emotions.

I believe this was also the start of our first codependency. I relied on Sarah's judgment in all things social, which allowed me into her Connecticut family and its privileged world. And Sarah felt secure because I was a smart, successful young man whom she was proud to marry. We gave each other validation. Was she in love with me? I think her emotions were just as jumbled as mine. We needed each other emotionally, for sure, and there was definitely love and tenderness, but I think "being in love," the absolute merging of souls, the Hollywood version of head-over-heels obsession, eluded us. Without either of us knowing it, ours was also a partnership with responsibilities and duties.

Less than a year after we were married, Sarah's mother called out of the blue. She told us that she had just packed her suitcase, and would be seeing a divorce attorney in the morning. She didn't want to explain, but when we pressed her, she said she was tired of living with a man whose ego was far too big, and who was oblivious to her needs. She'd been unhappy for years and had only been waiting for Sarah to get married before flying the coop. Sarah and I were in shock. This couldn't be happening, not to her family. Sarah tried to talk her mom out of her "drama," but with no luck. Even today, more than thirty years later, Sarah has difficulty acknowledging the full impact of her parents' divorce. The perfect family—the couple who never argued, the couple who wanted me to talk about my feelings—wasn't so perfect after all.

Sarah was deeply hurt, yet it was against her upbringing to admit that life was anything less than rosy. Her self-definition was to be just as perfect as her mom. If that meant keeping secrets like her mom had, and putting a premium on appearances, she would do it. The ultimate effect of the divorce was to make Sarah want to be even more perfect. Whether this was to make up for her mom's "mistake," or if it was some kind of competition with her mother, or if she needed to feel loved in order to salve her wounds, I had no idea. But Sarah would suddenly go out of her way to be liked—not unlike my own behavior, or my mother's—by virtually everybody.

One evening Sarah and I were supposed to meet at a club for dinner. She showed up two and a half hours late. She couldn't understand why I was upset. She explained she was having a drink with an old friend of her father's. She arrived

late and didn't want to be rude by leaving too soon. I don't think
I ever begrudged her her need for validation, not directly, but
the more Sarah was there for everyone else—helping them
solve their problems or offering advice or just being social, just
being liked—the less time I felt she had for me. Whenever I
grew upset, she would swear that it would never happen again.
She also reminded me of how much she hated fighting, and
that I had promised her not to get into arguments.

Yet Sarah continued losing track of time and breaking
promises, and that became another of our patterns. She would
get me upset—I would let her get me upset—and then she
would make me feel better by fixing me a special dinner, or
making love, or buying me a present. And I liked it. I liked being
taken care of. Sarah could be warm and intimate. Our
lovemaking was terrific. I remember holding her afterwards in
my arms—there was no better feeling in the world.

Any man raised by a controlling mother might, in the beginning, be attracted to a strong-willed partner, as Tom is to Sarah.
He repeats in his adult relationship the patterns he established
with his mother, yet takes it to another level. In Tom's case, he
allows Sarah to get him upset, but he also lets her make him feel
better afterwards in a way his mother never did. At some point,
Tom needs to focus less on Sarah's shortcomings and take responsibility for dealing with his own emotions and behavior: all
the anger he felt toward his mother, as well as himself for living
a repressed life. To a large extent he lets Sarah control his emotions. He lets her heal him rather than learn to heal himself. In
turn, this allows Sarah, by repeatedly coming to Tom's rescue,
to feel secure in a false, unhealthy way. Maybe Sarah's deepest
fear is that Tom will one day divorce her, so she does everything
in her power not to let that happen.

In our first years of marriage I worked terribly hard, and not only at my public relations job. I would rise at four every morning to work on a novel. Even if I had a master's degree in business, I had learned writing skills at Stanford and wanted to try my hand at fiction. I was disciplined and determined to be successful at whatever I tried. In the ambition department, however, Sarah was right with me. This was the seventies, and women were suddenly flooding the workplace. Sarah decided to go to law school and was accepted at NYU. She studied incredibly hard, yet managed to keep our social lives intact. A drama major, she had an obvious talent for theatrics, so in her third year, when she announced that she was going into criminal law because she liked the idea of arguing before a jury, I knew she'd be a natural.

While there was one private side of Sarah—the sweetness and innocence of a child (the side I loved the most), there were two public personas. One was cheery, generous, empathetic, and loyal. Sarah could make anybody her new best friend. Like her mother, she could turn on her personality like a thousand-watt bulb. Winning new friends, or just making a strong first impression, was a way for her to get validation. This is not to say she was insincere. Sarah really did like most people, and she could be a great friend.

Sarah's second persona was more complicated. This was someone who acted supremely confident, feeding off the power of the women's movement, challenging anyone in her law class, and later her firm, with her ideas and ambition. This Sarah could be highly competitive, controlling, and secretive. Even though she didn't like to fight with me, she would willingly take on someone at work. She was not one to back down. She was good at disguising this side of her—maybe she wasn't even aware of it—because her other persona was so dominant. With her charm and an infectious ability to please or persuade, Sarah could usually get people to do what she wanted. But if charm didn't work, she could be tough too.

When she started as an associate at a prestigious Manhattan firm, she worked even harder than she had at law school. I began to see that her work ethic and drive for success were even stronger than mine. Yet if you paid Sarah a compliment, she would brush it off. If someone remarked, "Sarah, what a terrific job you did preparing that brief," she would answer, "It was okay, but the next one will be better." She often made herself the center of attention, yet too much scrutiny or praise made her uncomfortable. This has been a habit most of her life. To me it reveals Sarah's core insecurity. She must have figured out that playing the role of the perfect daughter in the perfect family was somehow wrong, that she'd been taken in. She knew she wasn't perfect. Yet she didn't know what to do about it, except not tell anyone and keep playing the role.

After seven years in Manhattan, Sarah told me one weekend that she was tired of New York and wanted to move west. I was mystified until she revealed that she was having a major disagreement with her boss, and that New York had begun to feel claustrophobic. Then, with a huge smile, she also told me she was pregnant. We were both ecstatic. We'd been trying to have a child for a couple of years. Being a father—a good and caring father—was extremely important to me. When I thought about it, I didn't mind the idea of a move. I had now published a couple of novels and had quit my public relations job. Two of my books had become minor best sellers, and both had been favorably reviewed in the Sunday *New York Times.* I saw a career ahead of me.

After an exploratory visit to Phoenix and a job offer from a law firm there, Sarah couldn't wait to move. I wasn't as sure. Phoenix was another metropolis, I argued. We could go anywhere—why not somewhere near the ocean? We debated it for a couple of weeks. In the end I went along with Sarah's wish. Looking back, I wish I hadn't agreed so quickly. I had fallen under Sarah's persuasive spell, and this was to become another of our patterns. Too often I would do what Sarah wanted rather than express my own will. None of my behavior in those days makes me proud, but it was conditioned behavior from my childhood: accepting familial authority, especially female authority.

For Sarah, leaving New York fulfilled another emotional mandate. Both her parents were now remarried and she continually remarked how strange it felt to visit them in different households. I think the little girl in her still fantasized about her fairy-tale past. Because that was now all but wiped out, perhaps there was only one solution—get away from it all.

We bought a house in Scottsdale, and basked in the warm weather. Once our son Robert was born, Sarah wasted no time going to work at her new firm. She put in long, exhausting hours, and I did most of the child care, while also writing my next novel. Neither Sarah nor I complained about our new lifestyle, as taxing as it was at times. Sarah's assertive personality, incredible work ethic, and natural leadership abilities brought success at her firm. Within three years she was billing almost twice the hours she'd billed in New York. We also had our second child, a beautiful daughter named Alice. This didn't slow Sarah down. Because she insisted on nursing, Sarah went to her office every morning carrying Alice in a bassinet.

I was proud of Sarah. I was a believer in the women's movement because I thought all efforts at pushing gender equality were positive. Besides, my wife earning a good salary took some pressure off me. While I had published my third and fourth novels without difficulty, I was struggling on my fifth. After getting a dozen rejection letters, my agent diplomatically suggested I start another book. I did, but I couldn't get that one published either.

As she grew more successful in her law practice, Sarah's old patterns of lateness and broken promises resurfaced. "Sorry, I was busy with a client," became a common excuse for showing up late for dinner. Because of the setback in my writing, my self-esteem was hardly flourishing, though I pretended to Sarah that I was just fine. I pretended to myself and friends as well. Because I was in professional turmoil, I felt I had to carry my share of the load by being a particularly diligent parent, and responsible for everything around the house.

Another pattern in our relationship surfaced around this time. Sarah was becoming embroiled in a growing disagreement with some senior partners. Because Sarah did not always get along well with authority, I wasn't surprised when she told me she would be leaving her firm and starting her own. Then came the bombshell: she wanted me to join her. My MBA and experience in finance would come in handy. We would be a team. This would be "our" firm. We'd only have to hire a couple of attorneys to make the venture profitable. She asked that I really think about it. I wouldn't have to do that much, she said, just keep the office running, maybe a couple hours a day. I looked at our financial needs with two young children to raise and accepted her proposal. We could use every extra dollar, to be sure, but money was also important to me psychologically, just as it had been to my parents. But it wasn't everything, I knew. Sarah and I agreed that once we made a certain amount of money, I could leave our venture and go back to writing, or whatever else I wanted to do.

My habit of accepting Sarah's ideas had already started with the move to Phoenix. Really, it had started with our first argument outside the restaurant. I would capitulate to Sarah many more times in the future: to grow our law firm despite our promise to keep it small, to take on more overhead, to put in more hours. Years later, long after we had reached our financial benchmark and I was free to leave, I stayed on. I'm honestly not sure why. Did money—and the power and respect that came with it—become more important to me as I got older? Did I lack the confidence and the will to go back to writing? Struggling with the fifth and sixth books definitely felt like failure, and I didn't know how to deal with failure. There had been no real precedent, and no role models for me. If you come from a family where love and approval are tied to being successful, failure becomes a real problem. In order to feel successful, wasn't it just easier to stay with the law firm?

The goals of money, success, and feeling in control as ex-pressed in Tom's story represent other components of his mas-culinity. Focusing on externals, such as material comforts, allows Tom to hide from his deeper emotions. For a lot of men, when money and acquisitions become their yardstick of success, and they see other men, including their role models, subscribe to the same values, it's easy to believe they're doing the right thing. Conformity is a strong lure for anyone who lives with a lot of fear. Fear also becomes the foundation of a false masculinity—a masculinity that is as much about things men shouldn't do as things they should. *Don't show your weaknesses; don't surren-der; don't trust your competition; don't compromise unless you have to; don't feel sorry for yourself; don't let anyone too close because they might want something from you; don't let anyone see you sweat; don't admit your pain. . . .* For a man, there are more thou shall nots than in the Ten Commandments.

Anyone reading this story can probably guess its climax. Sarah was persistent in her pursuit of excellence and validation. In the next fifteen years, the firm expanded to twenty partners and twenty-five associates. I went from working three or four hour a days to ten or twelve. I never matched Sarah's tireless energy at work, but I became the primary caregiver for Robert and Alice. Even though we had live-in help, out of guilt I would dash from the office to take the kids to soccer or ballet, then out to dinner, then back to the house to help with homework. I felt I could never do enough for them. Then I'd run back to the office for details that needed attention before morning.

Life became so crazed that I forgot how to think or breathe or do anything but be on call 24/7 for either our firm or for Robert and Alice. I was in adrenaline mode. How else did one get by? Amazingly, when I look back, this went on for a period of almost fifteen years. Sarah couldn't help at home as much as she wanted, because she was too busy with clients. Whenever she was home, however, she was a conscientious mom. Every birthday was memorable. For holidays she pulled out all the stops. But as much as Sarah loved Robert and Alice and they loved her, their memories of growing up mostly involve me. I think Sarah would admit today that women pay a huge price for trying to balance a career with motherhood, and that it just might be an impossible juggling act.

There was virtually no time for me to write anymore. Still, I would try, rising at four in the morning again, and every now and then I published a book. But I no longer had the focus or energy I coveted. And there was a second, even stronger frustration building in me. While Sarah enjoyed the public limelight, I was buried in the office, solving myriad behind-the-scenes problems. Whenever Sarah saw how overburdened I was, she would promise extra help and say that I could soon get back to writing full-time. Her speeches cheered me.

Down deep, however, the validation issue began to trouble me. While Sarah had become a marquee name in Phoenix law circles, most people hardly knew my role. The attorneys in our office appreciated me, and I enjoyed working with most of them, but Sarah had the habit of jumping in and solving administrative problems that were supposed to be my responsibility. Whenever I confronted her, she would say defensively, "Tom, I'm only trying to help." I sometimes felt she wanted to prove to the world she was Superwoman. Yet she seemed to have no idea how this was making me feel.

Part of our problem was that we were both perfectionists and overachievers. We were competing against each other without fully acknowledging it. We would tell ourselves we were being supportive of each other, but it was an unhealthy competition that, looking back, obviously had a lot to do with control. My one undisputed power in the company was over the finances. Sarah cared about money largely because it was a yardstick of her success, but she didn't want to read a profit-and-loss statement or balance sheet. All that was left to me, including investing our savings, which I did successfully. Like my father, who had pored over his ledgers in his study, combing through financial statements and watching over our investments made me feel secure.

After too many drinks at a party one night, I commented to one of Sarah's female friends that I sometimes felt overshadowed by my wife. Even though I worked sixty-hour weeks, no one knew what I did. I was only trying to be honest and let some of my frustration out. The woman cocked her head and said I had way too big an ego. I was being unsupportive of Sarah who, after all, had started the law firm from scratch and was largely responsible for its success and our very comfortable lifestyle. I had a typical male ego, insecure and competitive, afraid to give women their due, she said.

When I repeated the conversation to Sarah the next day, she pretended that none of it mattered, and changed the subject to a vacation we were planning. I looked away. I had begun to feel I was no different than a client in Sarah's eyes. I was someone who had to be stroked and mollified at the right time before she went on to solving the next crisis. If I started an argument, Sarah reminded me that arguing was unproductive, that it reminded her of the pain of her parents' divorce. There was nothing I could say that Sarah didn't have an answer for. I began to feel invisible. Clients would phone all evening and Sarah unfailingly took their calls. Memories swept over me of childhood dinners and the patients who called my father, and how angry my mother would get.

Somewhere around this time, Sarah and I stopped looking into each other's eyes. And because I didn't vocalize my unhappiness effectively, Sarah, the eternal optimist, assumed everything, while stressful, would ultimately right itself. But it didn't. By the time I turned fifty-five, I began to unravel. I became sloppy in helping other attorneys. I didn't return phone calls or e-mails. My energy and love for my work was no longer there. Both Alice and Robert were away at school and when they called home they seemed to be enjoying their independence. I had the feeling that if I disappeared tomorrow, no one would miss me. One weekend I told Sarah how I felt and why. In a calm voice, I said I was miserable and that my problem was perhaps one she could not solve. She presented herself to the world as happy and self-sufficient, but perhaps she was as insecure and out of touch with her real feelings as I was. I told her I was tired of being a "we." I wanted to be an "I" again, or perhaps the "I" that I'd never been. The loneliness and desire to be one with someone that had pushed us—or at least me—into our relationship were now pulling us apart. I think this happens to a lot of men with lost childhoods, ones where they never had a voice. As I talked, at one point Sarah burst into tears and then grew angry, as if she had been holding something in for a long while. She accused me of being emotionally disengaged, indifferent to her accomplishments, and for criticizing her as her father had done. Then she accused me of wanting to divorce her, to cause her more pain.

I didn't want a divorce necessarily—I was too confused to think clearly—but a separation was definitely called for. I moved into the guesthouse on our property. About this time, my mother, still in California, was diagnosed with dementia. My brother and I put her in the best assisted-care home we could find. In her moments of clarity she let us know how unhappy she was. Sarah was supportive of what I was going through, but her head and heart were still in her work. My old abandonment issues resurfaced. I was frustrated by my helplessness. Why couldn't I solve my problems? I could solve everyone else's. My self-respect began to slip away. I slept two or three hours a night, took to eating most of my meals alone, and jumped in my car and made midnight drives to nowhere.

The label of "midlife crisis" seems to get pinned more on men than on women. This is certainly not because women don't have crises, but perhaps they are more aware of the changes in their emotions, hormones, and bodies as they approach and go through menopause. Because of this self-awareness as well as support from friends, women may be better prepared to confront a crisis because they see it coming. Men, on the other hand, are often unwilling to deal with their childhood issues, buried emotions, and relationship issues until a crisis hits them over the head. Often several crises come at once, as they did for

Tom: his ambition peaks, his virility wanes, he is no longer needed as a father, and he loses respect for himself because he fears he has lost the respect of others.

When Tom's universe begins to unravel, he first seeks validation the old-fashioned way—though traditional masculine outlets of work, money, and achievement. When he realizes he's still deeply frustrated, however, and that blaming Sarah isn't an honest answer, he'll begin to look to himself for a solution. For a lot of men like Tom, having a breakdown, admitting their lack of self-love, is the first step to healing. The second step is to acknowledge that seeking validation from others is a losing game. The third is to shed all fear of failure. Once that is accomplished, the fourth step becomes possible: to be completely open to, and trusting of, yourself and, if she's still hanging in with you, your partner.

The accepted wisdom that men are not communicative, especially about their emotions, is challenged in Tom's story. As we'll see, when Tom gets a handle on his issues, he can't stop talking or thinking about them. Part of his frustration with Sarah is centered on her inability or unwillingness to listen to him, and to be forthright about *her* feelings. If men have multiple personas, women can too. In Sarah's case, the confident, hardworking, goal-setting attorney is in conflict with an interior self that is defensive, vulnerable, and fragile, just like her husband. Why does it take them so long to figure out their commonality? Why can't Sarah find the courage to speak up? Perhaps they are both too busy still seeking validation from the rest of the world.

That summer my mother was rushed to the hospital with kidney failure. My brother and I were at her side in less than twenty-four hours. While she was still conscious, she kept looking at us but didn't say much. I told her that I loved her, but she didn't offer any "I love you too," nor that elusive compliment or hug I'd always longed for. As I watched her die, I couldn't believe it was happening this way. I took her hand, met her stoical gaze, and then she was gone.

I thought that her death would finally release me from the past. Instead, I felt more angry, hurt, and alone than ever. I went back to my habit of taking midnight drives and staying away from the office, hanging out with friends instead. I didn't care about eating or taking care of myself. I lived moment to moment. I knew I was having a breakdown, but it turned out that it wasn't an entirely negative thing. As I grew disengaged not just from Sarah but our series of codependencies, I felt a burst of powerful new emotions. I could be reading a book and suddenly have a new insight into my life or become overwhelmed by childhood memories, and the next thing I would be in tears. I was awash in emotions I hadn't felt in decades. The trust and intimacy I had been unable to access in myself as a teenager now came welling up. It felt unreal and unpredictable, but great.

When Alice and Robert came home from school, they knew something was up, but Sarah reassured them that everything was fine. I was more forthright. To work with your spouse day in and day out for two decades, come home together, wake up together, and still have a romantic, loving relationship, I told them, was not an easy thing. I also tried to explain my childhood issues, and the series of codependencies that bonded Sarah and me, and then about my breakdown and all the revelations I was having. I don't know if they understood. There was a huge amount of surprise and sadness in their eyes, but there was also acceptance—they didn't expect or even want us to be perfect parents. And in the end they wanted to stay clear. This was our problem, not theirs.

Sarah and I agreed to try a marriage counselor. By now the

whole office knew of the friction in our relationship. Tongues wagged. There was so much new gossip every day that I didn't want anything to do with the firm. With the help of the marriage counselor, Sarah and I both raised good points, but ultimately little seemed to get resolved. I then went into several months of private therapy. When I suggested to Sarah that she and I had similar issues with validation and perfection, she resisted the idea. The more I delved into my emotions, and the more I admitted to myself the destructive patterns of my life, the more unsettled she grew. Sarah blamed me for not only hurting her personally, but jeopardizing all the success we'd achieved together.

But with time, to her credit, Sarah slowly came around: to understanding my point of view just as I came to understand hers; to going into therapy to deal with her own issues; and to stop obsessing about success and being liked by the world. Around the office she held her head high. She came to learn what I had already accepted: that people who gossiped and judged you were the most insecure people of all. After another year of living with the demands of her career, and simultaneously accepting how her personal world was changing, she decided to retire from her field. I have since become involved in other business ventures, while Sarah is considering her options. Being free has been a huge adjustment for her, but a healthy one. We now hold nothing back from one another, and have given each other the freedom and trust we should have bestowed decades ago.

What have I learned from this journey? When you get overwhelmed by your emotions, especially if you've repressed them for a long time, it is extremely hard to have clarity on anything. You keep waiting for the issues to resolve themselves, but they rarely do. You have to worry to resolve them. Looking back on our turbulence, I think neither Sarah nor I had strong identities, despite what our clients, friends, children, and peers thought. We had strong personalities but not clear identities. A personality is something that other people relate to. An identity is something you relate to. Our lives were based on achievement and not on understanding who we really were. I think that many people in middle age stop growing, questioning, exploring, and challenging themselves. They settle, rest, and compromise. Perhaps they also find comfort in the pursuit of the false gods with which they were raised, as I certainly did for a while. Just because you reject those idols intellectually doesn't mean you escape them emotionally. If you grew up aware that your parents believed that money, material acquisitions, and social status were worth pursuing, the emotional connotations you place on those goals just don't go away. And if you fail to achieve them, the affliction of failure weighs on every part of your life—until you force yourself to change.

Tom suddenly wakes up in middle age to realize he's not happy, that his life feels like a fraud, and that he has little respect for himself. A psychologist would add that Tom carries around a significant amount of guilt for not measuring up to his mother's expectations, and reexperiences those feelings whenever he disappoints Sarah. He's one of those emotional time bombs that, when it goes off, scatters the fragments of his life in all directions. It's not clear whether Tom actually fell out of love with Sarah or he simply fell into a deep relationship crisis. It was as if he found himself in a car with no brakes, careening down a road he's never seen. Memories and emotions from childhood come welling up, first in a tidal wave of frustration, then, slowly, with Tom's hard work, they begin to sort themselves out. He realizes that giving up his definition of masculinity—the idea that a man always has to be responsible and hardworking, that he has to be in control—is a necessary transition to getting away from his guilt and anger.

There were many reasons Tom's relationship with Sarah was failing: a lack of self-love in both of them; getting lost in work and addicted to power, money, and control; not being a candid communicator; and confusing their codependencies with intimacy. Tom recognized what was happening before Sarah did. Yet, not fully accepting the lessons he learned, or unwilling to admit failure, he was slow to communicate. When he finally does communicate, he pushes Sarah to do her own exploration. As she discovers her other persona and the need to be honest with Tom and herself, their relationship begins to improve.

As Tom recognizes, a man's need to be whole, to be healed, and to be one with another soul is a galvanizing force and can be defined as one way of falling in love. But when the bonds begin to dissolve, and the intimacy and unification he was once seeking slip away, he will tear away from his partner, often in an attempt to find the happiness that eluded him in childhood and adolescence. To Tom's credit, he doesn't take the easy path and desert the relationship. He works through his issues and reestablishes, even deepens, his bond with Sarah. This is a hugely creative act that follows a period of desperation and destruction, and for men, a not uncommon means of redemption.

6

George's Story

Misery and shame are nearly allied.
—Samuel Johnson

The most likely place to find George in his free time is riding his motorcycle. Thirty years old, single, a self-employed writer, musician, and filmmaker, he has "don't fence me in" written all over him. He wears his hair long, favors a leather jacket, and is more comfortable in work boots and jeans than anything fancy. His face is long and expressive, and his skin is pale. His life is driven by a strong intellectual curiosity about politics, the arts, and social values; the struggle to grow comfortable with his emotions; and an effort to balance his life between loving someone and seeking a Thoreauvian independence.

An only child, George was born and raised in an isolated town in southern Michigan. There was a small population of Saginaw Chippewa Indians nearby but most families were Caucasian and blue-collar. Most fathers worked at the paper mill, the town's largest employer. Definitely a company town, and not a particularly happy one because of periods of high unemployment and the chronic fear of being laid off, George remembers. There was no such thing as high culture, he adds dryly, unless you count hunting and fishing. George describes his small-town environment as being as soul-crushing as Michigan's interminable winters. He doesn't romanticize blue-collar life. Growing up, it was considered cool by his friends to bash anyone who went to college, and no one was ever caught dead in the library after school. "If you didn't start drinking beer by age ten you were judged a freak," he says. "I don't like looking back at my childhood—it was tense and volatile—but I do so in order to understand where my life is today. I call myself a free-thinker, a liberal, and an antiauthoritarian in every healthy way. Social injustice and poverty make me queasy. I wasn't born until the seventies, but my attitude and idealism belong to the sixties."

George was one of the few in his peer group who did make the jump to college. Being different in an environment of overwhelming conformity made him grow up quickly. Self-esteem, he says, didn't come without surviving a period of adolescent depression. Later, a Kerouacian journey with his girlfriend across the country turned him into a self-described existentialist. The basis of his "male values," he says, is a confluence of childhood lessons and a strong sense of self-preservation.

My mother was a professional bookkeeper, and even though we needed the money from her work, she committed to staying home with me until I was five. My mom is funny, witty, sharp as a tack, and in some ways tougher than a Sherman tank. We've always gotten along. Dad worked in a nonmanagement job in the paper mill for thirty years before it was shut down in the orgy of downsizing in the nineties. When he was forced to retire, he never did get the full pension he was entitled to. Even before that, he was disgruntled and angry for most of his thirty years at the mill. He truly hated his job—yet, paradoxically, he was devoted to it. He couldn't stand being sick or missing a day of work. But whenever he came home he looked miserable. His temper was explosive. Without warning, he would throw chairs, go off on tirades about the people he worked with, or belittle me for the slightest perceived infraction. He was a cruel father even though I don't think he meant to be.

One of my worst memories is an incident that took place one weekend when I was passing my father some bricks off the back of our pickup. He was pounding them into the ground to make a walkway. Each pair of bricks was either horizontal or vertical in relation to the line of the sidewalk and they alternated according to position. I was supposed to be setting the bricks on the tailgate in the correct position so Dad could just grab them and automatically put them in place. Apparently I set them up wrong. He glared at me. "Nine years old and you can't even take a simple direction, can you?"

I also remember him on weekends, just sitting at the kitchen table, chain-smoking, brooding over his coffee, making lists of things to do. I think he liked to keep busy to keep his anger at bay—and to avoid interacting with Mom and me. He was so straightlaced and uptight that he didn't even allow himself the luxury of an occasional beer. He was obsessed with work. He burned the concept of a work ethic into his brain— and mine. He would always work at least fifty hours a week, sometimes sixty, and once or twice he put in ninety hours. It was insane, yet if he'd been asked to work even harder, he would have said yes. Work was his validation. In his thirty years, except for vacations, I believe he missed maybe four or five days because of illness. It was as if his job, which I only later came to understand was the cause of much of his anger, was something he couldn't leave unattended. He couldn't allow himself to fail. As I said, he was tormented by his job, yet it also defined his self-worth.

I have friends today who, every time they've lost a job, experience a sense of defeat that affects their relationships with their partners and children. You start to think that if you screw up in this one pivotal way—the role you were born for— you wonder if something is wrong with you. Your confidence and self-esteem are shaken, and inevitably you take it out on other people.

It was only much later, when his position at the mill was eliminated and Dad spent more time at home, that I really got to know him. I was sixteen or seventeen by then. He suddenly opened up to me, as if he realized that that was one of the things he owed my mother and me after years of shutting us out. I began to see where his rage had really been directed. He had had a Dickensian childhood. His father turned out to be already married when he married my grandmother—that kind of dysfunction set the tone for the family—and there was never enough money. My dad was the oldest of eight brothers and sisters, and to a large extent he was responsible for raising them. When the slightest thing went wrong, he was blamed by his parents. He never had a chance to speak up or defend himself, or just to be a kid. That same shame-oriented environment was duplicated at the paper mill, a hypermasculine, high-stress workplace where you never spoke back to your boss. Also, Dad was so much more capable and intelligent than the work he was assigned. So the rage just built and built and had to come out somewhere. As Anaïs Nin wrote, "Shame is the lie someone told you about yourself."

My dad's life taught me that what society expects of men, at least working-class men, is far from human. The stoicism, the obedience, the groupthink—it's all this pseudomasculinity. If those concepts are taken too much to heart, they wound you and wound grievously. Because of what happened with my father's life, as well as what I learned on my own, I came to see how undemocratic most democratic institutions can be. I will always have a strong distrust of authority. As symbols go, flags, jails, churches, and courthouses are scary to me. I'm suspicious of anyone who blindly follows the common wisdom and doesn't think for himself. At my core I guess I'm something of an anarchist. I hope I never grow out of it.

As he grew up, George was confused about his feelings for his father. Whether he hated him or loved him, or admired him but felt alienated, or wanted to love him but couldn't because his father's anger pushed him away, he was deeply frustrated by having a father who was so lost and defeated. George's life is also a manifestation of the internal conflict of every hetero-sexual male from a traditional family who struggles to "feel like a man"—sexually and otherwise—but internally identifies with his mother because the father is emotionally absent and his mother so accommodating. George comes to understand and accept what or who his dad is, in part because he longs for iden-tification with a strong father figure. But this intellectualization belies his emotional self, which is still angry and hurt.

There are no statistics on how many men truly dislike their jobs as George's father did, but of the men I spoke with, at least half wished they had different careers or bosses. The irony, as George points out, that a man can detest his job but still be de-voted to it, is explained either by a definition of masculinity or simply a fear of getting fired. So many men define themselves by what they do and nothing else. When losing their job is para-mount to losing their identity, they don't know how to redefine themselves unless it's by getting another job.

For four years my parents sent me to a Catholic elementary school. Even at that young age, while I could recite the required liturgy in the required robotic voice, I never felt spiritually elevated or that I was part of something bigger than myself. If anything, I felt more alone and isolated. In my view, the Church was just one more institution to be leery of. I'm not hesitant to say that today I'm an outright atheist.

My mom was to some extent my salvation. And not because she coddled or overindulged me to compensate for my dad's rages. If I got in fights with kids and came running home, Mom told me to go right back outside and "take care of it." That meant go back and kick the crap out of someone. That wasn't easy. I was small for my age, socially awkward, and not especially aggressive. But Mom knew that in my neighborhood, if you back down, you'll always be picked on. I did what she told me. In many ways it was my mother, not my father, who taught me to embrace my masculine side. Mom also had a great sense of humor and I adopted it as my own to get through many family crises.

Mom also encouraged me to read and learn as much as I could. I remember subscribing to *Discover* magazine when I was in the fourth grade and loving everything about science. This didn't fit with my more sports-oriented, library-hating friends, and by the process of elimination, I suppose, I was soon labeled a geek. I garnered attention by reading the ingredients on the labels of whatever god-awful food we were served in the school cafeteria. It doesn't sound like something to brag about, but being able to read "partially hydrogenated animal protein" in the fourth grade secured my reputation as a brain.

My first real role model was Indiana Jones. The Harrison Ford character in the movies was exactly who I wanted to be:

strong, quick, and deadly, but driven by a quest for knowledge rather than a desire to be rich or famous; basically a geek who no one wanted to tangle with. Later in my life I would take up martial arts and became good enough to make money teaching it.

When I was around nine, my dad developed an interest in commercial dogsled racing. Because a kennel wasn't allowed within city limits, we had to move to an even smaller town, twenty minutes away; it might as well have been another planet. When I entered fifth grade there, I was greeted like the outsider I looked like. Already I kept my hair long and my choice of clothes wasn't the usual blue-collar wardrobe. I was rechristened a geek, but not a helpless one. In Catholic school I'd learned to defend myself with my fists, so being picked on didn't worry me. My concern was that it was hard to make friends with people I found truly interesting; they tended to snub me. I suppose they couldn't get beyond my appearance, or that I was the new kid in town. This, by the way, seems like one of nature's cruelest tricks: how do you meet people if you're introverted but still need friends? I developed a pattern that I maintain today; I have two or three very close friends whom I trust implicitly. While I'm polite to everyone else, I keep them at arm's length.

I was an unmotivated student in junior high and, whether it was cause or effect, adrift emotionally. My dad still scared the hell out of me at this time. We got into ferocious arguments about the Gulf War, drugs, the government—anything I could think to pick a fight about. I found my own temper flaring irrationally. I did the same thing Dad did. He let people walk all over him without saying a word, then suddenly, two or three weeks later, he'd explode at some innocent party. There were moments when I wanted to physically hit my dad because I was so angry with him. But nothing is one-sided. I picked up on some of his positive traits too. While he couldn't express his own feelings, he'd make a point of being there for somebody else when they had a problem. His brothers and sisters often called him for advice, and my mom, as tough as she was, relied on him for nurturing as well. To this day I credit my more sensitive side to my dad, as well as my work ethic.

I just wish for Dad's sake that he had those thirty years at the mill to live over, to become a more enlightened and happier person. He missed out on so much. Somewhere along the way I think a lot of blue-collar men turn into "grinders." The shadow of Calvinism still reaches the width and breadth of America. Today a lot of men (and women too) are the reincarnation of the Organization Man of the fifties—they work themselves practically to death and leave little time for anything else. God knows why. To prove they're invincible? To avoid their emotions? To make tons of money? Whatever, it's pretty sad.

While in high school I discovered that I had something else in common with my father. I suppressed my feelings and desires, often to cater to the needs of others. I liked to be helpful to friends and acquaintances. Maybe that was my way of getting some attention, or making new friends, or maybe it's just my basic nature. But ignoring your own feelings comes with a price. I began to have this tormenting sense down deep that my sexual appetites were on the unorthodox side. I just wasn't aroused like most boys by lurid pictures of the female anatomy, or the prospect of getting laid. When I focused on what did turn me on, it tended to revolve around sadomasochistic fantasies. If my tendencies meant I was a sadomasochist or bisexual, so be it. But I kept my thoughts and feelings secret. This is not something you casually mention in your typical small-town Michigan bar. You don't even tell your family. You *especially* don't tell them. So I tried to persuade myself that I wasn't bi or kinky, as if that would make the "problem" go away. And to prove I wasn't as weird as I thought I might be, all I had to do was concentrate on girls.

George is forced at an early age to deal with the dilemma of being different, not just sexually but intellectually. Walking the line between conformity and acceptance, and following his own ideas and desires, leaves him feeling misunderstood, friendless, and wondering how he'll ever escape his provincial environment. Living two lives, suppressing a lot of his emotions, he faces the same fear that haunts many adolescents, male and female—first, that he's some kind of fraud, and second, that no matter what he does, he'll always be an outsider. Popular culture romanticizes the rebel, but in reality being different and swimming upstream is about as glamorous as having a migraine.

As a son, George is the product of a traditional couple: a rigid, responsibility-obsessed, critical father, and an accepting, fair, and loving mother. This dynamic does not allow for a genuine male identity to form. Instead, it leads George to heavily identify with his supportive, comforting, and accessible mother. Because his deeper self identifies with his mother, his sexual orientation also comes from her.

George is open about his feelings but often in an abstract way. He can philosophize and intellectualize about who he is and what his emotions mean to him, but on an intimate level there's still guilt and secrecy about being bisexual, homosexual, or a sadomasochist. As we'll see, his sexual crisis begins in high school when he "couldn't feel anything." The depression he will experience is probably protection against his growing awareness of being "different," and his self-described numbness is an effort to distance himself from it.

lost my virginity at age sixteen to a brunette named Emily in a cold, wet ditch after a graduation party. We were both drunk and inept. It was a pretty miserable experience. My more romantic interpretation is that I actually lost my virginity twice. The second time was to a beautiful girl, Gloria, who was athletic and smart and liked to come to me for advice. She knew I stood apart from jocks and the lesser lights in the classroom. One time she actually asked me for advice about sex. I was no expert, but I acted like I was, and I could convey enough empathy that I soon won her over. The discussion was also exhilarating and erotic. This might have been the first time I was conscious of falling in love with someone, or coming close to it. I had an incredible crush on Gloria. I was more her confidant than boyfriend, but Gloria and I just clicked. And we did have some physical intimacy, which was terrific. Our relationship didn't last more than a few months, yet it was a huge boost to my self-esteem.

I took up the guitar in high school and was part of a band that got some local gigs. There were drugs, of course, and girls, but I also developed a reputation as a decent musician. Music is still one of the driving forces of my life. It certainly helped me get through high school, though it wasn't quite enough. Suppressing my unhappiness, and especially my sexuality, I lapsed into a state of depression around my junior year. It wasn't that I was lost in some deep funk and walked with my eyes continually cast down; I just couldn't feel anything. It's a hard thing to convey to someone who hasn't suffered from depression. You feel like you're not tied to anything. Life is something you watch but never participate in. You can be talking to a good friend and at the same time watching yourself, wondering who the hell you are.

I'm sure part of my depression was due to the guilt I carried inside me. As Tori Amos laments in one of her songs, I had enough guilt to start my own religion. Guilt about my sexuality, about not working hard enough, about not living up to my dad's expectations, about not knowing what to do with my life. I knew I was smart, but that didn't seem to get me anywhere or answer any key questions. I tried recreational drugs, conventional sex with women, and more sadomasochism. If I kept some things a secret from the world, I was still open to finding out who I really was.

I moved to Minneapolis the summer after high school, worked odd jobs, and qualified for enough student loans to enroll in a small state college. This was a major statement of ambition for a kid from a blue-collar family. I skipped most of the liberal arts curriculum and focused on sociology. Coming from a small dot on the map, I desperately wanted to know what other cultures were like. How different am I, and is there anything that passes as a definition of normalcy? I loved my courses and professors—for the first time in my life I was intellectually challenged—but I was still wrestling with my private demons.

In my sophomore year I met and began living with a woman named Grace. We slept together, experimented with drugs and various modes of sexuality, and traded confidences. In my gut I think I knew there was something "off" about Grace, but because I'm the kind of person who feeds off intimacy, I confided in her about my bisexuality and sadomasochistic tendencies. She was only the second person to whom I'd admitted the truth. The first was another girl I dated and who accepted me without judgment. But Grace turned out to be different. She decided to share my secret with the world at large.

Overnight I lost just about every friend I thought I had. I became extremely isolated and, given that I was already prone to spending most of my time alone, I would now hide from the outside world for weeks at a time. Insomnia became a chronic problem. I really thought I was losing my mind. I went into therapy, was prescribed an antidepressant, and lost myself as much as possible in academics. The therapy helped in that it gave me insights into myself. From my mom I'd learned how to pick myself up when things got tough. I was still not ready to come out of the closet, but I suddenly was making new friends—intellectual types that I'd never been exposed to. To this day I'd rather have one scintillating conversation with a stranger than ten dull ones with acquaintances. Having to make small talk while trapped in a car with someone is one of my visions of hell.

Like a lot of men, George exhibits a strong need to be liked and loved. However, his search for validation is undermined by his fears. His primary issue is his sexuality, but in a broader context it is the fear of not living up to expectations. Even when they have a problem in their lives or their relationships—and acknowledge that honesty is called for—men are still slow to look for support. George says he likes to have a couple of close friends but feels no need to confide in anyone else. If he holds nothing back from his friends, he's in better shape than a lot of men, who are too competitive and distrusting to share their problems with one another. The Steven Spielberg *Band of Brothers* vision, where men stand tall as caring comrades in times of adversity, is ennobling, but hardly an everyday occurrence. Perhaps it does show what emotions men are capable of if daily competition—and living in a fear-based culture—were replaced to some degree with empathy and support.

One day at school I met a girl named Roni. I didn't know it at that moment, but looking back, my life changed in a heartbeat. I would have to call Roni the love of my life. She was, and remains, stunningly beautiful. Half Korean, half white, she was born in the Midwest but with an otherworldly soul. She has a body that might have been designed by a horny teenage boy, but I was even more attracted to her wit, sensitivity, intelligence, and sense of humor. I mean, she could have been a chubby half Korean with a weird face and I would not have loved her any less. Roni liked to talk about politics, the environment, human rights—and she could do trigonometry too! Even more astounding, she appreciated me for my brains and sensitivity, things I liked in myself. We didn't hold anything back from one another, except in one crucial area. In our five-year relationship she would prove to be my greatest teacher, as I was hers. Not to tip the scales of sentimentality too far, but we covered so much territory emotionally, endured the agony of ironic fates, and wove our lives around each other with such texture that if I were Shakespeare, I would have written Roni a sonnet every day.

Falling in love is less of a process than falling out. Falling in love is spontaneous, out of control, compelling, enthralling. It starts with infatuation, which is so powerful the first time you experience it that the depth of emotion stays with you forever. In fact, it haunts you because the second time you fall in love, infatuation doesn't have quite the same grip. And the third time, if there is one, the power is even less. With Roni, I didn't want to be one second, one breath, without her in my presence. We could make each other laugh. We could piss each other off. We could make each other insanely lustful. It was beautiful. For a while I thought my issues and my confusion about my sexuality were over. I was a straight male after all, and I decided not to tell Roni about my past forays. Why should I, I reasoned, if they had no bearing on the present. That decision would turn out to be a devastating mistake.

When you're first in love, you don't really know who you're in love with. You think you do, but the real discoveries, both positive and negative, only come with time. I think that staying in love for a lifetime—at least in the romantic, early-phase definition, the one where "spark" rules—is almost impossible. With Roni I never thought about a future, certainly not at first. I was totally absorbed in the moment. When I had to drop out of college because I could no longer afford the tuition, Roni dropped out with me. We decided, poring over a map one day, that we would become explorers, travel the country, and be the captains of our destinies. We had had similar childhoods, deprived and fear-based (the Korean culture can be even more repressive than my Catholic blue-collar one) and we now empowered each other to be free.

Like other men who struggle with strong female identification, George was attracted to a strong, confident, even dominant woman in Roni. If one accepts that real gender is often disguised, Roni played the role of the male and George was more of the traditional female, dependent and often clingy. He embodies the sexual confusion, vulnerabilities, and defensiveness of many men. George wants or expects—despite the blend of having a close, loving bond with his mother and a negative, distant relationship with his father—to emerge "all male." The difficult dynamic of being raised by two contrasting parents makes George confused, self-punishing, and in need of validation. Growing up in a masculine, blue-collar town that he despised, he had nowhere to acquire the identification to feel, on a gut level, that he was the man he'd like to be.

Despite confusion about gender roles, there is no doubt that George's deep feelings for Roni are genuine, and they give him some sorely needed confidence. The relationship provides the foundation for giving and receiving affection that all men need in order to escape the perceived requirement that they always have to be proving themselves. A good relationship is a refuge not only from the world of competition and judgment but, certainly in its early stages, the opportunity to grow and move in ways that cannot be undertaken alone. As we'll find out with Roni and George, the crucial test of any relationship comes when the infatuation wears off.

For the next five joyous years we traveled here and there, took dead-end jobs, endured some humiliating family visits back home, and learned new things about the world together. We also taught each other about emotions and happiness. We ended up in San Francisco, where I landed a writing job with a newspaper, covering the arts and music scene. Even though I had no journalistic experience, I was good at it, and unlike my father, I now had a job that I really loved. Roni didn't have to work because she got a tip from her cousin about a tech start-up. That paid for a year of leisure, reading books, self-exploration, and indulging herself for the first time with a few material acquisitions. We could have been mistaken for a straight, aspiring middle-class couple.

And we might have pulled it off, if one night Roni hadn't come out of the closet on me. She said that after a lot of painful soul-searching she knew that she was gay. In her year off from work she'd found the courage to be herself. She gave me some credit for giving her that courage. I should have seen this coming—things Roni had said or hinted at during our years together—but I was totally blown away. I was hurt. I was angry. I never yelled at Roni and my most aggressive moments were the angry silences I learned from my father. Of course, all that anger was basically coming from confusion over my sexual identity.

When I told Roni that I was bi, only a few days after her revelation to me, it was a catharsis for me on the one hand, but the end of our relationship on the other. The irony, of course, was that if I'd been more honest from the beginning, or if she'd said she was bi as well, and not gay, maybe our relationship would never have unraveled. To this day I regret that I didn't have the courage to be more honest. When you live in fear, nothing goes right.

Sometimes I wonder if our uncertainty over our sexuality wasn't part of the initial attraction process, something working on a subconscious level. I kind of believe that. But what can bring two people together can in the end tear them apart. Ultimately you can't be in love with someone, or stay in love with them, if your sexual orientations are different. That may seem obvious to some, but it's still one of the "whys" that I grapple with. Our souls were so entwined—wasn't that enough to keep us in love? I honestly believe that nothing can be deeper than a soul connection, but without a physical connection—when your sexual orientations are pulling you in opposite directions—it's impossible for a romantic relationship to survive. When Roni actually started dating other women, I felt hurt and abandoned all over again. My biggest fear was that we would become strangers.

It was an awkward, confusing situation for me. To some degree I'm still in it. Roni and I moved together to another town, and for a while we saw each other at least once a week. Actually, we slept together a couple of times. What was that about? Perhaps I couldn't let go and neither could she. Yet, with time, we began to lead separate lives. To survive emotionally I began to will myself out of love. Some part of you has to die to make room for something else to be born. But it takes a long time to recover. In the middle of the night I'm still capable of memories of Roni that are so powerful that I can't go back to sleep. I suppose, if one will allow for an elastic definition of love, Roni and I are still very much attached. I've

never come to love her any less; it's just that the nature of that
connection has changed. People have far more dimensions
than three, and a couple has way more than six. That's one of
the lessons she and I learned from our breakup. And I wouldn't
have learned it if we hadn't broken up.

So Roni changed and I changed. The nature of our love
was now built around openness, respect, and liberation.
We'd always had those qualities, but they grew in importance.
Through Roni I became exposed to the postfeminist movement
which, as far as I've seen, relies more on self-realization than
male-bashing. Another positive was that I stopped being in
the closet. I finally learned not to coddle other people's
insecurities. It's a far worse thing to lie than to present
someone with something they may not be equipped to cope
with. You have to be true to yourself. Thank you, Shakespeare!

Even though George displays lots of confidence at times,
it's not enough to hide his insecurities. Once his secrets are
exposed—deliberately or unintentionally—he has to deal with
his anger, shame, and humiliation. Unless his partner is understanding and supportive—Roni, caught up in her own liberation, seemed to have a mixed response to George's news about
his bisexuality—a man may begin to pull away from his partner
when rejected at this crucial juncture. A lot of men I spoke with
said rejection is one thing that pushes them out of love. "If a
woman is not attracted to me anymore," one man said, "I'm
going to kill all my emotion for her, even if I had been deeply in
love. Some women want you to adore them forever, like they're
goddesses, but that's not very realistic."

Popular culture—and the billion-dollar industries that revolve around fashion, beauty, and romance—perpetuates the
myth that something is wrong with us if we can't find our soul
mate. As George points out, loneliness is the great bogeyman.

We fear it almost more than death. Indeed, we treat loneliness as a kind of death. But loneliness should not be confused with aloneness, or the validation that comes with taking private journeys and personal risks. Being different, being without a partner, can be okay for many people. A lot of women have been liberated from the mind-set that to be whole they have to be part of a team. Most men have not. If you don't have a woman at your side, what kind of man are you? Are you gay? Are you depressed? Do you have self-esteem issues? The sad irony is that men often cover up for their lack of self-esteem by hiding in their relationships. Men could learn from women, especially the under-thirty generation, about flexibility, strength, independence, and letting go. It's what George was finally striving for in trying to separate his identity from Roni's.

The Quest for Validation
Conclusions

Many men I spoke with said they felt confused, and at times overwhelmed, by the multiple roles they're supposed to play—problem solver, breadwinner, understanding husband, intuitive lover, wise father, compassionate friend—and the expectation that they should be good at all of them. They thought this is how society validates them as men, even if they secretly felt more conflict and anxiety than satisfaction. Yet they were afraid to complain because they were sure they'd be labeled inadequate or thought of as not being "real men." They were especially perplexed by the myth that if you're a man you can do almost anything because men have always had it "easier" and have more freedom and more choices than women. More freedom and choices, they agreed, but easier, no.

One man I interviewed talked about the first time he felt that his life was going to be harder than his sister's. He was nine years old when his father, a Vietnam vet, told him that the government could reestablish the draft whenever it wanted and he could be called upon to die for his country. He felt heroic and fearful at the same time. If there is danger in the world, a man learns early on, he is the one expected to sacrifice himself to protect others. By logical extension, if he doesn't make sacrifices for his family, surely he's letting down those who count on him.

Being pulled in too many and often contradictory directions leaves men with the idea that they are being set up for criticism. The quest for validation and self-esteem is in part an attempt to avoid the failure label and to support the definition of masculinity as one of duty. Is there any way out of this box? First, many men would be happier—and feel less burdened—if they stopped trying so hard to prove themselves. Second, it would be helpful if they verbalized to their partners the pressures they feel, and delegated some tasks or simply cut back on their roles. Third, if they recognized that their culture is riddled with fear-based behaviors and this is partly attributed to men who run from the stigma of failure—and subliminally pass the message on to their sons that it's okay to run—they could reeducate themselves to become better role models.

For most of us, self-discovery and the motivation to change don't happen until a serious crisis enters our lives. Even when we admit to a crisis, our first attempts at a solution are often superficial. Women, if fearful their partners are falling out of love, will probably start going to the gym, try a new diet, pay for cosmetic surgery, throw out their old clothes, or embark on some other makeover. They think that men become dissatisfied with them because they have lost their physical appeal, so they respond to a crisis with external solutions. This idea is reinforced by a culture that not only lauds women who look thin and sexy, but stereotypes men as a gender that is largely stimulated by a woman's appearance. While the latter may often be true, it doesn't automatically follow that men fall out of love because of a sudden or gradual loss of physical attraction to their partners. In most cases, the reasons for falling out of love are deeper and reflect feelings of anger, powerlessness, or fading of attraction due to a woman's manipulation, control, or marginalization of her partner.

Perhaps if they acknowledged the importance of a man's emotions, women wouldn't be at such a loss about what to do when their relationships run into trouble. Strip away the pretenses of masculinity, and men are looking, just as women are, to be loved, understood, and accepted, to express their emotional needs, and to feel comfortable with themselves and their partners. Listening and accepting is the healthiest kind of validation one partner can give another.

In tracing the roots of self-esteem, many men, if they're truthful, will admit to feeling failed by their mothers or fathers. To use corporal punishment on boys, to refrain from nurturing them, to urge at an early age that they "become men," to teach them that success and achievement are the quintessential male values—this gives a boy the hidden message that love is conditional. *If you do what I tell you . . . if you follow the prescribed path . . . if you're a good boy, I'll be so proud of you.*

While the origins of self-esteem are in childhood and adolescence, its further development in an adult relationship—for example, the capacity to accept criticism, to recognize and deflect harmful messages, to forgive one's partner as well as one's caregivers—is a necessity for the relationship to grow. Continued growth and awareness also may help in balancing the power structure of a relationship. Leverage in any partnership is rarely fifty-fifty, but when it becomes too lopsided, both partners suffer. The one who is dominant often becomes critical, indifferent, impatient, or cruel. The one who is submissive is insecure, clingy, and feels powerless and unworthy. For Bill, Tom, and George, each is overly dominant or overly submissive—or vacillates between the two—without knowing how to find the center.

Tips for Avoiding This Relationship Buster

1. Define what you want and need from a relationship before you become involved with someone, then reality check your list with a good friend. What may seem reasonable to you might be a case of overexpecting, and an indicator that you need to mature before you can sustain a relationship.
2. Look more to yourself and what's in your life than to your partner for validation. A good partner should be a great listener and empathizer without being your enabler.
3. Recognize that full-time relationships are no more a guarantee of happiness than living without a partner is a stigma. For a lot of healthy people, validation and self-worth come principally from work, friends, and individual passions.
4. Work through your own validation issues—discover where they come from and what needs to be done—not just to help yourself, but to recognize similar patterns in, and be able to help, your partner.
5. For men, accept that healthy masculinity is not about denying failure but embracing it as a cornerstone of growth, and a means of opening up and becoming more intimate with your partner.

The Perfection Impulse

t's debatable whether the perfection impulse is a more pervasive demon in men or women. As hard as men are on themselves, perhaps achievement-oriented women self-inflict pain with even greater depth and accuracy. For women, the unanticipated price of liberation four decades ago was a new self-scrutiny and self-criticism that men had been living with, without much benefit, for a long time. Women seem no more certain than men about how to deal with this anxiety, except to keep striving to look younger, thinner, and sexier, be more successful in the workplace, or be the perfect mother or homemaker. A lot of us think we can't be perfect enough, because trying to be perfect is what we think makes us happy. Trying to be perfect is how we validate ourselves. It's also how we impose a semblance of order on the chaos we feel is caused by those around us who are less than perfect.

Of the men I interviewed who described themselves as perfectionists, most were professionals on the achievement track who defined their "mission" as working as hard as they possibly could, and being more successful in life than their peers. Their motives for perfectionism were either getting respect, recognition, and love, feeling good about themselves, or running from something in their pasts. All of them had a strong need to feel in control of their lives. Indeed, for almost all men, but especially perfectionists, masculinity *means* being in control. If you're a perfectionist, you need to feel in control not just of your own life but often those around you, and you become judgmental or intolerant of those who fail to meet your standards.

Other themes covered in this section include:

- Why an excessive focus on ambition, achievement, and perfection are sometimes the result of a "loser" or deprived childhood, and why being highly successful, while a topical fix, never addresses the deeper issues of anger, loss, and abandonment

- How some men hide in their perfectionism, giving them an excuse to reject women, and avoid real intimacy, by claiming their partners don't meet their expectations

- Why those who try to be as perfect as possible, in order to be liked and validated, don't realize that most people are turned off by overachievers

- Why even if we feel happy and secure when we are successful, there is an underlying anxiety that we are still being judged and scrutinized—and we are somehow inadequate—because we can never be successful enough

- How perfectionism is a relationship buster not only because it leads to the need for control, but the failure to achieve goals can mean loss of self-respect (and blaming our partners in the process), and eventually falling out of love

7

Barry's Story

Sixty-three percent of men expect women to make an effort with
their appearance, including firm breasts, a toned stomach,
and cellulite-free thighs. Ninety-two percent of women
expect the same thing of themselves.
—Daily Diet Tracker

While Steven has his argument with Renee in New Mexico,
and Bill contemplates the night vista from his Los Angeles pad, in Denver we meet Barry, thirty-eight, as he walks his
dog back to his expensive condo. An executive headhunter,
Barry is over six feet tall with dark, floppy hair, a big smile, and
a purposeful gaze. There's a bit of the fraternity rat about him—
a fun, prank-loving guy—but there's a seriousness underneath
his carefree demeanor. It's Saturday night, he thinks, and what
am I doing? I'm walking my dog! He laughs, more dismayed by
his reality than depressed. Recently divorced, Barry is dating
several women, but none of them really interests him. Rather,
they interest him at first, but it's only a matter of time before he
finds something he doesn't like about them. He knows his standards are high, but after his disastrous first marriage he's not

going to settle for just anyone. The woman in his life needs to be close to perfect, at least for him, or he's not going to be happy.

Maybe he should just drive to the office tonight and do some catch-up work before Monday. Imagine, working on a Saturday evening, he thinks, but he doesn't mind. Barry's barometer for self-esteem is money and professional success, and he pushes himself harder than most of his peers. Because of his ambition, Barry has a high degree of sensitivity to, almost an intolerance of, criticism. He works his butt off and resents anyone who says differently—an echo from his childhood, where no accolades came his way, only taunts for being a loser. He has come a long way in his life. He has slowly fashioned a lifestyle that minimizes any chance for failure by carefully controlling his social and work environments. Control is very important to Barry, as is the idea of perfection. He will not compromise his professional goals any more than he will his standards for the women he dates.

Barry thinks of himself as a fairly complex person because he lives with several internal contradictions, and not a small amount of guilt. Growing up, he was the kid chosen last for the baseball team, had no social skills, no friends, and zero self-confidence. What he had in spades was anger. "Getting left out or left behind all the time does that to you," he says. Then he was sent to Catholic school, and that turned out to be a mixed blessing. The discipline and structure were a positive, but emotionally the school felt dehumanizing. Barry was taught that the Virgin Mary was the quintessential mother figure, the role model for women in all walks of life. The nuns drilled this into his head. "Somewhere along the line," he says, "you develop the notion that not only should you strive for virtue and perfection in your own life, but the woman you're ultimately seeking as your wife has to be perfect too. Someone on a pedestal, someone with all the 'assets.' Not that Britney Spears should ever be confused with the Virgin Mary, but in some ways Britney and other divas take her place today. Men are always looking for the perfect woman, the '10' that Bo Derek represented a long time ago."

The "perfection dream" holds true for a lot of guys. They want to make over some girl in exactly the image that suits their needs. Maybe this is because as our world grows increasingly complex and unpredictable, the idea of control becomes increasingly important, and linked to our happiness. Also, men are acquirers by nature, and many guys think of women as another acquisition. (I know this is politically incorrect, and you don't dare say it in public because some woman might shoot you in the kneecaps, but a lot of men still think this way.) Ultimately, your relationship will be doomed to failure because women, or men, don't want to be made over into anything. When the relationship crashes, you initially blame your partner but in the end you feel responsible. And if you're Catholic like me, you never stop flogging yourself.

Yet idealism dies hard. Even after my divorce and all the lessons I learned from it, there's a part of me that still is searching for the perfect woman—my perfect woman—as I begin to date again. I go through women relatively quickly, saying good-bye when they disappoint me, but on the other hand, I've been tossed out of some relationships too. If a woman thinks of me as too critical and demanding, that's okay, she's not my type anyway. I tell them half-seriously that I'm a Virgo, and Virgos are first and foremost hardest on themselves.

Does the perfect woman or man exist? Of course not, but that doesn't stop either gender from setting the bar pretty high. Partly I blame the media, especially those reality-TV shows. If you check out shows like *elimiDATE* or *Blind Date,* you might say, come on, this is just entertainment; it's supposed to be about degradation and cruelty. But there's a subtext that is taken seriously by viewers. The subtext is that this is a competitive, judgmental world, and you better be as perfect as possible if you want to find your dream partner, if you don't want to be rejected or stigmatized. What you do with your looks, how witty you are, how funny, how appealing—this is crucial because we live in Judgment City. And if you're not close to perfect, you're more or less thrown in the trash heap. The singles scene is one of the circles of hell that Dante forgot to include in *The Divine Comedy:* peaks of pleasure alternating with valleys of rejection, pain, and despair.

When you marry the woman of your dreams you never know what's going to happen. You're in love, and you hope you're also compatible and comfortable when that rush of love wears off. In addition to being in love, I thought my marriage offered me comfort and security. Sometimes the sex was good, sometimes not, but that wasn't as important to me as the feeling of being accepted and wanted. My marriage lasted ten years, eight of which I would call prosperous and generally happy. Then came as unexpected a deterioration as I could imagine. I didn't want my marriage to die, and even today, more than a year after my divorce, I feel the breakup was my fault. Divorce felt like a huge failure to me. I look at my parents—they've been married for almost four decades—and I ask what happened to me.

Failure is something I've been conscious of most of my life. In fact, it's one of my greatest fears and a motivator in my professional life. I can't stand to fail at anything. Growing up on the East Coast, I was the oldest of three kids, but the one with all the problems. I looked like a dork with Coke-bottle glasses, and I was awkward socially. Physically, I was a lumbering giant who had few if any real friends. The neighborhood scapegoat, I had no protectors, and no witty comebacks of my own. I simply could not think on my feet. Today, I dislike silences and tend to fill them with words rather than to stand there and be judged a dummy. I had learning disabilities too, and not much help in diagnosing or correcting them. Even if they didn't say it, I always thought I was a disappointment to my parents. My life was the perfect storm for low self-esteem, chronic anxiety, and unfocused anger.

My family did a lot of moving around as I grew up because Dad kept climbing higher on the corporate ladder. He was a loving but absent man, though now, in his retirement, we get along well. Both my parents were incredibly supportive of me during and after my divorce. When I was growing up, however, my mom turned to religion to keep from going crazy while raising three kids. Catholicism gave her a lot of solace. When we became teenagers, she went extreme, even speaking in tongues. She was the quintessential true believer. She thought being devoutly religious would cure her of all the anxiety, frustration, and stress of trying to be the devoted, perfect wife and mother. In the end, she learned that extremism cures nothing, and she now takes a more centrist position about her life and her religion. Both my parents have learned over the years that personal growth does not come without some experimentation, risk taking, and pain. They are great role models for my siblings and me.

Growing up, I was a handful for my parents, because I was always in trouble. I may not have understood the impact of peer rejection at the time, but I felt it and reacted to it. Both Mom and Dad thought Catholic school would give me the discipline and confidence I sorely needed. In one sense, from first grade through high school, the nuns definitely gave me that gift. In the Church there is the sense of belonging to something bigger than yourself. For a time I even thought about becoming a priest. Catholic schools are run like the military-industrial complex, a bureaucracy where regimentation and procedure are an end in themselves. Rules mean everything. Without rules, there is only chaos. As an adult, I attribute a lot of my professional successes to a basic organization of my life and daily conduct that I learned in school.

But another side of me, the part that felt unloved and alienated from the world, was a rebel. As an adolescent, I became moody, with an unpredictable temper, and I was cynical or sarcastic about everything. I didn't know how to handle conflict and confrontation. I was as undeveloped emotionally as I was physically. Because I was in an environment where confrontation was not tolerated, I hung with the out-of-orbit clique. It was easy to slip from unfocused anger and discontent into drugs. I was messed up a lot of the time.

My views about the nuns gradually grew darker. There is a long-term effect on your psyche from an educational system run largely by women, a system that is unforgiving of anyone who breaks the rules. And I was always looking for ways to undermine the system. If I could buy a piece of candy on the outside for a nickel, I would smuggle it into school and sell it for a dime, because the school store charged you fifteen cents. That's how my mind worked—be clever and undermine the system. In school I ended up not only disliking and distrusting authority, I distrusted women because they were the authority. I kept a series of underground notebooks where I illustrated the injustices my friends and I suffered at the hands of the nuns. The notebooks were my revenge on the system. I passed them around to allies and sympathizers, which further enhanced my reputation as a rebel, which in turn became a foundation for my self-esteem, such as it was. You could say that my anger was my life support.

To the school administration I was a serious hazard. I broke the all-time demerit record in my sophomore year. At the end of my junior year I was asked by the head prefect not to come back. That's the moment I hit bottom. Mom and Dad made me realize that I had a choice: buck up and become responsible, or be labeled a screwup, disappoint myself and my family, and give up on my future. They never exactly said, "You're a failure, Barry," but the message was clear. I was not living up to my potential. I gave the issue lots of thought over the summer. Thanks to lobbying from my parents, I got reinstated, but not before I signed a special contract with the school with a "zero tolerance" clause. One mistake and I was out for good.

I have a serious side that wants to do the right thing, to be successful and respected (my parents' values, for sure), and maybe that seriousness started to kick in during my senior year. I started to enjoy learning, and I also excelled in music and choir. I even got the lead in the school play. I filled out to six foot three and two hundred pounds, and became a decent hockey forward. As I went from C student to honor roll, people who had once called me a loser now rallied to my side. I would wake up in the middle of the night, thinking, Hey, is this for real? For the first time in my life I had real self-respect. At graduation I was even singled out for an achievement or two. That validation meant a lot to me.

Describing his early adolescence, Barry says his anger functioned as his life support, which on a certain level is true, but his anger also kept feeding his distrust and cynicism. With help from his parents and school, Barry is able to reverse those patterns of negativity and tap into a reserve of talent that quickly boosts his confidence. At this point in his life he's not fully aware of how deep his anger and self-doubt run, but at least he has a positive glimpse of how his adult world might turn out. The conflict between dealing with childhood and adolescent traumas and the tantalizing possibility of success and achievement—being whipsawed back and forth between rejection and redemption—will drive Barry's need to feel in control and, ultimately, the search for perfection in his adult relationships. His perfectionism also comes from his parents—the father who keeps climbing the corporate ladder and the mother who wants to be the absolutely devoted wife and mother. As we'll see, Barry thinks that perfection will mean happiness both because it is a shield against criticism, and an emulation of the values of his successfully married parents.

got acceptance letters from several very decent, high-pressure colleges, but because my confidence wasn't that deep I settled for a state school. In college my behavior regressed slightly—no drugs, but lots of partying. I started out being attracted to almost any girl who gave me a lot of attention, so long as she met my minimum standards for attractiveness. Call it the quest for validation from someone who still feared he was a geek inside. Even if my looks had now blossomed and I was no longer awkward and lumbering, I was still insecure. I could be charming one moment, but with my temper I could blow up at someone at any time.

Because of that immaturity, I wasn't capable of committing to any one woman. I ended up cheating on several girlfriends, even though I knew it was wrong and I felt guilty. I got one girl pregnant and we had to arrange for an abortion, which did nothing to soothe my Catholic conscience. Morality, however, was no match for the emotional logic that said the more women I had relationships with, the more I was loved and validated, the more popular and desirable I would be, and the higher I could set the perfection bar for women I dated in the future. What amazed me was that most women couldn't see through me. As transparent, even desperate, as I thought I was, the women I dated got caught up in the externals. I was funny. I could dance. I was charming. I was a gentleman. What else is there in life when you're twenty years old and in the incubator called college?

The problem for perfectionists like Barry is that they are driven not just by the need to live up to someone's expectations, but by a fear of failure. Men can be so consumed with their image and reputation that they are slow to trust their own instincts, or listen to any internal voice that complains of unhappiness. In Barry's case, his anger and distrust of authority—the nuns in his school—eventually led him to a distrust of women. It's too bad his focus on perfection becomes a diversion from his unresolved conflicts, and a rationalization to keep him from real self-discovery. He says he's amazed in college that women can't see through him, but how well does he see himself? He knows he uses women for validation, but when that strategy fails, does he have any idea where he will look next? Barry, like a lot of men who are frustrated in their relationships when women don't make them happy, will turn to other definitions of masculinity to feel fulfilled.

Another downside of perfectionism is self-delusion. Men and women create in their imaginations, from their own needs, an idealized version of the opposite sex. The Prince Charming myth gives a little girl a sense of destiny—the notion that the perfect man is out there, waiting just for her—along with a sense of entitlement. At some level the myth stays in her consciousness forever. But that myth is no different than someone like Barry or his friends creating their list of attributes of the perfect woman. Men too have a hard time relinquishing their fantasies. Popular culture, especially celebrity worship, enforces the idea that one can never be beautiful, rich, smart, thin, or happy enough. As psychologists have pointed out, we push each other to impossible extremes to reach impossible goals, then tell ourselves something is wrong with us or our partners if we don't reach them.

At the end of my freshman year I fell in love for the first time. Zoey was my age, and—incredibly—she met all my criteria for the perfect woman. Not only was she a gorgeous, athletic blonde, she was empathetic, kind, caring, and totally accepting of me, rough edges and all. She had not a bone of distrust in her body. Zoey was an angel. I was too young to understand how lucky I was, too much on the prowl to settle down and make a commitment. I didn't even know enough to be sad about my loss when we broke up because I thought there'd be a million more Zoeys on the horizon, just waiting for me. I was so wrong. I don't know how many women I dated before I graduated, but none came close to Zoey. She definitely spoiled me. I was suddenly attracted only to tall, athletic, smart blondes who also had to be empathetic and kind. And of course they had to love me to death.

I want to stress the absolute importance of a woman's acceptance of me. At that time in my life I invested all my emotions in women. The only yardstick for success or source of self-esteem was who I slept with, ate with, went to the movies with, and to whom I revealed my deepest thoughts and feelings. One of the ironies was that I wasn't overly revealing to any woman because I had that old trust issue dating back to the nuns. I was very cautious about what I exposed of myself— never my fears, God forbid—yet women found it quite easy to talk to me and trust me. I thought that was the perfect template for a relationship—women opening up to me while I coyly hid my insecurities.

Although I didn't recognize it at the time, I had become in some ways quite controlling. I certainly fit the profile. If you've had a rough childhood, you know your pain spots and work hard to avoid them, consciously or unconsciously. If I had women trusting and confiding in me without me reciprocating—isn't that the ultimate control? Yet one of my contradictions, particularly after Zoey, was that I tended to fall for controlling women.

That was my frame of mind when I met Georgia in my junior year. She was even more physically stunning than Zoey, and I was pulled into the gravitational field that I would call her "feminine mystique." Georgia had one powerful aura. I fell in love with her right away. I would come to realize she was nothing like Zoey—Georgia was selfish and manipulative—but sex with her was beyond description. By that I mean its emotional connotations far surpassed any physical pleasure— God, this woman really wanted and needed me—and that opened the floodgates for my total devotion to her. I kept thinking that I didn't deserve this woman, and even when her darker side became evident—she was, for example, always driving a wedge between me and my friends—I couldn't say no when she wanted something. In retrospect, a classic case of fatal attraction. The more elusive or unavailable she was— deliberately so, I came to realize, as she broke dates or failed to keep her word—the more I chased her. That was her power, or the power I gave her. She ended up cheating on me, more than once I'm sure, but I didn't want to believe it. Georgia was even more insecure than I was, and playing the same validation game with the same tools. She had the charm, the good looks, the intuitive/empathetic insights that you offer your partner when the lights are out, but Georgia used them even more seductively than I did.

I don't think Georgia was even close to being in love with me, no matter what she said to the contrary. When I began accusing her of insincerity and deceit, she always had an excuse. More arguments ensued. I never did get her to admit that she wasn't in love with me. She could look me in the eye and lie with such grace and conviction that I wanted to believe her. I finally broke up with her, but I still felt like a fool for being used. No doubt this was my karmic payback for all the women I had cheated on and lied to. I was chastened. I told myself I had learned three huge lessons. One, don't abuse or lie to people, especially someone you're intimate with, and think you can get away with it. Two, don't be too dependent on women; don't let them be your measure of success or validation. And three, using a combination of their sexuality and emotional reasoning, women have an incredible aura, a power that few men possess. Men are great bullshit artists but that "talent" doesn't compare to a woman's bag of tools. She can manipulate and persuade you without your even knowing what she's doing. Sometimes she doesn't know either. Men may be liars, but they usually know what they're doing. Women exaggerate (they rarely call it lying), but I think often subconsciously.

Many perfectionists beat themselves up, and sometimes blame their partners in the process, if things don't go exactly their way. In Barry's case, growing up Catholic and believing in the ideal of the Virgin Mary, coupled with his perfectionist parents and the desire to overcome his "loser childhood," make him almost inflexible in his pursuit of success.

Barry's tendency to fall for controlling women might mean that he really wants a woman to take care of him and make him feel better. His own controlling nature comes from a fear of being hurt and taken advantage of, but if he interprets control in his partner as care, indulgence, and nurturing, or just a feminine aura, he gladly surrenders to her as he did to Zoey and Georgia. The women Barry really likes are those who "love (him) to death," a blind adoration that seems to draw inspiration from Mary and Jesus. Only when the motives of the adoring/controlling partner become obvious, as they did with Georgia, does Barry realize he's been taken advantage of. This pushes him back to a state of deep suspicion where he has to feel in control again. Until Barry finds a middle ground, where trust becomes more important than control, it's unlikely that he'll have a stable relationship.

After my Georgia experience, I began to date with a lot more caution. I no longer looked for an outrageous beauty with all the cards. I looked for a woman who wouldn't threaten me. Often I found myself attracted to wounded souls. These were women who had had a bad childhood or, like me, had been scarred in a relationship. I would help them solve their problems, at least give advice, and be around when they needed someone for comfort. If you're with someone who's hurting, it's easy to play lifeguard, the wise father, the fixer . . . whatever is necessary. This made me feel great because I like to be counted on and looked up to. I think my hero complex goes back to my underground school journals—the rebel as hero—because it's me slaying all those authoritarian nuns and righting the world's wrongs. So here I was, adored and validated once again. It was a safe strategy for me, like going to state college instead of trying an Ivy. None of these women could reach my emotions because most were too vulnerable or needy to make that effort. Once again I was resorting to one-way relationships. I had plenty of fun and companionship with these women, but I didn't fall in love with any of them, or even care to. Falling in love, I figured, might take away my power.

Rather than dating a lot, I put my energy into my fledgling career as a bank loan officer. This meant fifty- and sixty-hour workweeks, but the results were superior performance and accolades from my boss. I was feeling much better about my life. Everyone respected me. I had transferred my validation needs from women to work. The bank was a place to feel safe, and as competitive as it could be, the reward for honest, efficient labor was straightforward. I think, in general, men are much happier, and more productive, in a masculine work environment, as banks usually are. When a woman is the boss, or most of your coworkers are female, communication in general is a lot more emotional and circuitous, a lot more complex. You need a higher level of intuition to do well in that environment.

Barry's jump from women to his profession in order to find deeper satisfaction in his life—and less volatility—is not untypical of the men I interviewed. The world of women is complex, filled with nuances, and its emotional rewards are often seen as transient. On the other hand, a male work environment such as Barry's is linear, predictable, and usually rewards someone who puts in long hours. However, one of the more destructive assumptions of masculinity is that men need to work hard, to lead, and to make lots of money in order to feel in control, as well as to be liked and respected. Barry talks about his idealized self-image as a hero, and being loved. If he can't get that from women, he thinks he can get it from his male peers and bosses. But in the end, no matter how hard he works, how much money he makes, or how in control he feels, his pursuit of perfection will turn him back to women. For a lot of men, starting with their mothers, women are the ultimate source of approval. Barry fears his life will be incomplete and imperfect without a successful relationship.

I met my future wife, Danielle, when I was twenty-seven and had just switched careers from banker to executive headhunter. Within a year I became as adept in my new field as I had been in my old, but now I was making close to a six-figure income. If work is your validation, money can be your supervalidation. Like Zoey and Georgia, Danielle was a blonde but hardly a "10," and not especially athletic or even a great dresser. What she offered was a winning personality, sincerity, friendship, kindness, self-confidence, and humor. She didn't exhibit very many weaknesses. This was a turn-on for me, and another one of my internal contradictions. While I am attracted to women who need me and look up to me as a hero, as well as to women who control me, sometimes I'm simply drawn to confident, independent women who treat me as an equal. The equality ideal brings out respect for one another. It feels healthy.

As exaggerated as it may sound, Danielle became my own private vision of the Virgin Mary. As we got to know each other, her beauty radiated from within and I fell in love with her, not with head-over-heels adrenaline as I had with Zoey or Georgia, but slowly, as I came to feel secure around her. Trust was now a very big part of my search criteria. It was what ultimately made me decide on marriage. During our courtship there wasn't one incident of deceit, or even a case of Danielle letting me down. She was in love with me, she said, and she would always be there for me. Unlike Georgia, Danielle showed she meant it time and time again. I realized how lucky I was. Maybe this is a Catholic response, but I thought I was getting more than I deserved.

When I got to know Danielle's family, I knew right away that fitting in was not going to be easy. These were brilliant but strange people. Her dad, an engineer, was a cold, unfriendly hermit who had the first nickel he ever earned; he was too tight to put air-conditioning in their home. I had the impression that in his eyes I wasn't good enough for Danielle, but at the same time he treated her with such indifference that I knew I would be a lot better for his daughter than he was. Danielle's older sister came across as friendly, but there was something "off" about her; eventually she'd be diagnosed with a mental disorder. Danielle had two brothers. The older one was a Ph.D. and a ringer for the old man in his coldness and hoarding. The younger was socially immature. I learned that their mother had died when Danielle was only twelve.

Danielle had no trouble blending in with my family. My parents and brother and sister adored her. We didn't talk much about her family—it wasn't a subject she was comfortable with—though in the back of my mind I wondered how she had survived her teenage years in that crowd. Danielle was so responsible and self-confident I assumed she had somehow taken over the role of mother for her younger siblings, and being responsible had kept her sane and out of trouble.

After we were married Danielle and I went about our lives with great focus and happiness. We had different sets of friends but everyone mingled comfortably. I don't think we had a serious argument in those first eight years. Danielle worked as a financial consultant and I did increasingly well as an executive recruiter. Money was never an issue for us. We got along on every level, including agreeing on things like who put out the trash (me), who balanced the checkbook and paid the taxes (Danielle), who went grocery shopping, washed the cars, and made house repairs (me), and who cleaned house (Danielle). While we talked of having kids, we were in no hurry.

We traveled, lived well, had passionate sex, and thought the world was made of roses and daffodils.

If there was a dominant person in the relationship it was probably me. I think it wasn't intentional, it just sort of happened that way because Danielle looked to me whenever a real problem or crisis came along. And being a man, I thought that was my role. She would never really thank me for coming to the rescue, and that bothered me at times, but I didn't dwell on it. I just assumed that this was what a man did—take charge, solve problems, show some leadership, even if I didn't always know what I was doing!

Because they often don't like to lead or compete in areas where they aren't competent, men can be reluctant to try new things. Even in areas where they are competent, most men, like Barry, prefer a routine where the rules for success and failure are clearly defined, including the roles of each partner: who washes the cars, who makes the beds, who does the dishes, who pays the bills, who drives the kids to school. From a male point of view, all tasks need to be defined, assignable, and consistent. Logic and a linear order must rule the day. If he does his job well, a man thinks, he not only escapes blame and judgment, he wins praise. When his partner tampers with the rules and routine of the relationship, as Danielle will soon do with Barry, a man will either fight back or, frustrated and resenting his loss of control, begin to disengage emotionally.

As we'll see, besides his quandary about how to perceive Danielle, Barry also may be confused about how he sees himself. He wants to have a positive self-image—someone who's jumped from immature loser to respected businessman. Yet he sets himself up for disappointment—and being perceived as demanding—by putting himself on a pedestal. Because he has to be perfect, everybody around him feels the pressure to measure up too, especially Danielle. Barry would like to get some nurturing from women, but his negative experiences have led him to believe he can't count on the opposite sex because women have their own agenda. Ironically, by putting himself in the perfection box, by being afraid of risk, his chances of staying in love, as much as he wants it, are greatly diminished.

et us fast forward. After eight years of a contentment that I thought would last forever, something happened. The first sign of trouble was hardly noticeable. Danielle began to get up in the middle of the night to make sure the doors of our house were locked. Or she checked the kitchen to make certain the oven was off, the lights were out, and the car had been put in the garage. At first I attributed her behavior to fatigue and her admirable habit of responsibility. When she began to check the door or oven two or three times in one night, however, I began to wonder. At restaurants we would pay the bill and leave, then Danielle would rush back inside because she was sure she had left her purse behind (it was in the car). On several occasions she was sure she had lost her keys, earrings, or driver's license, and became very nervous until they were found. She began looking into my wallet every morning to see how much money I had. When I inevitably came home with less, she demanded to know how I had spent it. Old friends, she complained, were standing her up for lunch dates. I didn't know what to think of this bizarre turn in her behavior. For a while I thought she was just frustrated with her job, or wanted a change in her life, like starting a family. Whenever I asked what the problem was, she said, cheerfully, "What problem?"

One night, however, Danielle tearfully confessed that she knew something was wrong. She said she wanted to get help. I was relieved. A therapist diagnosed her as suffering from OCD—obsessive-compulsive disorder—and put her on some serious medication. Obsessive-compulsive behavior, as I would learn, is all about control, and usually springs from deep-seated fears that you are not in charge of your life, or some pain or unhappiness that lurks below the surface. OCD is often seen in people who strive for perfection, and at times I wondered if I wasn't obsessive-compulsive as well. What was hard for me to understand was where her paralyzing disorder had come from, and why did it spring up after eight happy years of marriage? I knew her family was bizarre, but I had always believed Danielle had escaped that connection. I looked critically at my own behavior. Over the eight years I had definitely become the dominant personality in our relationship. Was I suffocating her? Did she think I was too controlling? Danielle never really said anything. In the meantime her meds made her moody and depressed. Worse, she became convinced that by taking drugs her OCD was now fixed and her life would return to normal.

Our lives did not go back to normal. Danielle's behavior grew worse. If I tried to help her clean the house, for example, she grew upset because this had always been her role. But cleaning now took on a new meaning. Every piece of furniture and knickknack had to be in one place and one place only, and she alone had to make the choices. If she didn't like what she'd done, an hour later she would rearrange the furniture, then feel anxious and paralyzed about having made the wrong choices. After I put out the trash, Danielle would get up in the middle of the night and bring it back in the house, sorting through it to see if I'd thrown out something that I shouldn't have. Her medication also caused her to gain weight. Soon she didn't want to leave the house. She didn't look or feel good, she said, or she needed more time to get organized. When she did go out, I would catch her bringing home strange and useless objects—pieces of string, rubber bands, stacks of newspaper—

that she'd hide in drawers and closets. She would never say a word, as if none of this was happening, or maybe somehow I wouldn't notice. For my part, I just rationalized that things would somehow get better.

But Danielle's behavior became a nightmare. Had the bizarre behavior that ran in her family, particularly the hoarding, distrusting behavior of her father, or her sister's mental illness, had some impact on her life? The therapist couldn't give me a clear answer. There seemed to be many reasons for her fears, he said, implying that the process of ferreting them out could take years. I didn't have years. Danielle said she couldn't stop her behavior and begged me for help. And I wanted to help. The old role of playing hero to wounded women was familiar, yet so different this time. This time I didn't have any solutions. Comforting Danielle only went so far. So did imposing my will. Danielle grew suspicious, if not hostile, when I stopped her from bringing trash into our house. She also grew increasingly antisocial. One evening I invited over our closest friends, hoping that would improve Danielle's mood. She sat passively in a corner, barely talking. By now our house was a rat's nest of odds and ends. Our friends kept looking around the house, then to Danielle, then me. I could see the dismay in their eyes, like, "What the hell is going on here?" As they said good night, they pulled me aside and asked what was wrong. I fumbled for words, claiming that Danielle simply wasn't feeling well. They urged me to get her some serious help.

I was determined to hang in with Danielle because I loved her and took my marriage vows seriously. I also wanted to prove to myself that I wasn't the immature kid I'd been in college who fled at the first sign of trouble. I know a lot of men who run away emotionally when there's a serious problem, but I was determined to be different. We tried a new therapist, and

Danielle began to speak in darker tones about her family, yet still told me nothing specific. When I pushed for more information, she pushed back. A wall went up around her. I grew increasingly frustrated, but never more so than when she tried to claim again, with her new doctor and new meds, that everything was back to normal. Her wishful thinking, her denial, seemed like the easiest place for her to go. I remember one evening asking her if she'd gone that day to her doctor, or paid our bills, or run specific errands—all promises she'd made that morning. She said of course, asking why I would ever doubt her. When I checked the next day, I found that nothing had been done. (I later learned, during our divorce, that she hadn't filed several years of tax returns.) She'd grown into a compulsive liar because that was part of her disorder.

Even though I understood that her illness was controlling her, Danielle's lying and deceit were the triggers that brought out the most intolerant and controlling part of me. I sat with Danielle many evenings, trying to reason with her, but by now any rational communication was almost nonexistent. If I couldn't control this situation, if I couldn't be of help, then what was the point of sticking around? That's how I began to think. Despite my vow not to do a disappearing act, I was about to do that very thing. If the roles had been reversed, I wondered, would Danielle have stuck with me—or would she have bailed? Those are the issues I still wrestle with today, long after the divorce.

When mental or physical illness occurs in a relationship, the wild emotional swings in the healthy partner may bring more instability to the relationship than the illness itself. Barry runs the gamut from sympathy to disbelief to guilt to deep frustration. He never quite knows how to treat or think about Danielle—is the person he relates to in the past, or the present?—

and no doubt his vacillation makes Danielle feel more insecure. He tried hard to stay the course, but when Barry eventually gives up on his relationship, one reason may be that he loses respect for someone who is weak, or that he sees Danielle as an obligation. Does he actually fall out of love, or just decide to leave out of frustration? Barry isn't sure. The under-forty generation tends to believe that a relationship should not be based on duty, but on attraction, pleasure, and emotional fulfillment. If something doesn't work out with one partner, you're entitled to find happiness with someone else. The idea of committing to commitment is almost a foreign concept.

I honestly believe I could have stayed with Danielle if her lying hadn't become epidemic. Where once I had trusted her implicitly, I was now in a state of suspicion about almost everything she said and did. My frustration only fomented the same emotions in her. We virtually stopped talking to one another. In bed we slept back to back and never touched. I'm sure she thought I was the coldest asshole since her father. Each day the arguments and accusations grew in intensity, along with Danielle's hoarding and paranoia. Finally, I told her I couldn't live like this anymore. I knew she couldn't live with herself either, and that filled me with guilt. I still wanted to be the hero and save her. There was just no solution that I could think of. We tried a couple of separations, but each time we got back together, our old patterns resurfaced.

By now I was frustrated, angry, and tired of being blamed. Why couldn't she blame her problems on her illness? Instead, she told our friends that I was cold, insensitive, and uncaring. As she turned herself into the victim, I felt sorry for her, but I didn't feel love anymore. When we agreed on a divorce, I thought most of my stress would be behind me. Then I found

out Danielle hadn't filed our tax returns for the last three years.
She told her divorce attorney that her lapses were due to my
bullying her.

Since our divorce, Danielle has been in and out of a couple
of romantic relationships, and is working with yet another
therapist. She admits to being unhappy, and still sees me as
the villain. What hurts most is the way she judges me. In
Danielle's eyes I suddenly had been a bastard from the day we
first got married. All my actions and motives were now
described as controlling, selfish, and cruel. She suddenly
couldn't find a speck of good in me.

As I've begun dating again, I've had a half-dozen fairly
serious relationships. In my city the singles scene is pretty
wild, but I imagine it's the same in most big cities. At any given
time there are five or six "hot" clubs where everyone hangs out.
You see the same faces over and over. The ritual gets pretty
familiar too. Your first date is almost always "the interview."
You feel under the microscope from the first hello, and most
times you only get one chance to get it right. I always overdo
the intro—making a big splash to win the woman's attention
before I really know what or how I feel about her. I want to be
accepted, of course, but I also want to know that she likes me
before I venture out on a limb and make the effort to get to
know her. I also want to pass her test because rejection is so
painful to me.

After my divorce, I got myself in shape physically, bought
new clothes, and tried to look as youthful as possible. We all
have mental checklists when we go out, but I think for most
women their list is longer and more rigorous than a guy's. It's
certainly a different list. For example, while looks are important
to women, I think it's just one item on the list, while for most
guys it's at the top. Women have a longer list, and it's got

nothing to do with emotions, not in the beginning. Instead, a lot of women take one look at you and a half-dozen questions pop into their heads. Does he have a secure job? Is he generous or cheap? Does he open the door for me? Does he make me laugh? Does he have a lot of confidence? Did he win the NCAA tennis singles championship? As difficult and demanding as I can be, most women I have dated were even more discriminating and judgmental.

Sex is definitely part of that test. Maybe not on the first date, but if you get a second or third, and the woman trusts you, you're onstage. I was shocked at how many women wanted to go to bed before they decided whether they wanted to develop a relationship with me. Were they thinking that if I wasn't good sexually, I wasn't worth a relationship? For a guy, jumping into the sack sounds like heaven, but it's not. I did it because I was afraid of disappointing the woman and getting kicked out of her life, failing another test without even taking it. The whole experience is awkward and self-conscious. I felt one woman was evaluating me as she would a glass of wine: first there's the smell, then the initial taste on the tongue, then the body of the wine as it swirls in her mouth, and finally the aftertaste. You know the *Wine Spectator*? It's almost as if a guy gets rated in the same way. There's so much anxiety. After your "performance" you want to scream out, "How did I do? How did I do?" I was judging her performance too, but it took a backseat to wondering how I did.

Drugs, particularly ecstasy and pot, are prevalent on the singles scene, and so is Viagra. Women carry Viagra or Cialis in their handbags just in case you forgot yours. For many women, the idea is to get smashed in a romantic restaurant, make the guy pop a sex pill, then go somewhere to screw your brains out. Most women over thirty know how important and strategic sex

is. Sex is their resource of choice for winning over a man.
That's certainly what Georgia did to me. Few men I know can
resist. It's not just the testosterone thing. You feel this
incredible acceptance—dear God, she's letting me into the
most intimate part of her body!—and like the Sirens singing
from the dangerous shoals, you have to tie yourself to the mast
of the ship not to be pulled in. But who does that?

Barry's depiction of the nightmare of being single and trying
to find a new relationship is the same for women and men. Perhaps, as Barry says, women are more focused on what they
want, but both genders have a deep fear of judgment, especially
regarding their bodies. Men may put some pressure on women
to look as attractive as possible, but the greater pressure comes
from women themselves. The same fear of judgment extends to
sex. Worries about performing adequately and meeting expectations in bed affects both genders, but it particularly affects
those, like Barry, who are driven to succeed in every endeavor.
Men like this become their own worst enemy. It's almost as if
Barry is setting himself up for failure. In his marriage, the pressure he put on Danielle to "get better" probably helped doom
their relationship. While Barry says he wanted to be understanding and patient, his perfectionism led to an attitude of intolerance. Could he have fought harder to get Danielle more
help? Presumably that's where a lot of his guilt comes from.

Despite the temptation, I'm leery of entering an intimate
relationship prematurely. Once you begin to have sex with
a woman, the fundamentals change. Communication between
you moves from a plane of logic to one of emotion. I can't
explain this alchemy. Maybe the woman is thinking, Hey, I've
shared the most intimate part of me, and I want the same

intimacy back from him. But she doesn't mean just sex. The intimacy she wants is a lot deeper. After having sex, her expectations and needs change, and the man is held to a higher level of accountability. You often feel "owned" by a woman. Then there's the unwritten "exclusivity contract" that women demand after three or four dates and going to bed with you. They want you to date only them. Maybe this is a dark definition of intimacy because part of me likes this possessive quality in a woman; to me it means that I'm special, accepted, and she's taking care of me. Yet another part of me is wary. I want to be possessed but I don't want to be owned. I know my current girlfriend defines our relationship as much by the future as she does the present. I look at it more as a day-by-day phenomenon. She is a wonderful person, and I'm beginning to fall in love with her (she says she is already in love with me) but I don't want to rush into a commitment. When I explain what happened in my marriage to Danielle, that I need time to heal, she acts sympathetic, but in the next breath she lets me know she won't wait forever. Does a man ever get out of this squeeze play?

In terms of commitment, there is a strategic difference between men and women. I know Freud is famous for asking "What does a woman want?" As brilliant a psychoanalyst as Freud was, the answer escaped him. If he were alive today, he might be asking "What does a man want?" Because for women today it's pretty clear. Most women want long-term relationships. That, and having or raising children, are their primary definitions of security and happiness. They want commitment and emotional fulfillment. Some women want it all—if you believe romance columnists, they want to be adored, possessed, and protected—so no wonder they get so frustrated. No man is going to give them all that. But that doesn't stop a lot of women from expecting the moon.

On the other hand, men don't define what they want. They just don't know, or they're all over the map. Among other things (like a lifetime pass to Yankee Stadium), I believe they'd like multiple relationships. If they have a really, really good marriage, they will restrict their extramarital activities to fantasies. But the truth is men aren't wired for monogamy. Maybe the younger generation of women aren't either. Whatever women want, they are a lot clearer and more insistent about getting it. Men simply go along because they're not as focused, or they're too afraid to stand up for themselves.

Of the generation of working women in their thirties and forties, some have borrowed a page from the male playbook that equates perfection and control with happiness. By ascending to positions of authority or achieving high levels of success, many believe that men will migrate to them—and some do, just as women are attracted to men with power—but most men I spoke with said they wouldn't trade places with any of these women. Indeed, they thought most would have to learn the lesson that men have already learned about the demon of perfectionism: it leads to exhaustion, frustration, and an abiding sense of never being perfect enough. Although there is a difference between achieving and overachieving, between a quest for excellence and one for perfection, the line is so vague that many never realize when they cross it. Once crossed, it's hard to go back.

Men value goals, independence, and being a go-getter as their definition of what one should do in order to achieve happiness. Women's values—presumably Danielle's—have more to do with support, closeness, and connection. These are what make women happy. Unfortunately, a lot of men regard women's values as inferior to their own. Men have little chance of genuinely connecting to women until they accept that both value systems are valid. Creating a bridge between the two worlds takes consciousness and effort. While men tend to give up more quickly in this endeavor—and become frustrated in their relationships— women should stop blaming men if they haven't first tried to teach them basic communication and relating skills.

8

Benjamin's Story

The first problem for all of us, men and women,
is not to learn, but to unlearn.
—Gloria Steinem

Benjamin is a successful forty-eight-year-old artist, recently divorced, and shares custody of their teenage daughter with his ex-wife, Andi. When it comes to his art, he is a painstaking perfectionist, planning and anticipating every last detail before putting one brushstroke on a canvas. He defines himself by his discipline and ability to analyze. But with women, at least in the past, emotion has eclipsed analysis, and impulse overshadowed prudence and planning. In falling for women, he thinks, his judgment has always been clouded by a romantic sense of destiny. He gets too emotional. Once in the relationship, however, his pragmatic, problem-solving side takes over, but often too late. He doesn't see a problem coming until it's on top of him. There is a gentleness in Benjamin's face and demeanor, and he has an animated speaking style when he feels passionate about something. An intellectual, Benjamin can talk on almost any subject. He likes to dress casually, wears glasses, and while he carries some extra weight around his middle, he never worries about his image. He admits to having "straight-arrow" values, reflecting his Midwestern upbringing and the lessons of his immigrant parents.

Benjamin acted purely on emotion when he became infatu-ated with Andi, a beautiful brunette who was totally his oppo-site in almost every way. They were married for almost two decades. Believing in the infallibility of his Midwestern values and a man's ability to be a master problem solver, it took Ben-jamin 18 years to accept that his wife didn't love him and that his marriage was something he could not fix. Even as the rela-tionship deteriorated and he felt increasingly abused, his sense of denial was strong. It was Andi who finally asked for the di-vorce. What sustained Benjamin after the divorce were male friendships and a lot of self-exploration. His emotions turned out to be more layered and complex than he knew. He had mis-taken infatuation for love, a mistake he believes that many men make because they don't know what they want from a relation-ship. How can they, he wonders, if they don't first know who they are and what they want from themselves.

From my experience, women like to think of themselves as the more special of the two genders. They see themselves as exotic, mysterious, inscrutable, sensitive, intuitive—even sublime. When you read *The Da Vinci Code*, you learn about the "sacred feminine." I'm told that women readers devoured that book as much as men. They love the concept that Mary Magdalene was not only the wife of Jesus, according to the novel, and the mother of his child, but that she's really the Holy Grail. It's the goddess label they love. Most women I know treat themselves well because they think they deserve it. Maybe that's why they love designer fashion labels: you're the best so treat yourself to the best. I think of the L'Oréal ad—"Because I'm worth it"—and how that must resonate. High self-worth is great, but can any woman explain how she gets that label? Does she just give it to herself? Is this an assumption that runs with the gender? If a man were to proclaim that he were a god or somehow ineffable, he'd be laughed at.

It's not a stretch to argue that in the last few decades our society has become increasingly matriarchal. There's little doubt that, in some industries, in terms of salaries and authority, men are still the dominant gender—but who shapes the mores and social values of our culture? I think women have that power partly because they market themselves better than men. Eavesdrop on conversations at Starbucks, at the workplace, in the movie theater lobby. Women see themselves as smart, caring, open, fair, and when they make a mistake, misunderstood. Men are perceived as needlessly jealous, possessive, distrustful, hypercompetitive, and often deliberately hurtful. Somehow, women have labeled themselves with the "good" emotions and men often get stuck with the "negative." And when men get those labels, they often don't know what to do about it, so the labels stick.

I don't know many women who like it when men analyze them. They like to believe that men can't truly understand their complex and subtle natures. Their exotic essence is one of their "secrets." Only women can understand women. On the other hand, continuing with this metaphor, men are easily understood by women because they are not nearly as complex or mysterious. Men are just men. Their emotions are not as evolved as women's. They are transparent. Yet, while women may claim to understand both themselves and men, I have had psychologists tell me that men don't understand men. As supposedly linear and transparent as we are, we are often still clueless about what drives us in life. And because men are so lacking in self-awareness, they need women to help them through life.

A lot of women believe that myth and, unfortunately, men do too. I certainly did for a long time. It's only in the last two years, since my divorce, that I've realized that for men to have power and autonomy they're not going to get it from relationships. They need their own separate world. I don't just mean some male hobby, but a psychological world where happiness is a perception that they control. If I perceive that happiness means getting along with other people, then I get along with other people and I'm happy. If I perceive that my happiness has nothing to do with other people—if it means just getting up in the morning and working on a canvas or getting the oil changed in my car—then that's all I have to do. I decide what makes me happy, and I have the flexibility to change that perception anytime I want. I think that's what women do all the time but men have such difficulty. Men are just not as adaptable or flexible as women.

From my own relationships, and from the men I know, we're drawn, at least initially, to a woman's physical attributes. Men stare at women as they walk down the street, in the supermarket, or waiting at a traffic light. They all have their favorite part of a woman's anatomy. Why else are we seduced by the sleek, feminine lines of a car, a boat, a plane, a computer, or piece of furniture? Women know how important looks are. Most will do anything, and spend lots of money, to make themselves look as attractive as possible. They don't just do it for men. They do it for themselves, often in competition with other women. Whether the issue is self-esteem, cultural pressure, or the desire to "pull in" a man, clothes, cosmetics, shoes, perfume, and plastic surgery are as crucial to a woman's existence as food and water.

Benjamin gives women proper credit for being emotionally more developed than men. He thinks, with some envy, that they give themselves more latitude than men in defining and expressing themselves, and are more articulate about what they want for themselves and from men. By taking relationships more seriously and writing the rules for the nest, they acquire a certain power and entitlement that men rarely challenge. If men complain about women who are controlling, as Benjamin will, it's because most men acquiesce to being spear-carriers on the domestic stage. Even if they don't like their role, they are too busy doing other "masculine" things, or they're lazy, or they simply don't have the social skills to handle the tasks that women perform. But by not being assertive, or just because he is unclear about his feelings, as we'll see, Benjamin finds out how lopsided and unhealthy a relationship can become.

'm from the classic school of Midwest conservatism. Growing up in the fifties, I was a scruffy, outdoorsy kid who could have posed for a Norman Rockwell painting. I was a "boy's boy" who had lots of practical and mechanical skills. I was taught to be patient and thorough with every assignment or job I tackled, to do it right, and see it through to the end. I'm also an optimist in the sense that I believe almost every problem has a solution, if you just think hard enough about it. I also developed a sense of individuality as I grew up. I have rarely cared about social conventions, judgment, or gossip. I remember going to grade school wearing a coat and tie and toting a small briefcase because I wanted to look like my father. Kids made fun of me, but I just blocked out the noise and kept my eye on the prize: good grades and learning as much as I could.

I went to Catholic schools and toed the line in every respect. In second or third grade the nuns showed our class a picture of a man standing on the edge of a cliff. He was in a business suit with a briefcase and a hat (that could be me one day, I thought), and his family was clustered behind him. An angel was pointing down toward a bottomless abyss; one poor guy, briefcase and all, had already teetered off the edge and was diving into the flames of hell with this horrified look. I've never been able to forget that picture.

My dad was from a working-class family in Germany, and around 1935 emigrated with my mother to the United States. Like a lot of immigrants, he associated the American Dream with a ceaseless work ethic and material success. He put himself through med school, became a practicing doctor, and later acquired an engineering degree as well. He worked fourteen-hour days, six or even seven days a week, and had little to do with raising me and my three sisters. I was the second child but the only boy, so maybe it was natural that my dad was my role model. Excellence through diligent, hard work. That became my marker for masculinity.

While I had great respect for Dad, he was an emotionless, authoritarian man whose focus was on winning respect, wealth, and social status. I felt I was often an underperformer in his eyes. While Dad was a perfectionist and so am I, I don't mind my failures so long as I've tried. Failure is a great teacher. Dad was less forgiving of himself.

Growing up in our very regimented house was easy in the sense that my sisters and I knew the rules, and that there were no exceptions to those rules. Everyone had a role. Father was the breadwinner, children did their chores and homework, and Mom wrote the book on housekeeping. A typical immigrant's wife, the house was her kingdom and she was determined to administer it at the same level of excellence that my dad applied to his medical practice. But how many times can you scrub a bathtub? My older sister remembers Mom bleaching the hell out of everything she got her hands on.

My mom was a problem solver more than a nurturer. I wouldn't ever call her warm and fuzzy. Looking back, I realize that my father never gave my mother much latitude for personal growth, and perhaps her anger at her repressed life showed both in her obsessive housework and in her strict discipline in raising us kids. I think a lot of boys bear the brunt of mothers who are really angry at their husbands but take it out on their sons. There was almost zero physical affection in our house, and a fair number of slaps across the face for breaking rules or acts of disobedience.

Down deep, I loved my mother, but I can't discount the fear factor. A lot of men, if they feel safe enough, will tell you they have mixed feelings toward their mothers. My wife had lots of childhood issues and anger toward both her parents. I think that's why she picked on me often and without provocation. I wish I had challenged her about who she was really mad at, but my own anger was so repressed that, rather than speak up, I just buried my resentments.

When you're a child you're aware of none of this, of course, including the seeds of discontent and rebellion that are planted in you. If you're lucky, as I was, you escape for a time into play and fantasy. Because my folks lived in a rural area, I had hundreds of acres of meadows, forests, and streams as my backyard. My friends were all boys and we did the Daniel Boone thing. At age twelve I built my own minibike out of scrap parts. I gravitated easily to Cub Scouts, then Boy Scouts, and as an Eagle Scout I was honored at one of the national jamborees for my achievements. Life wasn't all seriousness. My friends and I loved playing practical jokes—but deep down there had to be purpose to most things I did. Equally important, I was never boastful about my accomplishments, in keeping with my Catholic, Boy Scout, immigrant upbringing. Eventually I became valedictorian of my high-school class, scored 1590 out of 1600 on my SATs, and was admitted to more than one Ivy League college. Yet I never talked about any of it, believing that modesty was a virtue.

Most men I interviewed whose parents shared Depression-era values—a strict work ethic, repressed or unspoken emotions at home, fixation on success and respectability—produced children, particularly boys, who were unsure about their emotional values. The "virtues" of modesty and self-effacement are reinforced in Benjamin's case by his Catholic schooling and a repressed mother and father, but what he really learns is that the importance of emotions pale in comparison to intellectual and professional achievement. Benjamin says he was lucky to escape into fantasy and play, becoming a boy's boy. However, because his emotions are so underdeveloped, his early relationships with girls will expose his naïveté and innocence. Lacking self-awareness and emotional armor, Benjamin gets hit hard in high school and college, and worse, isn't sure what lesson he's supposed to learn. Is it about women's sophistication or men's naïveté? What is he supposed to do about it? He has no father or close friends to trust to tell him how to avoid future knockouts.

Modesty can be code for lack of self-knowledge and courage. Not speaking up for yourself, I believe, begins with not defining or exploring yourself internally. If you don't feel safe speaking up as a child—if your parents fail to give you that special space—you won't develop a voice for your emotions. It doesn't matter how intelligent you are, if you don't understand your emotions you're still going to be ambushed in later life. Maybe I just followed my parents' lead of quiet stoicism, but for most of my adult life I've had difficulty getting things off my chest. That weakness played a key role in undermining my relationships with women, especially my wife, Andi.

In high school I had only one girlfriend, and we went steady for three years. When I first laid eyes on Marjorie I knew I wanted to be with her and only her. I've had this pattern with women all my life: while I'm very selective, once I'm attracted to someone I go all out—flowers, lunches, love letters, poetry. My second pattern is, once we're in a relationship, I stick with a woman through thick and thin. I am impervious to temptation. Is it my fear of violating the Seventh Commandment or just my habit of being single-minded? Then there's the family history. Not only have my parents never been divorced or separated, but my grandparents on both sides exhibited the same fidelity. Monogamy is only one of several "ideals" that I have been drawn to throughout my life. I think that's part of my romanticism—if I'm scrupulously faithful to my ideals, if I'm perfect, I've always believed my life will be fine.

While we were not quite karmic twins, Marjorie, my high-school flame, was very similar to me. She was brainy, a cheerleader, a student-body officer—in brief, an overachiever extraordinaire. She was also drop-dead gorgeous, and more than any of her other characteristics, it was her beauty that I focused on. I didn't lose my virginity until we'd been dating for two years. This was before the sexual revolution, so we moved from first base to second to third at a snail's pace. My friends and I believed you didn't sleep with a woman unless you intended to marry her.

I thought Marjorie and I made the ideal couple. I assumed that because we were so compatible and because I was in love with her that we were going to get married. It never occurred to

me that eighteen years old was too young, because I basically
envisioned life as a series of duties. Once you found the right
woman, you married her and moved on to your next duty—
college, career, whatever it was. In our senior year, while I was
wondering where and when we would tie the knot, Marjorie fell
in love with the star basketball player. I was dumbfounded. I
could barely breathe. Cool as ice, Marjorie told me, "He's just
better than you, Benjamin." Today Marjorie has both law and
medical degrees, and has been married and divorced three
times. I think no achievement is ever enough for her.

Losing Marjorie was my first experience with deep
emotional pain. Her unexpected rejection was like a right hook
from Muhammad Ali. I didn't share my grief with anyone, nor
did I try to understand it. I just let it grow inside me like a
tumor. I was so devastated that I didn't date again for two
years. By then I was a sophomore in college. I joined an eating
club, which at our school was the equivalent of a fraternity.
Women were not permitted to join most eating clubs at that
time. This allowed for sharing thoughts and feelings with just
men, creating our own male universe without worrying about
what to say or think in front of women. Men act differently
when women are around: they're less forthright, more
artificial, more cunning, more prone to jealousy-inspired
competition. I developed terrific male friendships during this
period, many of which have lasted throughout my life. College
was a great four years for me. My friends and I devoured the
seminal novels of the fifties and sixties—Kerouac's *On the Road*
was my bible—and we all dreamed of being free to challenge
bourgeois conventions. My summers involved tough manual
labor, including work on oil fields and in coal mines. I loved it.
The money was good and I made friends with roustabouts,
cowboys, hobos—tough, independent men, uneducated but

very smart in their own way. I'm an unabashed romantic when it comes to the outdoors, traveling around, living the rugged life, using my ingenuity, being independent—that's a big part of my definition of manhood. But I also have a pragmatic side that helps me with day-to-day reality.

Later, when I studied different cultures and their initiation rituals, particularly those of the American Indian, I was drawn to the fact that there were specific tests for bravery, honor, and survival. You passed the tests and you never worried about your self-esteem again. You had made it! You were a man! One reason I loved the Boy Scouts was that there was a relatively clear path to maturity. There were skills you acquired and that were validated with each merit badge. Skills defined manhood. Where else in American culture do you find this clarity?

A lot of Benjamin's perfectionism comes from a fear of making mistakes. As in the painting from Catholic school that he'll never forget, he comes to believe that the price of screwing up is one kind of perdition or another. He defines his life by believing in various ideals and duties—a value system reinforced by his parents and Boy Scouts—and carries those values into his relationships. Once he's in love with Marjorie, he's not even tempted to look at another woman. He just assumes they'll always be in love and live happily ever after. His naïveté, while it ultimately causes him pain, is indicative of an unusual and liberating mind-set. Unlike most men I interviewed, Benjamin is no more hung up on success than he is bothered by failure. As long as he gives one hundred percent of himself to a project, he feels good about himself. His interpretation of masculinity is flexible and determined by his role models—men who live in the outdoors and make their living with their hands, or who prize their intellect and the world of ideas, or who choose spiritual solutions when rationality doesn't work. Open-minded, Benjamin is likely to take his own middle road in a culture that is usually defined by polarization.

While men are usually portrayed in sitcoms and commercials as bumbling, clueless, and self-centered, on the other end of the spectrum they are seen as brainiacs, philanthropists, or fearless leaders who strive to both improve themselves and the world—and also beat their competition. Particularly in business and athletics, mere effort is not enough; men need to be validated by their successes. Not everyone can be a master of the universe, but most men feel a need to be recognized for *some* skill or accomplishment. If he doesn't get acknowledgment from his peers, his boss, his life partner, or his children, he has a problem: either he has to work still harder to find approval, or write himself off as a failure. Or, like Benjamin, make his own path without worrying about judgments and benchmarks.

In my junior year at college I met a coed named Isabel and zeroed in on her. Isabel's looks were even more stunning than Marjorie's, she had an incredible work ethic, and what started out with innocent intellectual discussions ended with my falling in love with her. We had a three-year relationship and this time I did talk about marriage. I told Isabel I wanted to spend my whole life with her, and the next one too. Isabel said she liked that I wore my heart on my sleeve. She also liked my sense of humor, my art, my intelligence, and my imagination. She said she wanted to get married too. I realize now we should have talked a lot more. I took Isabel at her word, instead of picking up on little warning signs that flashed in the last year of our relationship: missed dates, broken promises, moody behavior. Was I just being horribly naïve again? One night I went to her dorm to surprise her with flowers and found her in bed with another guy. Another right hook from Ali!

Days later, Isabel showered me with clichés—she was too young to marry, needed to grow and find herself, sorry she hadn't had time to tell me, and of course she still wanted us to be friends. I don't think she had any idea of the pain she caused me, and somehow I couldn't tell her because I just buried it inside me. Dumping me meant little more to Isabel than a change of mind, a practice every woman in my life has handled with great facility. I know men can change their minds too and cause plenty of pain (and are quickly branded as assholes), but when women do the breaking up they seem to forgive themselves more quickly and are largely spared social judgment.

After graduation I took a high-school teaching job in a small California town. Removed from the Ivy League pressure cooker, I happily occupied my free time by hiking, camping, working on my motorcycle, and successfully building a plane with a friend. This was a very specific, self-explanatory world where I felt safe and validated. During these years I was into music, writing, and my art. I also read voraciously about the Chumash Indians, who at one time represented a thriving culture in California. By now I had abandoned Catholicism, but I still considered myself a very spiritual person. The Chumash believed in sweat lodges, the importance of visions, and they had a concept of the earth as mother goddess, not unlike other ancient cultures. I began to think of women in this positive role, not just as goddesses, but as protectors, guardians, special beings of sentience and warmth. I even said a prayer that I could meet a woman that had those characteristics.

The next day, right after my prayer, I met my future wife. In every serious relationship I've been in, the woman has to be physically attractive. She certainly has to be more attractive than I am. I was so blinded by Andi's beauty and femininity that I barely considered her character, background, or mood swings. I trusted that my strong attraction to her femininity would be enough to keep us together. Trust has been my downfall with women. Once I fall in love, I trust a woman implicitly.

Like other men in this book, Benjamin confuses a magical moment—the fact that he prayed to meet a spiritual earth goddess and, the next day, he ran into Andi—with a sense that this is destiny and that falling deeply in love with her is inevitable. This infatuation was so strong that even when we watch his relationship with Andi begin to disintegrate, he still clings to the hope that the magic will resurface and rescue him. Men are hopelessly romantic in an impractical, almost destructive way. Benjamin implies that once he falls in love, he is virtually putty in a woman's hands. It's as if men connect to their emotions in the most simple and primitive way, defying normal male rationality, because they lack the sophisticated emotional circuitry that women rely on.

Except for being stunningly beautiful, Andi was very different from Marjorie and Isabel. There was nothing hardworking, self-effacing, or overachieving about her. Andi had little ambition. She was a college dropout who was the quintessential California babe with her vintage sports car, a deep tan, and a sparkling personality. She lived moment to moment, day to day. That's not to say she wasn't intelligent: she was as clever and intuitive as anyone I've met. After we were married, when we began to argue, she ran circles around me with her debating skills.

I didn't know what she saw in me, and I didn't particularly want to ask. I just wanted Andi. Her sexy smile, the way she dressed, her perfume—it was all part of an irresistible package. While I was normally a careful, patient, and organized man, Andi was spontaneous, freewheeling, and unpredictable. We were living proof that opposites attract. It was her wildness that I found so liberating, the perfect escape from my straightlaced past and the pain caused by overambitious women.

As our courtship progressed, Andi took me to parties, bars, all-night clubs, homes of her crazy friends, and ultimately to meet her family. Unlike mine, Andi's family had a history of multiple divorces and remarriages. She was from a wealthy and (as I would eventually learn) highly dysfunctional family, but for the first year of our relationship I was blinded by my infatuation. Was I finally breaking out of my old, repressed self? I was spellbound by her family's wealth. Everyone dressed well. They were incredible athletes. They even had their own plane. It was hard to keep track of all the stepbrothers and stepsisters, uncle and aunts, with everyone coming and going. There was so much unsettling change and chaos around Andi. It didn't seem to bother her like it eventually upset me. Even with my infatuation, I wondered in the middle of more than one night if I wasn't in way over my head with Andi.

After dating for a year, Andi showed up at my studio one afternoon and announced she was moving in. Just like that. This was the same studio where my friend and I had built parts of our plane—our sacred male space, if you will—and the moment Andi entered it with her suitcases, declaring her intentions, everything felt different. I was upset by her arrogance, yet I was too hooked on Andi ever to turn her away. She said she found my digs "different and exotic." I knew they were really quite plain.

By now it was clear what Andi saw in me. I was her port in the storm, the only stable thing in her kaleidoscopic, chaotic life. Trust was very important to her, she confided, almost tearfully. I would always be there for her, wouldn't I? Yes, I promised, I would. When she told me stories of past boyfriends chasing her for sex or money, I understood that I was supposed to save her from all this. And being the quintessential Boy Scout, not to mention the lapsed Catholic who was nevertheless still aware of the dangers of hellfire, I was prepared to do exactly that. Was there a merit badge for this? Yes, I would save Andi from herself.

Our first year of marriage was special. A year of great sex, fun, racing around in her sports car—Andi saving me from geekdom, I suppose, and me saving her from her aimless, destructive ways. (Sex later would be anything but great. It was either nonexistent or it felt forced and mechanical.) I got to know her family better and Andi opened up to me about growing up with unloving parents, health issues, sibling rivalries, bitter divorces, betrayals, and damaging gossip. I tried to shield her from that past. Determined to have our own life, we bought a small house together. Andi took some courses and qualified for a job with a state social agency, counseling people in abusive relationships (something she already knew well). We talked about having kids. We were happy. Maybe, I thought seriously, my prayer of finding the perfect woman for me had been answered. I could never live without her, I thought.

I could, however, easily live without her complex and agitated family. Andi's many relatives were forever visiting us, often unannounced. Even though she didn't get along with many of them, she would never ask anyone to leave. Despite all our intentions, Andi and I had little privacy. As it turned out, the more chaotic things were, the better Andi liked it. Without my consent, she invited her father, recently divorced, to live with us. And I put up with it all.

After our honeymoon year, I think, something in Andi changed. Maybe she thought I wasn't quite the Rock of Gibraltar she had first envisioned. Or maybe she didn't covet or need that stability as much as she thought. Or perhaps she just surrendered to her wild side and didn't want me to cramp her lifestyle. But all of a sudden I felt she didn't love me. Somehow I was still useful to her—companionship, advice, and the ever capable handyman—yet there were many times I felt I was on the outside of our relationship looking in. With her verbal skills and sparkling personality, Andi was deft at convincing me of her needs while also convincing me that my own needs weren't as important. And Andi had lots of needs—for attention, flattery, friends, or just activities. She made a big point of saying she valued her independence, but if I ever brought up the same issue for me, wanting to spend time with my friends, she was annoyed.

As things cooled between us, Andi began to drift back to an old boyfriend. First it was just lunches and dinners, then she'd be gone overnight. This happened more than once. Rather than risk a confrontation, I just let the matter go. When she was home at night she drank wine, stayed on the phone, or isolated herself in a room. She began to complain that I was a really dull guy who never took her to exciting places. Yet when I tried to spend time with her or be intimate, Andi would push me away. I didn't probe further. I wasn't good at dealing with hidden emotions. And frankly, I didn't want to believe our problems were insurmountable. I was brought up to believe that every problem could be fixed. That's what a man does: if something is broken, you find a way to make it work again. That's one definition of perfectionism.

Benjamin is astute in his observations about gender behaviors and the psychology of women—almost in inverse proportion to his awareness of his own situation with Andi. He was lured into his relationship by the powerful mystique of Andi, but he didn't recognize that the beginning of most relationships is the accommodation phase, where a woman pleases a man to gain a foothold or even control. He also didn't pick up on Andi's methods of communicating. Creating crises, intimidating him, or storming out of the house after a fight is perhaps a manifestation of her anger over not being able to control Benjamin, or make him respond to her need for boundaries. Instead of admitting her vulnerabilities, she just walked out on him on numerous occasions. Leery of confrontation, Benjamin by his silence unintentionally encouraged her behavior. This may be why she got tired of him.

As we'll see, part of Benjamin's frustration with Andi, besides not knowing how to communicate, is not knowing how to deal with the consequences of their fights. He is a disillusioned perfectionist who will expend his energy trying to control and repair the damage, rather than prevent the fights from happening again. Benjamin, like many men, doesn't know how to process or learn from his pain, so his avoidance of it almost guarantees that he won't uncover the root causes of their conflict and that the fighting will continue.

Andi loved to provoke arguments, and not just with me. While fighting wore me out, it energized Andi. Arguing was the outlet for her anxiety, which seemed to come out of nowhere. I had now learned that this was her family's way as well. There was lots of yelling and screaming, threats, and tantrums. When I came home from work there was inevitably a knot in my stomach because I could never anticipate Andi's mood. She could find fault with anything—the way I was dressed, how her family treated her, the lack of flowers in the house, or the wine I'd brought home. If I argued back and raised my voice, even one decibel, she would snap back, "Why are you yelling at me?" She could go from aggressor to victim and back to aggressor with lightning speed. While I stumbled from one defensive position to another, Andi had her endgame in mind from her first word. She always knew what she wanted out of our arguments, usually some concession from me, even if it was just to agree with her point of view. Why couldn't she come out and say clearly what was on her mind? Everything had to be complicated and charged with drama.

Language is an art form, and I believe women have a genetic head start in that department. Andi's skills were formidable, as were Marjorie's and Isabel's. I've read that when girls are born, they are more open than boys to receiving information and emotions, and I would guess that somehow the two—information and emotions—get intertwined neurologically. I've also read that mothers with newborn daughters make more eye contact and talk more to them than they do with boys. If you combine a woman's body language with her voice inflections, and the nuances and subtexts of her messages, isn't a man automatically at a communications disadvantage?

I think Andi's temper and penchant for arguing ultimately became a form of abuse. The more inept or passive I was in arguing back—sometimes I was just too exhausted to fight with her—the more confident and bolder she grew. One time she was so angry that she didn't use words—did she think I was no longer listening?—but threatened me with a beer bottle. Another time she took a swing with her fist and broke my glasses. Once, out of spite, she vanished for a whole month from the house and never called me. If I were smarter, if I hadn't been in such denial, I would either have walked out and called a divorce attorney, or at least figured out that somewhere in her past, Andi had suffered from some kind of terrible problem and needed help. Her low self-esteem was camouflaged by her femininity and big personality, big enough to fool me and many other men in her life, and to help her get away with some pretty outrageous behavior.

The way Benjamin was raised by his Depression-era parents, he thought it was irresponsible to give up on any task. In analyzing his relationship with Andi, Benjamin feels his wife took advantage of this trait. If he saw himself as the problem solver, and the quintessential stoical male who never complained, this gave Andi license to abuse him not just because she knew he wouldn't fight back, but because he would ultimately blame himself. Many women criticize men for being too withdrawn and not intimate enough, only to end up exploiting those qualities, as Andi does with Benjamin. Do women really want their partners to change, or does male passivity offer them the chance for control? Many men I talked with believe that for a woman, the issue of "controlling her man" is paramount in a relationship, even more important to her than feelings of love. The same men also pointed out the fine line between being "taken care of and nurtured" and "controlled." Once the line was crossed, they said, the impulse in their partners was to take control of almost everything. This may be no different than a man assuming "ownership" of a relationship through male methods of control, such as intimidation and bullying, but in either case it's an invitation to fall out of love.

Andi also had what I call the goddess complex. Perhaps like a lot of women, especially women with big careers, incredible beauty, or great talent, she really thought that men should worship her just because she was this special, inscrutable, mysterious being. A friend told me he was watching the show *The Big Idea* and listening to a high-powered woman executive elaborate her views on men. She said, without a sliver of irony, "Every man lives to make a woman happy. Every man loves to serve us, you know." That was how Andi felt. It's hard to imagine a man saying those exact words today, about women being born to serve men.

The long and short of it was that I treated Andi like the goddess she thought she was. I gave her total empowerment. No matter how abusive she was, or how many times she stormed out of the house, I always was happy to have her back. Was it because I was so in love with her beauty and femininity? Was my loyalty a kind of self-abuse? Relationships are complex and organic, and for all the arguments and misunderstandings, sometimes there are periods of real love and contentment. During one peaceful interlude, Andi and I conceived a child, a girl who is thirteen today and a source of joy to both of us. But after our daughter was born, Andi's behavior grew even more erratic. She could be warm and nurturing one moment, then narcissistic and aloof. More than once she went into her disappearing mode, sometimes for weeks at a time, leaving me with most of the child-rearing duties. While it was lots of responsibility and a juggling act with my career as an artist, any time alone with my young daughter turned out to be a blessing. If I had a choice between going to work every day or staying home and being Mr. Mom, I'd choose the latter.

Andi hides behind the goddess label, claiming full privileges to act as she pleases with seemingly complete exemption from blame. Unlike a lot of women, Andi *likes* being on the pedestal. For many men this would be a huge turnoff because they fear they'll get blamed whenever their partners fall, just as Andi blames Benjamin for her various crises. That Benjamin waited

twenty years to be free—and only because Andi finally forced
the issue—may seem inexplicable, even to him, until he looks at
his childhood and the lack of nurturing. Lack of nurturing leads
to an adult male who doesn't know or trust his emotions, and
lacks self-confidence. Perhaps that's why men like Benjamin
cede authority and control to their partners. For Benjamin, giving control to someone who is out of control seems illogical, but
there was an emotional dynamic that kept him and Andi together in a dark way. Andi needed someone to beat up, to vent
her frustration on, while Benjamin lacked the self-worth and
confidence to stand up to her. Also, Benjamin simply assumed
that when things went wrong it was somehow his fault, or at
least his duty to make them right. As we'll see, no matter how
abusive Andi's behavior becomes, Benjamin, the perfectionist
and idealist, toughs it out. While he is more than entitled to
leave the relationship, *his* controlling nature is to fight that impulse and to pretend that everything will be fine.

No matter how much comfort and joy my daughter brought
me, however, I couldn't ignore the problems in my
marriage. After one petulant explosion, I told Andi she had to
get professional help because she was damaging her
relationship with our daughter. To my surprise, Andi listened to
my plea. For a while I felt some hope as she began seeing a
therapist. The problem was, she never told me what happened
in her sessions. She insisted they were private and confidential.
When I tried to insert myself into the equation, thinking that I
could help her solve any problems, she would sometimes grow
furious. "How could you possibly understand me?" she
demanded. "How could any man understand a woman?" She
ultimately quit one therapist and tried another. I was
sympathetic and understanding but that wasn't enough to help

Andi. It was as if too much damage had been done in her past for anyone, including me, to unwind. I had clearly disappointed her because I hadn't saved her, despite my "mission," and ultimately no therapist could help her either.

Andi had several reactions whenever she became overwhelmed with stress or anxiety. One was to explode with rage, often at me. I was to blame when things went wrong or she careened from one crisis to another. Another was to keep herself in motion, running to or from something, or working long hours at her job. The third was to go out and buy a haute couture wardrobe at Saks, take her friends to expensive restaurants, or splurge on new furniture. But she wasn't the only one with multiple personalities. I kept flipping back and forth as well.

One side of me was the romantic, emotional guy who was still hooked on Andi's feminine mystique; the other side felt rejected, abused, and helpless. Andi was drawn to chaos like the proverbial moth to a flame. I eventually understood that there always had to be a crisis in her life because she'd grown up with nothing but crises. I was from a steady, quiet, church-going family who rarely said a cross word to one another. Where we buried our feelings, Andi disgorged hers at every opportunity.

For all his weaknesses, Benjamin is one of those rare men who does not worry endlessly about failure. However, perhaps he took that attitude to an extreme by not acknowledging his painful reality with Andi. If he'd admitted early on that his relationship was breaking down—and why—he might have set the boundaries for Andi that she badly wanted from him. Her attraction to Benjamin was to someone who would save her from herself. As he gradually grew frustrated by that role along with her erratic behavior, Andi became vindictive because she thought Benjamin had betrayed her. What initially attracted them to each other—her femininity and his seeming stability— was probably not enough to sustain a marriage, certainly not without lots of communication and self-exploration.

was now keenly aware of problems in our relationship, and that my emotional needs were not being met, but I didn't know how to express that to anyone. I had no outlets. I never cheated on Andi or even thought about it. I was just as steady and dependable, and silent, as a plow horse. Even when I eventually attended some therapy sessions with Andi, I never got many insights into my own behavior and feelings because Andi was always making the therapist focus on her. Yet— another irony—she hid the truth from the therapist as adroitly as she had from me. She could giggle one moment and cry the next—how did you penetrate that kind of behavior? Either you embraced it or it repelled you. For twenty years I embraced it.

Today I sometimes feel ashamed of my long history of passive behavior. One or two good years out of twenty? How can I explain that to anyone, including myself? Was I just dependent on Andi, just like abused women are dependent on abusive men? She made me so happy in the beginning that I thought that even when things got bad we could find that happiness again. I don't know if Andi was ever really in love with me or just needed me, and ultimately she was the one who walked out the door because she had met someone else.

If Andi hadn't insisted on a divorce, maybe I'd still be married to her. I'd like to think not, but the truth is I let her get away with a lot of unacceptable behavior because, like my mother, she was the authority figure in my life. That was the pattern established in my childhood. I looked up to my mother with a certain amount of fear and blind obedience, and I did the same with Andi.

With my divorce two years ago, and lots of time for contemplation, I no longer blame Andi for the two decades composed mostly of misery. I let her do it to me, so I accept responsibility for that. I accept responsibility for my life. That way I become more cognizant of what I need from myself in the future (and from a woman): self-acceptance, space, respect, tolerance, and speaking up when I need to. I know that would make a very dull reality-TV show, but reality-TV is part of the problem. It distorts with adrenaline and instant gratification, just like Andi. What is truly real is more subtle, more powerful, and under the surface. Equally real is that I am now in a new, exciting, and fulfilling relationship that bears none of the hallmarks of what I endured with Andi.

When Andi formally ends their relationship, Benjamin finally comes to the realization that happiness for him lies in being less controlling and more assertive. Assertiveness reflects confidence and self-awareness, and represents true power. For many men, to release control is probably the smartest thing they can do for themselves and their relationships. It means abandoning a role they think they are supposed to play but generally distrust, because it brings so much stress and conflict. Too often men confuse control with power, when in fact the two are opposites. Having power means not needing to control anyone.

Like a lot of men, Benjamin throughout his relationship has an intellectual awareness of unhealed aspects of his masculine conditioning, but he can't seem to express that awareness on an emotional plane. The unhealed Benjamin is a good example of a man who adopts one identity or persona for his partner, while perceiving himself as someone quite different. Among other things, that gap is due to lack of (emotional) language skills in

Benjamin—the ability to let his partner know who he really is and what he really feels. Again, language and relating skills are taken for granted by women, but for most men they have to be learned. Understanding their multiple personas is also the key to men knowing how to heal themselves when they run into emotional pain.

9

Hugh's Story

How am I going to keep myself away from me?
—Counting Crows

In his mid-forties, Hugh is over six feet tall, with thinning hair and an intelligent face that always appears alert and eager. A stylish dresser, he keeps his car immaculate, his house clean, and the papers on his desk in perfect order. He is unfailingly polite, thoughtful, and articulate. He describes himself as ambitious and competitive, and gives the impression of thinking several steps ahead of everyone else. A sales executive who lists his goals as professional success and financial security, Hugh was married for almost twelve years before he and his wife Deborah divorced. Deborah, short and trim, is more than attractive, with strawberry blond hair, a quick smile, and blue eyes flecked with gray. But there is also a hint of pain in those eyes, and in the way her mouth sags when she's under stress. Today, Hugh and Deborah share custody of their only child, Cindy, a precocious eleven-year-old. Hugh attributes his emphasis on money and success to being an only child and having parents whose frugality denied him the opportunities enjoyed by other kids in his neighborhood. Deborah, whose parents struggled financially, shared Hugh's goals. Besides being in love, one reason they married was that they thought they were so much alike.

Without always realizing it, I think a lot of women want very much to be in control—in control of themselves, their romantic partners, their children, their overall environment. That was true for my wife, Deborah, and quite a few women I've known over the years. The more specific things they fear, the more control they want to exercise in all areas of their lives. Some women have a pretty long list: fear of fixing a flat tire, fear of violence, fear of any darkness in their past, fear of strangers, fear of not looking attractive enough, fear of being hit on, fear of not being popular, fear of not being good enough to make the cut. The list goes on, but just maybe their insecurities boil down to a fear of any task that a woman doesn't have the confidence or experience to tackle. For better or worse, our culture allows women to have their fears. That's why a lot of women make themselves into victims. Men, on the other hand, are expected by society not to be afraid. They're quickly labeled cowards or sissies if they don't step up to the plate. A woman can jump on a chair if a mouse scurries across the room. She'll be lampooned, but she won't be judged. A man jumping on a chair when the mouse runs by will be judged a pathetic wimp.

I think women channel their fears in various ways: by denying them, getting angry, filling themselves with entitlement, or blaming someone else. Anything but facing their fears head-on and saying, "Hey, I'm scared." It's so much easier for some women to go into that control mode, or pass the particular task on to a man, like fixing a flat tire, or figuring out how her BlackBerry works, or dealing with the spiders in the garage. Men, of course, have their share of fears—they especially fear emotional pain, and many, like me, fear conflict—but in the end, if they're honest, they admit their fears. A lot of women don't like to admit anything. They just won't. In my opinion, many women, like my ex-wife, are escape artists.

I didn't settle down and get married until I was thirty-three. Not because I didn't meet some terrific women along the way, or because I was into the stereotypical male sexual-conquest mode. I just wasn't ready emotionally, nor did I particularly want to give up the single life I enjoyed after college. That life could best be described as a sharply honed work ethic with a very fixed goal of success. I didn't want to marry until I felt secure in my career. I also wanted to be with someone who was equally secure, equally motivated and focused, and with whom I was in love. I was in no hurry. I wanted things to be right, to fall into place, and to be as perfect as possible.

I grew up in the suburbs of a large Indiana city, the only child of hardworking parents—my dad was a high-school guidance counselor and my mother was a housewife—in a predominantly white, middle-class neighborhood. My life was pretty conventional. My parents were loving but strict. I was pretty much a model child, as straightlaced as a choirboy. I knew I wasn't supposed to argue or talk back so I didn't. Why break rules unless you really have to? It's always easier just to get along. I had good friends, I was popular with girls, and I was a strong athlete, so I enjoyed peer respect. For most of my life I considered myself well adjusted, without any deep resentments or special self-esteem needs, but in the last few years, especially after the last year of my marriage with Deborah, I've done some reassessing.

While I loved my parents and respected their values, something gnawed at me as I grew up. My parents didn't have the means to send me away to camp for the summer, much less on trips to Europe, so I knew I was missing something that some of my friends were enjoying. There were also other things that made me think I wanted more from life than my parents had achieved. That's where my ambition came from. No doubt being an only child also shaped my values. I wanted to belong, to be accepted, yet I also wanted to stand out and be noticed. Sometime in high school, or at the latest in college, I became a very motivated student, and I put pressure on myself to excel and be the best I could at whatever I tried.

College was a terrific experience. I loved academics, especially literature and history, learning about worlds to which I'd never been exposed. I had different jobs during the summers, and lots of entrepreneurial ideas, even if I didn't act on them all. In addition to learning, my goal was to save as much money as possible during those years. Money eventually became one of my benchmarks for success and self-respect, as well as a criterion for respecting others. I realize now that on many occasions I was too tight with my friends, but I thought I had a good reason. I was on my own in the world— that's what being an only child growing up in a frugal household teaches you. How many times did I hear "Money doesn't grow on trees, Hugh." So I coveted it. Money was what made me feel secure. I think many women feel the same way. Money is something you can trust. Deborah and I shared that view.

Sometime during college I became pretty judgmental and critical of just about everything—politics, ideas, value structures, other people's behavior. It was my cynical phase. Not all idealists are perfectionists, but I managed, at least for this time in my life, to fit into both camps. I was hardest on myself, but also on the women I dated. Not in any mean or overt way, but it was too easy for me to find their flaws, give up on them without getting to know them, and move on to someone else. I didn't want to compromise. I wanted to have the "right" car and eventually buy the "right" house and always wear the "right" clothes and eat at the "right" restaurants and listen to cool music and do other cool things. And of course I wanted the "right" woman. And to have an idealized lifestyle you needed money, which only reinforced the idea that money was the appropriate benchmark for success and self-respect.

Like anyone who prizes discipline and moves toward his goals, I also had some control needs. To me it was all logical. The more you can control your life, the more focus you have, and the easier it is to meet your objectives. I definitely wasn't into controlling others. Even if I was critical of the women I dated, I didn't try to shape them into what I wanted them to be. I just said good-bye, walked away, and kept looking. I didn't want the chore of being responsible for someone else's life. I wanted to find someone just as self-assured and independent as I was.

Many perfectionists are goal setters from an early age. The need to accomplish something, to continually prove themselves, to be acquirers, and to control their environment, often stems from childhoods where, as in Hugh's case, they felt deprived or put down as boys and adolescents. In pursuing their goals, they become critical of themselves as well as others who disappoint them in one fashion or another. Hugh says he's not into controlling anyone but himself, but as we're about to see, he believes that setting and achieving goals with the woman in his life is an irrefutable bond, if not proof of their love. In fact, imposing his value system in the name of love will create competition, control, guilt, and distrust with his partner—"Why aren't you carrying your share of the load?"—and can easily tear this relationship apart.

Hugh talks about how both men and women have their fears, but in his opinion women are less than honest about them. They prefer to channel their fears by "denying them, getting angry, filling themselves with entitlement, or blaming someone else." As we'll see, Deborah does all of these. Hugh believes he is candid about his own fears and weaknesses, though from all my interviews, I came away believing that men were as much into denial, if not more so, than women. Responding to the male code, men know they're not supposed to be afraid, so they pretend accordingly. However, their fears, if not dealt with, can come back to undermine them and their goals. This is what happens to Hugh.

Hugh does touch on one issue—a woman's sense of entitlement—that a lot of men commented on. I was told that not a few women, particularly in the under-thirty generation, confuse entitlement for empowerment or even self-esteem. "So many younger women have no idea who they are or what they want from their lives," a perceptive, twenty-nine-year-old man said, "but they mask that by giving themselves various rights and privileges, such as the assumption of how men, if not the entire world, should treat them. Women will put up with very little, while they expect me to put up with a great deal. I have women friends who openly criticize and put down men. I generally find myself walking on eggshells around them. If I had more courage, I'd call them on it."

Once out of college, after a few hits and misses, I found a niche in sales at a large company. I enjoyed not just the people I worked with but the act of making a deal. The feeling of closure, of accomplishment, was terrific, as was earning a commission. By my late twenties, I was making good money and buying some of the possessions I'd always wanted, essentially living the life my frugal parents didn't, but one that I thought they'd be proud of. Being a success in your parents' eyes is what drives most men and women, isn't it? I didn't see how you could separate my need for money from my need for approval, security, and control. At that time it all blended together.

Besides gaining my parents' respect, it was important to me that I was liked by my peers and customers. I had decent looks and a pleasing personality, but that led to some problems. The first was I had a hard time with confrontation. In fact, confronting anyone and risking their anger, or any emotional turbulence, was a turnoff for me. It rattled me. You could say it was the epitome of loss of control, or a blemish on my idealized, perfect world, or maybe that's just how I was raised. So usually I would worm my way out of any conflict rather than be forced to deal with a difficult situation.

My second problem was that when I made a mistake, or an error in judgment, I got down on myself. A screwup meant I wasn't trying hard enough. Besides, I always found it easier to blame myself than to pick a fight with somebody, even if they were at least partly responsible for the error. That only led to conflict, which inevitably got in the way of meeting my goals. The less resistance, the better.

I met my future wife, Deborah, at a party in 1990, and we hit it off right away. In addition to the indisputable chemistry between us, Deborah met all my criteria for the ideal woman: she had been a Fulbright scholar, later was on the marketing team of a prestigious car manufacturer, and currently worked in sales in commercial real estate. She was a winner. The second oldest of six children, her family were third-generation farmers, hardworking, down-to-earth, and while financially they tended to struggle, they were the types to look you squarely in the eye and tell you what they felt. But they were also suspicious of the outside world. Her father would say to me, "You know, it's always the little guy who gets screwed." Contrary to her family, Deborah exhibited a kind of dazzling confidence and independence to which I was intrinsically drawn. She was a great dresser, she had a sense of humor, and she also shared my dream of upward mobility and material success. I suppose I saw my twin in Deborah, a safe emotional harbor for an only child who wanted validation for his idealized world. We got married fifteen months later. I was in love, I had risen even higher in my company, and I was in total control of my life. So I thought.

After we were married, Deborah's first piece of bad luck was to lose her job with her real-estate company. I was sympathetic but had no doubt she'd bounce back. Instead, she struggled for months to find new work. Nothing seemed to gel. For Deborah there was always someone or something to blame. The economy was still recovering . . . her interviewer didn't really listen to her . . . the job requirements didn't quite fit her talents. It took me time to understand that while outwardly Deborah was blaming others for her string of disappointments, she was really blaming herself. She didn't have confidence that she could land a meaningful job. She didn't think she was good enough. As the months went by, she'd let slip little comments that indicated she thought her life was rife with failures—setbacks in high school and college, in her family relationships, with friends, at her previous jobs—things she'd never told me before we were married and that utterly belied the aura of outward confidence to which I had been attracted. As these stray admissions grew in frequency, they affected her overall attitude and personality. Basically, she stopped believing in herself and her gifts. Deborah also became increasingly dependent on me—both emotionally and financially—and took solace in material comforts and acquisitions.

I didn't say much during this difficult period, except to give Deborah continual encouragement. But as she wore her mantle of defeat more openly, and her dependency on me grew, I became anxious. Our immediate problem was that we were about to buy a house and really needed two incomes. Deborah, finally giving up on the job market, told me she wanted to stay home and be a housewife. I explained that we couldn't keep up our lifestyle without both of us working. She essentially avoided the question about her confidence, and our crisis of overspending, and accused me of being too dramatic. Somehow she thought everything would turn out just fine. But I didn't have that confidence, and I couldn't hide my anxiety.

Whenever I pushed the issue, Deborah said I was trying to control her. That just made me more uptight. I resented the financial pressure that fell on me, and I also had difficulty with the idea that Deborah never dealt with her own issues. What suddenly made her so lazy, so entitled? As I got to know her parents and siblings, I could see that emotions were never part of any family discussion. They were nice, straightforward people, but their underlying stoicism and distrust of the world made me think that Deborah had never been given the opportunity to express herself. When I brought up that possibility to Deborah, she denied she had anything but strong feelings of love for her family.

The issue of control quickly rears its head in Hugh and Deborah's relationship, and neither knows quite how to deal with it. An anxious Hugh, whose identity is tied to making money, is only trying to protect their nest egg. Deborah, medicating herself (by overspending) from pain she hasn't identified to Hugh, is angry at her husband for not being a better provider, and ultimately making her feel bad about herself. Hugh doesn't understand the difference between confrontation, which he's afraid of, and assertiveness, so he never gets his point across to Deborah that her overspending makes *him* feel anxious. What comes across instead is his fear that Deborah is not doing her share to support their goals, and that she's letting him down. Deborah thinks he's attacking her for no good reason. But she fails Hugh for the same reason he fails her—by not being assertive and telling him where her lack of confidence comes from. Some couples who come together out of a commonality of goals fail to realize they may also share lots of fears and blind spots about themselves and that these traits, on a subconscious level, are also part of the attraction process.

To afford our new house and meet our financial obligations, we finally agreed it would make sense for Deborah to work for my company, where I now held a management position and could easily get her a sales job. For a while her spirits picked up and she made decent money. But her appetite for an even more lavish lifestyle grew, and despite our additional income, a monstrous renovation on our new house virtually depleted our savings. To make even more money, I left management and joined Deborah in sales. While we did bolster our joint income, the pressure of working together put further strain on our relationship. Deborah felt we were in some kind of competition. She was unhappy whenever my commission checks were larger than hers. "But all the money goes to a common goal," I told her. I was getting frustrated because I could never seem to please her. I was also worried not just about her overspending, but mine as well. That seemed to be another competition between us—who had the best taste and who would spend the most to prove it. From big things to little, we were like two junkies egging each other on. Who would find the most expensive china, the best lawn mower, the top-of-the-line lighting fixtures? My own discipline began to erode, eclipsed by this insane desire to be the perfect couple living the perfect lifestyle.

I can't say it was one single factor that loosened the first thread of the tapestry I had woven for my future. It certainly didn't happen overnight. But in essence, the Deborah I courted and fell in love with, the Deborah I thought I knew so well, turned out in many ways to be a front for a very different person. It was as if I'd fallen in love with a mirage. For a long time I never knew where reality was with Deborah, what was important to her, when she was posturing and when she was being sincere. Were my early perceptions of her simply incorrect—had I been blinded by love?—or did Deborah change? If the latter, did she know that she was changing, or was it something out of her control? Was I helping her or was I making things worse?

For Hugh, having a controlling, judgmental nature may have created in Deborah, at least in the early stages of their relationship, a corresponding submissiveness and desire to acquiesce. This may have started when Deborah asked Hugh to be a leader and make important decisions for them when she lost her job. Most men want to meet women's expectations and will assume the leadership role if asked. When Deborah came to interpret Hugh's leadership as domination, however, her own need for control became obvious. She had to do something to keep from feeling suffocated.

Both Deborah and Hugh hide from the pain of their pasts without realizing the harm that such secrecy can do to their relationship. It's the ultimate selfish act. Why don't more men—if they perceive themselves as leaders—speak up? Perhaps they are simply used to living with their fears, or believe its unmanly to divulge them. That Hugh wasn't more open with Deborah reflects the behavior of men who dislike a controlling woman but dislike confrontation even more. In the end, control in one or both partners becomes a means of not having to deal with their internal conflicts, which most certainly leads to even greater unhappiness and the likelihood of falling out of love.

One thing was for sure: our internal relationship was being replaced by an external one. One of our problems was that by ducking confrontation I also ducked discussing the touchy subject of our dissipating intimacy. I finally hinted that something felt wrong between us and that we should consider counseling. Deborah didn't really respond. She lived in this increasingly private world, to which I felt I was denied access. Her periods of moodiness grew more frequent. I ignored them, hoping that the problem, our problem, whatever it was, would simply go away. Our superficial solution was to become more wrapped up in our external world of parties and spending. In truth, we were both miserable. Even when Deborah became pregnant, what should have been one of the happiest moments of my life was tempered by my fading attraction to my wife. I was starting to fake all my emotions for her.

When our daughter Cindy was born, I hoped things would stabilize and return Deborah and me to some level of happiness. Cindy was colicky and never slept more than a few hours at a time. I wanted to do my share with the baby, but Deborah was insistent that since she was the mother, Cindy was her responsibility. Deborah was up at all hours, and with sleep deprivation her moodiness deepened. When I suggested she needed a prescription for a sleep aid, she coolly denied there was even a problem. Except for discussions about the health of the baby, our communication was dwindling down to subjects no more consequential than the weather. The subject of our still wobbly finances was never brought up. When we got into bed at night, we didn't touch each other.

Cindy seemed to take up all of Deborah's time. When I came home at night there was often no dinner because there was some issue with the baby. Deborah was too busy even to ask how my day was. I felt like a third wheel. When I grew more insistent that we seek counseling, Deborah became upset, even furious. Unlike me, my wife had no trouble with confrontation. Her behavior was cyclical—periods of pouting and moody silences alternating with out-of-control anger. Though I'd seen previous glimpses of her temper, now it came as a tidal wave of fury. What nerve had I touched? Was this just a case of sleep deprivation, or had Cindy's arrival stirred up some deeper issues? When I arrived home at night, if the slightest thing had gone wrong at home, Deborah would be screaming. Sometimes her voice grew so hoarse that she couldn't talk the next morning.

I often blamed myself during this period—even if I couldn't identify what I'd done wrong—because I thought that would pacify Deborah. Also it was my old habit to avoid fighting. But nothing appeased Deborah: not my apologies, not my offers to help her with Cindy. Deborah was so fixated on the baby's well-being that she developed frequent migraines and finally an ulcer. Still, it was hard to broach the subject of getting her help. She was playing the role of martyr all the way. Just as she denied that she was sleep-deprived, she denied that her physical ailments were anything to worry about. Maybe she thought she could hide them from me, from everyone, just like she hid from her fears. I would come to believe that my wife's fears, whatever they were, had such deep roots, and that her strategies for denial and masquerade were so ingrained, that she had little chance of ever seeing herself realistically.

Both men and women are leery of angry partners often without understanding where and how that anger originates. Hugh is so guarded that he doesn't let anyone know what's really bothering him. Faking his emotions for Deborah is symptomatic of how repressed he really is. Perhaps, like Deborah, he didn't develop his own voice in his strict, by-the-book middle-class home. His dislike of confrontation may really be a fear of being exposed or shamed, or a fear that his anger will come out and overwhelm him.

Looking at Deborah's life, her template for anger is the same as for a lot of men: a childhood where she never spoke up or got the attention she needed; an adolescence lost to the common family goal of labor and survival; the overriding message that you can never work hard enough or be virtuous enough; the defeatist attitude that the little man always gets trampled; and the rationalization that it's okay to be an impostor—pretending to be confident and happy, if not perfect—to impress your partner. Women are no different than men when it comes to putting up a smoke screen of confidence to gain a foothold in a relationship. However, while a lot of men will explode from their anger or run away, the majority of women will process their anger differently, according to most psychologists. It is often turned inward and manifests itself, for example, in eating disorders, obsessive-compulsive behavior, physical ailments (like Deborah's ulcer and migraines), self-mutilation, alcoholism, or anxiety disorders.

As much as I loved our little girl, I soon found myself competing with Deborah for who gave Cindy the most affection, who could be the most perfect parent. Deborah and I had competed before in the workplace, and now it was happening at home. Since I worked all day, no doubt Deborah's bond with Cindy was stronger. What was also clear was that Deborah and I had virtually nothing in common anymore except for our love for Cindy, and the same hollow, expensive lifestyle

that both of us clung to like a life raft. Once more I asked
Deborah to see a therapist with me. By suggesting counseling,
she said, I was implying that something was wrong with her. I
was invading her privacy. I didn't love her enough. I was, in
short, making needless trouble instead of enjoying our new
baby daughter and being thankful for all that we had. I think
she was mouthing what her stoical parents had told her. Do
your work, don't complain, don't make waves. Anyway, she had
a dozen reasons why our lack of intimacy was either
unimportant or my fault.

In the meantime, she became the perfect mother. I say that
with both admiration and jealousy. Deborah doted on Cindy
with such affection and joy that our daughter flourished
because of it. To say that I felt excluded from both Cindy's and
Deborah's universe was an understatement. For sure, there
were fun times when we both took Cindy on strolls and trips,
and Deborah, when she felt secure, could be as caring as she
was in the early days of our marriage. But she could turn off
those loving emotions in a wink, and I felt stranded again. I
resented always being at the mercy of her moods. At times I
got really angry about it. I wanted Deborah to recognize that I
had emotional needs too, that I wasn't just the great hunter-
gatherer who stoically, perhaps like her father, provided the
means to meet our material needs and that was all I was good
for. I wanted something more. I wanted attention and affection.

When I spoke up for myself, Deborah's eyes usually glazed
over. It was as if she had to make a choice between paying
attention to Cindy or to me—as if she didn't have enough love
or energy for both of us—and she chose our daughter. It was a
good example of Deborah seeking control over a very limited
world that was safe and secure and where no one could
threaten her. But if she'd paid more attention to me, if she'd
been honest about our lack of communication, trust, and

intimacy—if I'd been honest too—maybe the marriage could have been saved.

According to Hugh, Deborah hid from her darkest emotions and kept Hugh away from them too. She claimed the "complexity defense"—the allegation that Hugh couldn't possibly understand her—and therefore he couldn't help her. But apparently she didn't let her family or her women friends get close either, and did everything possible to keep her pain private. While Hugh did sincerely try to help Deborah, he was often an inadequate communicator. Like other men in this book, he didn't seem to know how to relate to his partner once she began to change. He wanted her to stay the same as when they fell in love. Even more naïve was Hugh's own prejudice—and Deborah's—that their lives had to be perfect, which ultimately made everything worse. Intolerant of mistakes, they reinforced each other's denial. Eventually, they got so caught up in their artificial, make-believe world that they became strangers to one another.

Hugh points out that women can be very selective when and with whom they share their emotions. He implies this is one of their primary tools of control over men, along with sex. Sex has always been a woman's basic trading card. Most women surrender sexually only when the card they get in return has real value, such as a relationship commitment, emotional support, or some material advantage. Bundling sex and emotion together—and the ability to withhold them at will—gives women an incredible leverage that men do not have. When men are shut off from what they crave and need—as Deborah does to Hugh by showering all her affection and attention on Cindy—women may not be aware of the anger and resentment this creates in their partners. Deborah may rationalize her actions as doing what it takes to survive, but men won't buy it in the long term. If the pattern of deprivation becomes willful and consistent, they will fall out of love.

For the next eight years, almost all our free time was so child-centered that Deborah and I rarely saw friends, went out to dinner or a movie together, or went away for an intimate weekend. Everything revolved around Cindy. There were so many toys inside, and playground equipment on the lawn, that it looked like we were running a nursery school. Deborah and I virtually gave up on sex. That should have been a clear warning sign that we needed to separate, but Deborah and I both ignored it. Cindy was the bond that would keep us together, she said once, and I wanted to believe that too. But in effect our beautiful little daughter was depleting the last dregs of energy and passion from our marriage.

As Cindy grew older, my perception of what was right for her changed. I suggested to Deborah that we were beginning to spoil her. Deborah grew defensive and put up another wall between us. Tired of futile conversations, I retreated into silence. That just emboldened Deborah to lash out at me and others when her mood darkened. She would repeat what her father had told her and the family: "The little guy always gets screwed." I think that's how Deborah felt. She was the little guy, the one the world tended to overlook or trample. Her bravado, her seemingly indefatigable confidence, that I had been so attracted to when we first dated, was turning out to be just a smoke screen. Whether conscious or not, it was a clever way to fool the world and me, and maybe herself as well. Underneath all that bravado was low self-esteem and the feeling she was never going to succeed at anything except being a mommy. Cindy was perhaps the only thing that kept her going.

Even if Deborah wouldn't join me, I knew I needed counseling. Why was I living with a woman who made me miserable? In therapy I learned a lot about my need for perfection and achievement and being validated by money. And that to admit that my marriage was a failure would be a breach of my perfect world. Also, maybe I wasn't the easiest person for Deborah to live with. She was comparing herself to me and thinking that she came up short. I didn't do enough to support her, and maybe that reflected my overly sharp focus on my own needs. I acknowledged to myself all my weaknesses and insecurities, and set out to work on them. If I could change, I thought, our marriage could also change for the better. But whenever I went home and confided to Deborah what I had learned about myself, how liberating it felt, I was greeted again by that faraway gaze. Either she thought I was suggesting she needed therapy too, or my self-revelations triggered unhappy memories of her childhood.

When I told my therapist about Deborah's background, more pieces of the puzzle fell into place. Because my wife was from a large farming family that struggled, she was imbued with a dawn-to-dusk work ethic that demanded everyone pitch in. That lifestyle also was characterized by an unflinching stoicism. One never complained, never whined, never asked for or received special attention. Along with not having a voice among six children, the work ethic on a farm makes you an adult before you're ten or eleven. I think Deborah felt she never had much of a childhood, even less of an adolescence. She had lived most of her life in a state of material and emotional deprivation. Her desire for an affluent lifestyle was more than understandable, along with a lack of self-confidence because she never had the opportunity to blossom on her own. It was easier for me now to understand Deborah's motives in raising Cindy with such affection and devotion. Besides wanting to be

indisputably good at something—motherhood—Deborah also
needed to lavish on our daughter all the love she thought she
had never received. I think she also believed that if she wasn't
overprotective of Cindy, something bad was going to happen to
her. Maybe that fear came directly from Deborah's father's
negative philosophy about the "little guy."

Deborah's anger was directed both inward and outward.
Her often explosive rages at Hugh were probably meant in part
for her strict and inflexible parents. Hugh doesn't say, but perhaps in Deborah's mind his passive, judgmental nature reminded her of her father. Deborah put added pressure on herself
by trying to be the perfect mother when it was clear that she and
Hugh were losing the title of the perfect couple. The future
raises some interesting questions. Desperate for validation and
investing everything in her daughter, what happens when Cindy
grows up and interprets her mother's smothering love and perfectionism as control? Just as Deborah felt controlled by her
family, will she pass that anger on to Cindy when she enters her
adult relationships? If she does let go of her daughter, what
emotional resources does Deborah have to fall back on?

As long as she had our daughter as her escape hatch,
Deborah wasn't going to choose to enter a world of painful
self-examination. So ultimately, nothing really changed
between us. To me it was incredible that Deborah could turn
from the most gentle and constructive play with Cindy, close
our daughter's door, and, in the privacy of our bedroom, lash
out at me for one infraction or another. During one screaming
tirade, she put her hands around my neck and pushed me
into the wall. Incidentally, we never fought in front of our
daughter. We gave Cindy the impression that everything was
fine between us, that her world was as safe and secure and

perfect as we all wanted it to be. We basically raised her with a
terrible lie.

I'm not trying to assign blame in this story. If anything, I put
blame on myself for not speaking up, and for perpetuating the
lie of our perfect universe. I have come to think that men
internalize blame and criticism more readily than women, and
that this is a conditioned response from childhood. A boy is
more likely than his sisters to feel a parent's pressure to be
mature, responsible and successful, and is held (and holds
himself) to a higher standard of accountability. It's the "You're
the man of the house" syndrome. Out of fear of criticism, or
trying to project an image of superman, a man tends to hide his
mistakes. He will even lie to hide them.

Long before Deborah and I were actually divorced, I knew
that our relationship had nowhere to go. I just couldn't make
myself tell Deborah. A divorce would mean the end of my
"Ozzie and Harriet" universe. And I think Deborah stuck with
the marriage for a similar reason. She had been raised with the
notion that you just don't quit or give up on anything. It was the
farmer's way: no matter what the adversity—your crops could
turn to dust and the bank could foreclose on your house—you
just hung in there with a poker face. In my opinion, Deborah
never understood what real happiness meant, unless it was
defined as the opposite of a negative—in her case material
deprivation. Women are supposed to be the ones who really
understand their emotions, but that wasn't the case with
Deborah. If they were under the surface, she didn't want to go
near them.

One day we both had just had it. Deborah asked for the
divorce first, but I was finally in the mental state to want it as
well. Many of our friends were shocked. Despite our internal
upheavals and Deborah's retreat from the world, we had

maintained the façade of the perfect couple. The divorce was relatively quick but emotionally tough on both of us. In my opinion, Deborah continues to be devoted to Cindy to the point of denying recovery for herself.

I don't know whether Deborah and I will ever be friends. I'm open to the possibility, but she has to want it too, and right now I believe there's too much anger and lack of self-understanding on her part. As for Cindy, I worry about her as well. She is eleven now, very mature, smart, but driven and perfection oriented. I spend as much time with her as I can. I worry if she can weather the trauma of her perfect world being cracked open like an egg. We had inadvertently taught her that perfection was not only the ideal to strive for, it was the norm. I hope as she gets older she can understand some of the issues and lessons that it took me decades to learn.

Instead of experiencing true intimacy while making love, many men—bored or frustrated in their relationships—fantasize about previous lovers or a colleague at work or even a stranger. Men do get tired of making love to the same woman over and over, but often these are men who have no autonomy or private world outside of their relationship. They feel stuck or trapped, and fantasy is their only empowerment. They may have given up nourishing their relationship on other levels as well. Naïvely, men think their sexual fantasies are a secret, but almost every woman sooner or later intuits that something is wrong. Sensing his emotional distance, she becomes increasingly dissatisfied, moody, or depressed—and one day she disengages too. This is what probably happened between Deborah and Hugh. For a lot of women, like Deborah, were it not for their economic insecurities or other dependencies, it's doubtful they would remain in their relationships when they perceive their partners as emotionally absent. A man might argue back, as Hugh would, that he wouldn't be so emotionally distant if his partner wasn't so controlling.

The Perfection Impulse
Conclusions

On the surface, perfection and control are about achieving happiness by excelling at what we do and not letting distractions get in the way. That perfectionism almost always leads to impossible goals, frustration, intolerance, guilt, and burnout is only one reason it's a relationship buster. For the perfectionists I interviewed—at least those who admitted this was a losing game—another problem was that they weren't really sure what made them happy, except for chronic overachievment, notice, and praise. Take away their ambition, many of them said, and their sense of masculinity was definitely challenged. Some said all they were left with was the message from popular culture about conformity and fitting in. If you looked and acted cool, you could get praise that way.

Perhaps popular culture's emphasis on conformity and status started in the fifties, and was soon identified in books like *The Man in the Gray Flannel Suit, The Organization Man,* and *The Lonely Crowd.* The sixties rang in an era of idealism, rebellion, and nonconformity, but for the next thirty-five years the pendulum swung back. Today, the pressure to feel "in," to buy the right jeans, to take that special vacation, to read the hottest book—to fear being different or to be singled out—has woven itself into the social fabric. Most of us don't allow ourselves to be misfits or rebels, and are distrustful, or jealous, of those who are. We take this position ostensibly to be happy but, in fact, many of us act out of fear. When it comes to relationship busters, fear and denial—the demons that often drive us to perfection and control—lead the class.

The media may be the main cause of our conformity, confusion, and sense of unworthiness. Stories and images of achievement and perfection meant to inspire us —like Lance Armstrong crossing the finish line with arms held high, or those beautiful models posing every year for the *Sports Illustrated* swimsuit edition, or Paris Hilton and her glam friends partying the night away in Vegas—instead, down deep, make us feel inferior and inadequate. Popular culture often motivates us to move in directions we don't want to go, but we feel left out, or something is wrong with us, if we don't go.

What else can we learn from Benjamin, Barry, and Hugh? They all seemed determined, especially when their marriages ran into trouble, to satisfy their interpretation of masculinity rather than to put the same attention and effort into keeping their relationships alive. This might be because "being a man" (depending on how one defines it) is less complicated than developing a lasting, satisfying relationship. For any man, masculinity is a double-edged sword. Sometimes it is a confusing burden—full of conflicts, hidden messages, and stress—other times it is profoundly simple. Getting involved with sports, cars, or computers, for example, or any pursuit that has a clear goal and doesn't involve ambiguity, has great appeal. This applies to more than just hobbies. Whether fighting in Iraq or supporting their families or just going to work every day, men see themselves as performing a sacred duty. In their eyes, they are behaving heroically and often sacrificing themselves for others. Compared to sustaining a relationship, particularly if one or both partners are perfectionists, the emotional dividends from masculinity are more dependable and immediate. Men don't understand why their partners get upset with them when they work a sixty-hour week and come home tired and irritated. They expect acknowledgment and praise. Criticizing or belittling men for their passions, or what they perceive as their duty, can create a wedge in a relationship and becomes a reason for falling out of love.

There's another theme conveyed in all three stories. After all the negotiating, conscious and unconscious, that turns a relationship into a working partnership, if one side ultimately feels he or she has been treated unfairly, the partnership won't endure in a healthy way. Recognizing that not all controlling behavior is negative—sometimes it's necessary for self-preservation—it's understood that control and leverage form the underlying foundation of any working relationship. Yet love, which presumably initiated everything, needs to be there too. Love means, among other things, the willingness to be flexible with your partner and renegotiate if either of you is unhappy. Yet some men have a hard time with flexibility, not because they lack negotiating skills but because they don't know how to relate to their partners in any way except in the masculine, linear, nonemotional fashion. Closing a real-estate deal or asking for a salary increase does not call on the same skills as negotiating for your happiness. Women, with their gift for "emotional reasoning," are usually more successful at getting, keeping, or changing what they want in a relationship.

Tips for Avoiding This Relationship Buster

1. Before you fall in love with a perfectionist, don't assume that his or her discipline and goal setting will translate to structure and security in your relationship. While perfection sounds like a positive, even noble, ideal, in an intimate partnership it can lead to conflict, jealousy, feelings of inadequacy, and guilt.

2. Understand that perfectionists are often those who mask self-doubt or low self-worth with excessive achievement, can never get enough validation, and sometimes have difficulty accepting that their partners can't be happy unless they're overachievers too.

3. Be aware that the need to control may come from a need to wall out one kind of pain or another, but unless those reasons are communicated to your partner, even healthy doses of control can be interpreted as selfishness and manipulation.

4. Understand that a lot of men, when they can't get the support and nurturing they need from their partners, and to feel in control, will turn to some definition of masculinity—such as pursuing a sport, or taking on new projects at work—to win praise from their peers or colleagues.

5. Realize that control and power are ultimately opposites in a relationship. True power comes from not needing to control anyone.

The Fading of Attraction

Despite the euphoria of falling in love and wanting it to last forever, despite the sanctity of wedding vows, despite all the best intentions, people do lose interest in one another and fall out of love. In almost all relationships, sexual attraction has a shelf life, and unless reinvigorated or reimaged over time, it needs to be analyzed in terms of its importance and manifestation. Physical affection doesn't always have to be sex, but some expression is necessary for most couples to be happy, even if it's just holding hands, giving hugs, or putting an arm around one another. It is an important link to the emotional bond that also changes with time, depending on the flexibility and creativity of a couple, and which provides the real nexus for staying in love.

From my interviews, the happiest couples were often those in relationships with a strong intellectual or rational basis; it was the mind that drove the emotions. These couples had experienced feelings of infatuation, and acknowledged how intoxicating those feelings were, but to sustain them, they said, meant having multiple relationships, either simultaneously or consecutively. They thought it was far easier and more practical to deepen one's love for a single person, provided that there was always attraction. Attraction, short- and long-term, was an indication of intelligence, they added, such as the ability to appreciate the quirks of your partner's personality, to empathize with his or her struggles and ambitions, to be intuitive and empathetic, to care and listen when someone needed sympathy or direction, and to know when to talk and when to listen. A lot of men said they were attracted to a woman if she cared about them and knew how to express it, either verbally or silently. They considered the quality of caring to be a primary definition of femininity. Most said that attraction was also based on their partner's character or integrity. Respect and trust ranked high among relationship "musts."

But no matter how intelligent or empathetic you are, or how much respect you have for your partner, attraction can still fade. For two people who begin to move in different directions, or who discover that their partner is not the person they ultimately want to share their life with, sometimes a breakup is both unavoidable and healthy. It may have little to do with childhood issues, the burden of masculinity, control and perfection, or validation and self-esteem. One man told me he lost interest in his partner because even though she was fun, sexy, and had a great sense of humor—attributes he prized in a woman—she became a "true believer" of a cause he strongly opposed. Their sudden intellectual differences became emotional—she cared for things that he didn't, and what he liked she found inexplicable. Though they tried to get along, ultimately neither could empathize with the other's point of view, and each ultimately felt marginalized.

Other themes covered in this section include:

- How the fading of attraction may have little to do with a partner's personality or physical appearance, or conflicts over money, raising children, or getting along with the in-laws, but rather, feelings of being upstaged, embarrassed, shamed, hemmed in, or being the target of anger or cruelty
- Why the argument "I just lost interest in him/her" is often used, particularly by men, as a catchall for heading for the exit without investigating the deeper reasons for one's unhappiness
- Why many couples lose interest in one another because they claim their needs are not being met, particularly in those relationships that began on a highly romantic note, but often these couples have never articulated their deeper needs, either to themselves or each other
- How popular culture makes it easy to believe that relationships are not meant to last forever, and if you're not happy, not only do you deserve better but there's always someone else to fall in love with
- Why losing interest in one another is inevitable for some couples, and rather than deny it, facing the problems behind it rationally and constructively, perhaps with the help of a mediator or therapist, increases the odds for better relationships in the future

10

Andrew's Story

We teach people how to treat us.
—Dr. Phil McGraw

ike Steven, Bill, and Barry who, in various parts of the country, pass their Saturday nights wondering about their relationships and what makes them happy, we find Andrew fixed on
similar thoughts in Seattle. It's the wee hours of the morning
and the fifty-nine-year-old psychologist can't fall asleep. Andrew is fair-skinned with fine, unkempt hair and soft brown
eyes. Of average height, he is for the moment on the thin side—
on a careful diet after surviving a health scare—and his expression is more somber than usual. Andrew describes himself as
extremely analytical, someone who's always peeling away another layer of the onion and never quite satisfied with what he
finds underneath. But there is also a softer, romantic side to Andrew, one that is on a quest for love and harmony with another
soul.

As he lies in bed, his thoughts drift to his sixtieth birthday,
coming in less than a week. Turning fifty was bad enough, he re-

members, and now ten years have passed in what feels like days. What's life all about? he wonders. Separated from his second wife, frustrated with his career, it's hard for him not to feel a certain loneliness. Despite earnest attempts with online dating services and networking with friends, he hasn't found anyone that he clicks with. Twice married, the doting father of two daughters and a son, Andrew still doesn't fully understand why his two serious relationships fell apart. Both Marie and Lucy were great women. They accepted and loved him. Why couldn't he love Marie and Lucy back? The simple answer is that he just lost interest in them. They stopped being the fascinating, nurturing, competent, or funny women that he first knew. In addition, they began to do things that annoyed him. But more than anything specific, there was a general, pervasive tedium in the relationships. Eventually, bored and restless—and responding to some internal compass—he moved on. All his life, he thinks, he's been searching for a deeper happiness that no woman has so far provided him.

Each of Andrew's marriages lasted over fifteen years. While athletic as well as brainy, Andrew has never been caught up in competition, and he shies away from any aggressive behavior. Quiet and introspective, he considers himself an existential romantic; at different points in his search for happiness he has taken up painting, gone into therapy, and steeped himself in the literature of religion, philosophy, and spiritualism. The older he gets, the more thwarted he feels by a lack of solid answers. He wonders if he is just too critical and judgmental, too much of a narcissist, or if he is on a search for some truth that is too complex and elusive to grasp easily.

When I was around two, I moved with my mother, at the time a housewife, and my father, an academic and economist, to Washington, D.C. My brother was born a year

later, and a sister two and a half years after that. My earliest
memory is of sitting with my grandfather on the edge of a
bathtub in our new home, hacking away with whooping cough
and having a terrible time getting my breath. My grandfather
couldn't help me, but I felt caring and compassion from him, and
his presence comforted me. I have many other pleasant
memories of Washington. We lived in a housing development on
the edge of a large wood. I remember hikes in what to me was a
slightly scary but fascinating forest. We caught snakes and
turtles, and there were always new areas to explore. My father
loved the outdoors and knew all about animals, birds, trees, and
plants. He was always teaching me about the things we
encountered. I remember one Christmas going out in the early
evening to find and cut down a tree for the house. The ground
was covered with snow. It was dark, but a full moon was out and
there was plenty of light to travel by. I was worried because I
didn't know where we were going, but I had confidence in my
father that he knew the way. We cut the tree and brought it
home by sled. It was truly a magical night. In those early days,
my father made my life exciting and I felt he cared for me deeply.

My memories of my mother in this period are less clear. I
had the sense of her caring and doing a lot for me, but it did not
seem as exciting as what I did with my dad. While my mother
loved me a great deal, I think she also wanted me to be well
behaved and to reflect well on her. She told me that she was
sometimes embarrassed when I was quicker and more capable
than some of my playmates, so she put an emphasis on me
learning to share with others. I think I took these lessons to
heart and worked at being well behaved. This kind of
obedience came relatively easily to me—I've never been a
rebel—so from a young age I developed a concern for pleasing
others and not showing them up. This pattern of wanting to
please has run throughout my life.

As I grew up, my male role models were hardworking, considerate of others, intellectual, and responsible. My father and both my grandfathers were this way. My own work ethic and pride in my professional accomplishments were seeded in my teenage years. I did not have any aggressive or strongly sexual role models that I can remember. In addition to my father, grandfathers, and some male teachers, probably my most influential models were heroes in books I read. In my early teens I was particularly drawn to Western novels and felt an affinity for the prototypical frontier hero: a tall, lean, strong, and quiet man, often a loner, who believed in righteousness and who suffered endless trials and pain before vanquishing the evil foes arrayed against him. In most novels there was also a beautiful woman to fight for, yet she was typically in the background, and often something like a goddess to be worshipped from a distance. These men rarely voiced their feelings of love and attraction to these women and acted almost as if that was not appropriate or manly. These novels seemed to be saying that when a man loves and cares for a woman, he should make a commitment to take care of her forever. Anything sexual came after that commitment, and usually after marriage. Sex without honorable intentions was inappropriate. This was my early concept of how a man was supposed to behave and to some extent it is still with me.

As an older teenager, I liked Ayn Rand's *The Fountainhead* and *Atlas Shrugged.* Both novels were thinly veiled stories to promote her philosophy of personal independence and responsibility, and striving for perfection. In Rand's universe, less competent or irresponsible persons were considered unworthy of compassion and undeserving of support. Love was highly prized, but even in a relationship it was crucial to maintain one's individuality and separateness. I believed strongly in this philosophy in my late teens, but by college it put

me in conflict with some new friendships I had developed. I
decided Rand's standards were too idealistic and I became
more accepting of the give and take that is necessary for any
friendship to grow. However, I continued to believe in striving
for high standards and always doing my best.

From an early age Andrew has a sense of his own vulnerability, and perhaps that's what pushes him as a teenager to his
romantic vision of the importance of virtue and responsibility—
by being a good person and working hard he can respect himself, and others, especially women, will respect him. Being
honorable toward women—not taking advantage of them for
sex, for example—is part of his romanticism. Like a lot of men,
he develops his male code based on role models, in this case
from books. Only when he gets to college and begins to think
independently does he reinterpret the world and modify his philosophy. He wants to be less idealistic and more practical, but as
we'll see, Andrew's early idealism is not just rooted in his role
models. It also springs from his shyness and caution—a fear of
getting hurt by the world—and for good reason.

To backtrack for a moment, when I was around seven our
family moved to Europe, because my dad got a job with a
United Nations agency in France. This was a bit of a shock for
me, as I had to make all new friends, and my teachers spoke
only limited English. However, I learned French quickly, and I
was an adequate student. I was somewhat shy, and though I
made some friends, I tended not to be very assertive in
socializing with others. Sometimes I felt on the periphery, but I
just took this for granted and accepted it as how things were. I
did notice that a few of my male friends were more sociable
and seemed to have a talent for talking to girls and making
them laugh. I was impressed but didn't think it was something

that was learnable. In my preteen years I got into thinking of girls as persons to avoid. That was the attitude most of my male friends were taking, and it seemed a natural thing to do at that time.

As I was growing up, my parents were consistently positive, and devoted a lot of time to me and my brother and sister. They rarely got angry. They gave us the message that anger was considered an inappropriate and socially unacceptable emotion. My younger brother was the only one in the family who became angry or provoked me or my mother. As we got older, he began competing with me more and more. This was a losing cause because, being three years older, I could easily defeat him in just about any contest, including physical fights. This did not deter him, however. He was jealous of me and wanted to beat me in games or contests and would get visibly annoyed when I beat him. In the end my parents insisted we stop fighting and learn to get along. So I got a lot of messages that fighting and being angry were wrong.

I think I gradually developed the belief that I shouldn't compete with people who were less capable than I was. My strategy with my brother was that as long as he didn't attack me physically, I would not attack him. He became adept at verbal insults and insinuations, pushing my tolerance to the limit, but I became good at restraining my impulses to respond. While this solved my immediate problem with my brother, it again strengthened my tendency to control my anger and think of others before myself.

At lunch one Sunday, when I was fifteen, my parents calmly announced to my brother, my sister, and me that they were getting a divorce. This came pretty much out of the blue. While I had recently noticed that my parents weren't getting along that well, they never argued or fought in front of us. I was frightened and overwhelmed by the news. I knew this meant

my parents had significant problems with each other, but I
didn't know to what extent and I was afraid to find out. My
parents also seemed to want to present the divorce as no big
deal, as if it wouldn't make much of a difference in our lives.
They asked us if we had any questions. I didn't have the
courage to say anything, but my brother asked what would
happen to the three of us. As if reading from a script, my
parents calmly explained how my dad would be moving out but
would continue to see all of us. Trusting my parents' judgment,
I was happy enough to buy into the notion that this wasn't such
a big deal, but I began to withdraw further into myself, to keep
my feelings private, and to believe that I ultimately had to take
care of myself. No doubt it was at this point in my life that trust
became an important issue to me. My parents did indeed
conduct themselves responsibly in keeping their promises to
us, but I did not feel comfortable opening up to either of them
ever again.

About a week after the divorce announcement, I
experienced my first migraine headache. It included numbness
in half my body and blurred vision. The doctor didn't know what
I had, so to rule out cranial problems I underwent a variety of
brain X-rays and neurological tests. He prescribed bed rest
for me for that summer, which was quite weird because, except
for the headaches, I felt fine. For a number of years I continued
to have periodic migraines, which I learned to endure in
solitude.

A year and a half later, my dad married my physics teacher,
which was another shock, and put my family situation squarely
in front of my classmates. In those days divorce was rare, and I
felt somewhat stigmatized by it, though at another level I was
able to maintain the belief that it didn't really change who I
was. Here again I just hid my feelings and felt I had to endure
these events with a stiff upper lip.

Any chance Andrew has of blossoming as a teenager and finding his own voice is undermined by the surprise announcement of his parents' divorce. He feels the typical range of emotions for a sensitive teenager: helplessness, anger, anxiety, guilt, and lack of trust. As manifested by his migraines, Andrew internalizes his pain and shuts down emotionally. There's no one he trusts to talk to about what happened; as if a self-fulfilling prophecy, he becomes more isolated than ever. Because he will fall back on his romantic interpretation of events—that it's almost his destiny to live in solitude, and to stoically endure whatever fate throws at him—he sets himself up for disappointment with girls. He starts from a posture of distrust, and coupled with his natural shyness, and little understanding of how women function emotionally, he is intimidated in approaching girls. But the deeper effect of his anxiety from the divorce is to create a huge, deeply romantic fixation on finding a girl who will love, nurture, and understand him—a woman who will never abandon him, and who will save him from himself, a common male romantic fantasy.

In high school I felt very confused about how to express my feelings of attraction to girls. As I mentioned earlier, in grade school, along with the other boys, I looked down on girls and sometimes made fun of them. Then I skipped sixth grade. By eighth grade, when most of my classmates were going into adolescence and starting to relate to each other, I was behind the curve. All through high school I was a year younger than everyone else in my class, and I had trouble catching up socially. I think my parents' divorce and Dad's remarriage had the indirect effect of making me even more shy and unsure around girls.

I did fall in love with one girl, and later still another. I thought about these girls all the time, but I never really

ventured to talk with them. I suppose it was a relationship I
carried on mostly in my head. The few instances when I
attempted to communicate, I bungled it badly and only made
myself look foolish. In my junior year, a new girl joined our
class, and briefly showed a lot of interest in me. But I felt
paralyzed with her, even though I liked her a lot, and she soon
moved on to another boy who was willing to show more interest
in her. I diverted myself with academics, developing a great
interest in math and science, and took pride in my
accomplishments. When I took my SATs, I did extremely well in
math and science, and that boosted my self-confidence, but it
didn't really help me in my confidence with girls.

Those last few years in France, before I left for college in
the United States, my mother became a stronger influence in
my life, and my dad, now in his new relationship, less so. While
I liked my stepmother, she was often quite emotional and it
took some adjusting to get used to her. My dad wanted to keep
her happy and didn't assert himself a lot with her. By this time,
my mother had for several years been taking classes to
become a psychoanalyst, and was starting to see her first
patients. Unlike when I was growing up, she was suddenly very
interested in talking to me about feelings and why people
behaved the way they did. This caught my interest on some
level, yet it scared me too. On a number of occasions my mom
asked me about my own emotions—for example, did I feel a lot
of jealousy toward my brother (I did not), and why did I think I
was so shy around girls? I didn't open up much—that was my
pattern after the divorce, and the answer to her second
question—but I appreciated her efforts. They helped me start
paying more attention to my feelings and how feelings dictated
so many of our decisions and actions. These are pretty obvious
observations today, but forty years ago this was novel stuff.

As much as I enjoyed Europe, I definitely wanted to get back to the United States. By going to college, I felt I was getting away from the embarrassment of my parents' divorce and could make a fresh start in my life. College really did give me a new beginning. I attended a prestigious all-male science college where I had the good luck to get in with a great group of friends who eventually became the leaders in our dormitory. This was a considerable improvement over high school, where I was not really part of the high-status crowd. In college I often ended up in some leadership position that I hadn't particularly sought, but I enjoyed the respect that it conferred on me. Along with being in my new group of friends, the leadership role helped my self-esteem considerably. I also discovered at this college (not known for its athletic prowess) that I was one of the better athletes, and I got involved in a lot of intramural team sports. More accolades came my way.

The downside of a male college is that it's hardly the ideal environment for meeting women. My interaction with the opposite sex consisted of blind dates or mixers at other colleges. I had several girlfriends but no relationships that really took off. With these girlfriends I tended to be tongue-tied and shy, and a number of them got tired of my timidity and moved on. While I had strong feelings for some of these women, I felt a great anxiety over expressing those feelings. I continued to feel that I had to be respectful of them (which translated in my mind into not making physical and sexual advances). Looking back, I was probably protecting myself from sexual relationships, which were both attractive and scary to me. I typically tried hard to be a "nice guy" because I thought that was what was needed to attract a woman and to sustain a relationship. I had little idea about how relationships worked, though I thought I did at the time.

During a sociology internship the summer after graduation,

I met a woman I liked very much, but she was dating someone else. Had I been more forward, I think she would have left him for me, but I ended up leaving for graduate school. My career interests had shifted in the last two years from the physical sciences to clinical psychology. I'm not sure of my motives for this change of heart. Perhaps my mother was a force, as well as my own need to better understand myself. I also found people's behavior interesting in general.

Graduate school was coed, but our immediate class was small and didn't have any women that I was strongly attracted to. There were lots of other women around campus, of course, but there was no easy avenue for meeting them. The summer after my second year of graduate school, however, while I was working as an aide in a psychiatric ward, I met Lucy. I liked her from the start. She had a warm, communicative side that I lacked—she brought me out of my shell—and as things progressed between us I developed my first real, deep, long-term relationship. Lucy and I went together for two years while I completed my Ph.D. and arranged for a postdoctoral internship on the other side of the country.

This impending move made it necessary for me to make a decision about Lucy and our relationship. In those days it wasn't common for a man and woman to live together without marrying. I thought I either had to marry Lucy or break up with her. I was pretty sure I was in love, and I felt very comfortable with Lucy. I also felt that Lucy was strongly attracted to me and that it would be very painful to both of us if I chose to break up. This thought—and the anxiety of moving across the country alone to a new place—ultimately led me to ask her to marry me. I can explain my actions by simply saying it was a combination of doing the honorable thing, getting married at the right time (for both of us), and expressing genuine feelings for Lucy.

In Lucy, Andrew finds his ideal mate. Not only is she "warm and communicative," she makes him feel comfortable and she responds to his romantic need to have himself rescued (simultaneously, he is also rescuing her). While he's not really sure he's in love, the thought of leaving Lucy behind is too painful, so he decides he must marry her. This is his perceived moral duty. Being honorable is Andrew's way of connecting to women. However, it's just a veneer that keeps him from expressing how he really feels. After experiencing the euphoria of having children, as we'll see, he slowly begins to give up on his marriage. Lucy is no longer attractive to him. She's just not exciting for a number of small reasons. Like picking at a sore that never heals, Andrew can't seem to get to the real source of his discontent: his inability to figure out his own emotions and how to open himself up. Instead, he takes the easy way out. He gets involved with another woman and romanticizes his exit from Lucy. As his story unfolds, Andrew will always vacillate between a romantic fixation on finding the perfect woman and the fear that the relationship won't last and his happiness will be taken away from him.

After we were married and I completed my internship, we returned to our original city. Our relationship was going well, and two years later we had our first child, Ann. Becoming a father turned out to be a wonderful experience. I really didn't know what it would be like, but I bonded deeply with my first daughter and I was delighted to spend endless hours with her. A great deal of my time and energy went into activities with Ann, as they did with our second daughter, Sue, who was born three years later. My relationship with Lucy remained good, but because so much of our time was centered on our daughters we had less time for each other. Over the years, our relationship lost some of its excitement and emotion. I would say that Lucy became less appealing to me, but we did not have any major conflicts.

Around the time Sue was born, I met a woman named Marie. We both worked at a large residential psych facility, and our paths crossed periodically. I gradually became more and more attracted to her and arranged my schedule to see her as often as possible. Initially I had no thoughts of leaving Lucy, but as I became aware that I was thinking about Marie day and night, I confided in Lucy about my feelings. She was very upset, but was later willing to discuss the subject with me. For a while I had the notion that I might be able to continue my marriage with Lucy and have a second relationship with Marie. This was the "open marriage" concept that had become popular in the mid-seventies. However, it soon became apparent to me that I was not emotionally able to carry on a relationship with two women simultaneously.

I really didn't know what to do, and for a while I let things slide, continuing to see Marie at work but not doing much else. Then I experienced an episode involving an irregular heartbeat, which like my migraines was no doubt another manifestation of stress. I was hospitalized for three days, and took medication to get my heart stabilized. I told my cardiologist what was going on and he strongly advised me to choose between Lucy and Marie, and then stick with that decision. I agreed with him, and entered a period of trying to sort out my feelings, which lasted another year.

Lucy had done nothing particularly to upset me. I was reasonably content in my marriage, but it had become mundane and routine. Marie was very beautiful, lively, intelligent, and friendly. She also did an excellent job at work and I greatly respected that. She seemed much more exciting to me than Lucy, although comparing the two was unfair, considering the very different roles they had in my life. I went to a couple of counselors in that two-year period, including a nine-month stint with a Gestalt group. Twice I moved out of the house and twice I returned to be with Lucy. Each time I moved in one direction I started to feel overwhelmed and changed my mind. Eventually I felt that I had damaged my relationship with Lucy to the point that it was not salvageable, and that there was no choice but to get a divorce.

I felt very guilty about the breakup of my marriage, in particular for the hardship and turmoil it created for my daughters. I worked hard to maintain my involvement with them. They visited Marie and me regularly and I volunteered weekly at their school. This led to some stress with Marie that, naïvely, I had not anticipated. I took a very strong role in setting the standards for how we treated my daughters, and didn't really discuss it much with her. In recent conversations she has told me she felt left out and sometimes criticized by me in dealing with Ann and Sue. Also, when they did visit us, she said, I tended to focus nearly all my time on them and neglected her.

For someone who becomes a clinical psychologist, Andrew's general naïveté about feelings and relationships, and his inability to act in a timely way, seems improbable at first blush. But his reliance on role-playing—seeing himself as the fallen hero who can't blame himself enough when things go wrong—is an example of someone who never learned relating skills as a child or adolescent. For most of his life he's seen himself as a fortress, believing that the enemy—the world at large—is on the outside, trying to get in to hurt him. But the enemy is already within. It's the pain of his parents' divorce and his overall feelings of helplessness and abandonment. Does he divorce Lucy before she can divorce him? Like a lot of men, the negative emotion he seems most comfortable with is guilt. As demons go, for Andrew, guilt is preferable to feeling abandoned.

Even before his parents' divorce, Andrew was a vulnerable, naïve young man who had difficulty expressing his feelings. The shock of the divorce only deepened his reserve, anxiety, and lack of trust. Until the surprise announcement, Andrew thought he had a very together family, and he certainly was a model teenager: selfless, hardworking, well behaved. He'd done nothing to break up the family. So why, he wonders, did this happen to him? Being an innocent victim is part of his romantic mythology, just like being the fallen hero, even if the two are opposites. After the divorce, it's inevitable that he becomes more guarded and circumspect, particularly around women, because they have the capacity to hurt him the most.

Nonetheless, I was very happy to be with Marie and had expectations of a deep and fulfilling relationship. We got along well, but from the beginning there were some issues that we weren't able to talk about. These included money and spending patterns, what love meant to each of us, and sharing our deepest feelings, as well as how to relate to Ann and Sue. We dealt with these topics mostly by avoiding them; we both attempted to "read" the other and do what we thought the other wanted. Looking back on it now, I don't think we always read each other very well.

After living together for a year or so, we decided to try to have a child. When Marie became pregnant, it seemed the appropriate time to get married. We were really happy. After a difficult pregnancy, Marie delivered a baby boy, John, and his birth brought us even closer together. While John's presence in the family mostly changed things for the positive, there were stress points too. The same pattern I'd experienced with Lucy appeared with Marie. Taking care of the baby left less personal time for Marie and me. When Ann and Sue visited us, how to spend time with them and John together became complicated.

Often it ended up with me doing something with the girls and Marie staying home to look after John. This wasn't very satisfactory to Marie, but it just became another issue we didn't discuss. When John was about twelve months old, I had a discussion with Marie about some plans; her response made me realize that she would be using John as an ally in some power struggle against me and Ann and Sue. I felt helpless and didn't know how to react. True to my pattern of denial, I didn't say anything to Marie. I did not want to pit John's needs against the needs of Ann and Sue, because I loved all three. But I also did not want to get into a constant tug-of-war with Marie.

Looking back, this began a long pattern of what I would call background tension and conflict. On the surface we continued to get along well, but there was still, for me, an absence of full trust between us. Marie has recently told me that she too felt a distance and lack of trust between us, yet neither of us talked about it in any depth. At one point, while John was still very young, I did tell Marie that one of my main hopes for our relationship was that we share all our emotions, even if they weren't always positive, and that we accept each other for who we were, faults and all. Marie's response was that she didn't feel a need to do this. I was surprised. I was trying to be open while Marie was choosing to go in the other direction.

Was I just too much of a romantic—maybe a demanding one—or was Marie reacting to being hurt and excluded in the way I dealt with my daughters? I felt rejected, and retreated into myself. I gave up further attempts to reveal my deeper feelings, or to expect Marie to be open. No doubt Marie felt rejected by me. I very much wanted to make this marriage work and spare John the family breakup Ann and Sue had been subjected to. I resolved to keep moving on and accept a relationship that was suddenly less than I wanted, and no doubt less than Marie wanted.

Sticking to his code of honor, Andrew decides to get married only when Marie becomes pregnant (instead of getting married because he's in love). Without being able to express his emotions, Andrew will soon set the stage for getting bored and losing interest in his new wife, just as he did with Lucy. This time, increasingly frustrated, instead of just blaming himself for not being a good communicator, he will cast some blame on Marie for being unintuitive and insensitive. Perhaps, on a subconscious level, this is what attracted Andrew to Marie in the first place. Perhaps he thought two people with similar emotional makeups might have a better chance at a successful relationship. This is in keeping with his idea that his life is a fairy tale, where fate rules, and is in some ways beyond his control.

remained married to Marie and we raised our son successfully despite many bumps in the road. Our relationship seemed to go through cycles of better and worse. After a while I became aware that whatever state we were in, it would eventually change—that is, if it was bad for a while it would eventually get better, and if it was good at some point, it would surely get worse. I took a certain comfort in the predictability of all this, that at least there was some stability to this pattern and that it never got too far out of control. It also gave me a reason to ignore some of Marie's complaints, believing that they would blow over in a few days. I realize that over the years I developed more and more the pattern of trying to anticipate Marie's reactions to what I did or said, and spent more and more effort trying to avoid antagonizing her. With the lessons learned from my childhood, I also believed that anger was unproductive, and I worked repeatedly and successfully to control mine. I had also made progress in learning not to blame others for things that might upset me. Overall, however, by repressing these feelings, I had diminished my other emotions and energy for life.

Another area of conflict between Marie and me was money management. I came from a frugal family and valued saving and looking for good bargains. Marie thought of expensive possessions as a way to judge one's confidence and station in life. She also believed that how much someone spent on you was a gauge of how much he loved you. On the other hand, I believed that saving money was a way to express love in a relationship. So we had a lot of divergent and entrenched feelings around money matters. It didn't help that in the early years of our relationship we didn't have a lot of money. After staying home with John for three years, Marie went back to work and eventually earned a good salary. However, we kept separate bank accounts and we never really worked out a good spending plan. I felt that Marie spent a lot of her money on herself and her interests and only contributed a limited amount to joint expenses. But any attempt on my part to discuss money or ask for an accounting of her spending resulted in Marie getting angry. This became another issue I learned to live with.

About fifteen years into our marriage, I resumed an old interest, oil painting. I had painted some in high school and college but was never very good and finally gave up because I couldn't really paint what I wanted. Marie gave me a book on drawing one Christmas and I went through all the exercises in the book. To my amazement, this gave me the ability to draw accurately in a way that I had never been able to do, and inspired me to take art classes. I found painting very soothing and comforting, a kind of therapy, and it became something of a refuge for me.

Part of Andrew's frustration in his search for a fulfilling relationship is due to his lack of real closeness to friends, family
members, and peers. He mentions nothing of his brother and sister or even his parents once he is married, nor any get-togethers
with male friends, despite having strong peer relationships in
college. Most of his free-time activities, like reading and painting, are solitary. They may bring him temporary comfort and
offer him some insights into himself, but he still lives a guarded,
self-protected life. Andrew not only shuts himself off from emotional nurturing (except, presumably, from his children), but his
fantasies of finding the right woman become too intense and
narcissistic to be realistically satisfied. And, as always, his romantic quest diverts him from dealing with the real source of his
problems.

Andrew mentions a difference in philosophy in dealing with
money. Almost everyone I spoke with said that money, at one
time or another, was a disruptive wedge in their relationship.
Getting into arguments over spending was often code for lack of
trust, or it brought out manipulation, control, selfishness, and
insecurity. Andrew says that Marie insisted on spending money
on herself (maybe, when she couldn't get enough affection from
Andrew, spending was a way of loving herself), while he believed in saving whenever possible. Whether his behavior reflects his general insecurity, or meets his definition of masculinity
by making him a protector and provider, it ultimately reinforces
his isolation in his relationship and provides another excuse for
losing interest in Marie.

Five and a half years ago I learned I had prostate cancer. I
was shocked because I had always been very healthy and
for some reason thought I would be immune to cancer. I was
frightened, but rapidly got into researching my disease and its
various forms of treatment. I consulted a number of doctors.

Marie was extremely supportive and accompanied me to these consultations. I eventually selected a choice of treatment and, while successful, the whole process was wearying, physically and emotionally. Facing the possibility of death was a mind opener. On the one hand, I could tell myself that I had already experienced a full and rewarding life, and could die without complaints. On the other, I felt a deep fear of dying and a strong desire to keep living.

It was probably three years from the time I was diagnosed before I had a fair degree of confidence that my cancer was gone. In this process I lost the feeling of invulnerability that I previously had, and I realized that there were things I would like to experience before I died. This led to me questioning how much I wanted to remain in my relationship with Marie. Should I leave her and explore the possibility of trying other relationships? Still, the thought of leaving Marie made me feel very anxious and guilty. We got along well on many levels—and she had been very supportive during my illness—but ultimately I was after some kind of happiness with a woman I had yet to experience.

I didn't take any immediate action. Marie and I continued to coexist in separate orbits. One thing I did do was spend more time on my art. I had gone to a half-time work schedule after I was diagnosed with cancer, and began working on a series of paintings which had to do with men and women. Most were about a man, a woman, and a convertible car (mostly 1950s cars), and expressed the attractions, longings, and fears that go with relationships. This was a significant outlet for my feelings of uncertainty about Marie and thoughts of possible relationships with other women.

Then, about three years ago, I began feeling quite attracted to a younger woman in my office. I had known Rita casually for several years, and we had gradually become friends. She was very lively and sociable, and had a sense of humor that I loved. She seemed to like me and welcomed our conversations. I began thinking about her a lot and looking for excuses just to drop by and talk with her. I reached the point where I began to think of approaching her for more contact outside work, to explore the possibility of a relationship between us. This thought frightened me because I felt I couldn't see Rita behind Marie's back. Just as I had done with Lucy when I first became interested in Marie, I decided to discuss my feelings about Rita with Marie.

Equally predictably, Marie was surprised and upset when I told her about Rita. But she really pulled herself together and made it clear that she wanted to work to resolve the issues between us. She didn't voice a lot of anger at me and really put some effort into being caring and understanding. We went to a marriage counselor for about seven months. In the beginning I was not optimistic, but over time Marie and I made solid progress, and I found myself losing interest in Rita. We stopped seeing our counselor and life seemed to be going well. Then about eight months later I began feeling an interest in Rita again. The intimacy that I had rediscovered with Marie seemed to be wearing off, replaced by my old doubts.

Andrew tries to do the noble thing by being open with Marie about Rita, and then by going to a counselor with Marie, but it's basically role playing on Andrew's part. At his core, he lives in a state of constant, low-grade anxiety because he can't quite forgive himself when things go wrong. Whether he is the perpetrator or the victim of the turmoil around him, any setback or rejection, even his prostate cancer, is taken personally. He also has a great fear of letting go or losing control, which is one reason his illness terrifies him. At first he says he doesn't mind dying because he's led a "full and rewarding life," but later he says he realizes there are many things he hasn't done. Terrence Real, author of *I Don't Want to Talk About It,* might say Andrew was suffering from covert depression; he knows something is wrong but can't quite put his finger on what or why. He dwells almost obsessively on his anxiety, guilt, and unhappiness.

As a psychologist, Andrew might be the first to agree that, particularly in men, there is often a difference between who we know we are and what we project to the world. To be assertive means narrowing that gap—being honest, proud of oneself, and not afraid to admit mistakes. Andrew has made some efforts to be assertive—from going to therapy to reading voraciously to expressing himself in his art—but one key problem is that he is an inconsistent communicator. On the one hand, he told Lucy and Marie of his interest in other women, but on the other he was largely silent about the anger and loneliness he felt from his adolescence. Like a lot of men who prefer or are simply used to emotional isolation, he lives a very self-protected, almost self-censored, life.

At work I felt Rita was showing an increased interest in me. She had been living with her boyfriend for two years and I had assumed that this, along with the difference in our ages (over twenty years), precluded any serious relationship between us. But when she showed a higher level of interest, it made me wonder if something might be possible between us. Through several coincidences at work, we found ourselves going out to lunch often. She confided that she was planning to get married to her boyfriend, yet simultaneously she conveyed how much I meant to her. There were also a lot of touches and hugs from her. What message was she trying to convey?

I chose a typically vain male interpretation: Rita somehow felt she had to marry her boyfriend, but he was lacking in the emotions and sympathies that only I could offer her. I soon

entered into a state of delirious euphoria in which I was
constantly thinking about Rita. Maybe I just had a crush on her.
I didn't actually know her well and, rationally, the odds against
a successful relationship were high. But at the same time I felt
that this might be my one chance in a lifetime for a great
romance and I didn't want to lose it. By now my new emotions
had taken control. I tried to suppress them but found that
almost unbearably painful. I came to believe that my
subconscious mind was giving me a powerful message that I
needed to do something new and different, that I had been
trying to please Marie and others for too long and it was time to
do something for myself, even if it was crazy. I felt alive and
energized in a way that had only happened perhaps two other
times in my life (both because of women, one of whom was
Marie). Finally, I told Marie what I was feeling and that I wanted
a chance to get to know Rita. She was again caught by surprise,
but she didn't fight me much. Maybe she too was
acknowledging that down deep our relationship wasn't
working. But I think both of us had a fear of letting go.

A few days later I found an apartment and moved out. When
I told Rita what I'd done and how I felt about her, she expressed
shock and dismay and reminded me she was planning to get
married. She said she hoped that my move to my own
apartment was inspired more by my problems with Marie than
by my interest in her. I felt a little stupid. Was it all a fantasy in
my head? Or had Rita been coming on to me, and had suddenly
gotten cold feet? Composing myself, I tried to explain that I
wanted what was best for Rita, and that I wasn't asking her to
give up her plans to get married. I was hoping, however, that if
she got to know me better, Rita might change her mind.

Shortly thereafter, I went on a preplanned ten-day vacation.
While I was away, a friend Marie had confided in called a
supervisor in my office. Marie's friend wanted information

about Rita. As it happened, the supervisor was a close friend of Rita's, and told Rita about the inquiry. Rita felt this was an attempt by Marie to orchestrate a smear campaign against her. Very agitated, Rita decided to protect herself by going to another supervisor and filing a claim of sexual harassment against me. I spoke with Rita by phone the day before I returned from vacation, and she told me what she had done. She said she didn't really feel I had harassed her, but that was the only way she could think of to stop what she felt were attempts to harm her reputation.

I was caught off guard, to say the least. I listened to Rita and tried to be sympathetic. I assured her that none of these machinations by Marie's friend had anything to do with me, and probably not with Marie either. I then tried to prepare myself to accept whatever came out of this situation. But never in my wildest imagination had I thought I might be accused of sexual harassment. Rita warned me that my supervisor would want to see me the next morning. She expressed regret again for all this chaos, but said she was also under orders not to have any contact with me. I said I understood and felt that things were over between us.

The next day my supervisor did call me into her office and informed me of the allegation that Rita had made. She told me I was to have no contact with Rita either at work or outside of work. She also expressed some sympathy for me. She doubted I had really harassed Rita, but warned me that this was a serious charge and any further allegations would lead to an investigation and potentially serious consequences. She also alluded to the fact that Rita had had similar situations in the past with other men, and that I should be very careful in dealing with her.

I carefully avoided Rita for the next four weeks. Then one day she called me, again apologized for the harassment

charges, and said she missed talking with me. She asked if I
would be willing to meet her outside of work. Clearly, she was
manipulating me, and I knew it, but I had a deep desire to see
her again. I felt powerless to stop myself. This led to a number
of phone conversations and having lunch together once a
month. Rita was always warm and friendly at these meetings,
hugged me, and expressed an interest in continuing to see me.
She got married as planned, but even after that she still called
me and wanted to get together. On several occasions she
talked about how her harassment charges against me were
wrong. She said she planned to withdraw them, but she never
did. I still felt a strong attraction to Rita, and I was very open
with her. I continued to be pretty direct about what I was feeling
and doing. I guess I was so needy that I felt I could trust her.
That my behavior was that of a lovesick adolescent didn't
escape me, but we don't always understand how powerful the
process of attraction can be.

About two months after Rita got married, I began seeing a
counselor on my own for Eye Movement Desensitization
Restructuring (EMDR), a therapy involving bilateral stimulation
of the brain. The theory is, roughly, that our early, strongly
emotional experiences are stored in the middle or lower parts
of the brain, which are not very accessible to the more mature,
reasoning parts of our brain at the cortex. EMDR somehow
connects these different parts of the brain and enables them to
work together to resolve early childhood patterns and conflicts.
In my case, I had some really strong and emotional
experiences with EMDR, and felt that I did gain access to a lot
of feelings and painful past experiences. These sessions
seemed to help me express my feelings more fully and also to
be more comfortable in expressing them. A number of my
family members have told me that I am now more relaxed,
spontaneous, and emotionally accessible.

After my second EMDR session, I felt a clear change in my feelings for Rita (though my feelings for her were not involved in that session). I felt like I had outgrown these feelings, that they were immature and no longer very important to me. In some ways I was upset to have lost the intensity of my feelings for Rita. They had energized my life, even though what had happened to my reputation was fairly disastrous for me.

Perhaps it takes both an illness and the humiliating setback with Rita before Andrew gets a wake-up call. The acknowledgment of his naïveté, juvenile romanticism, and the need to open up emotionally come relatively late in his life, but at least they happen. Besides self-knowledge, he gets some validation from family members for opening up. Still, with his vacillating feelings toward Rita, he is far from totally trusting of his emotions. The fact that he wasn't more outraged by her betrayal and manipulation indicates perhaps how deeply he has buried his feelings.

Andrew is strong intellectually—a strength that perhaps is in inverse proportion to his emotional resources—so it's natural for him to rely upon reason when he confronts his emotional problems. As we'll see in the last two chapters of this book, this is a smart approach, and women have been doing it forever. In Andrew's case, however, he fails to take his reasoning and analysis far enough. In his relationships, including with Rita, he must be thinking, "Look, I'm doing my best, and things aren't working, so what am I supposed to do? Nothing I do is ever good enough, and I end up getting screwed. Nobody really loves me." That defensive attitude reflects not only Andrew's romantic interpretation of his life (he's generally either a rescuer or a victim), but the tendency of many men to feel isolated in our gender culture. When the going gets tough in a competitive, judgmental world, the tough *do* get going, because there's no other choice. Support from other men is usually shallow, because behind any surface sympathy, men often judge their own successes against the failures of others.

Marie and I have now been separated for a year. In the beginning I did not have much contact with her, but after I started some counseling and doing EMDR, I began recovering some interest in her. More recently we have been seeing a different counselor together, and she has had us communicate directly about conflicts and feelings that we've hidden. I think we have both changed a good deal and are finally able to voice our differences without getting into a hostile or hurtful interchange.

During the time I've been separated from Marie, I have made many attempts to meet other women. But I realized after a time that I kept finding reasons not to get involved. Why I'm holding myself back, I'm not sure, but I suspect that I've come to the point in my life where I need more self-discovery. It may sound absurd at my age, but I really don't fully know who I am or what I want. In addition, I still feel some connection with and responsibility to Marie. I am not able to free myself from feelings of guilt about having a relationship with another woman. I am also worried about getting into a relationship and finding out I don't care for her, and then having the unpleasant job of breaking up. I still am fearful of conflict. I have felt very frustrated with myself for being unable to move in any clear direction.

I also realize that I have to find a better way to balance my own needs with those of others I'm involved with. I think for a long time I have downplayed my own needs to please others, especially Marie. The effect of this has been to take energy out of me and my relationships. I am clear that I want to express my feelings more fully and directly, and need a relationship with a woman who wants that as well. The dilemma I face is whether to return to Marie or maintain my separation. This brings me back to trying to figure out how I want to spend the remaining years of my life. I've been stuck in the middle of this conflict for some time, and don't see a clear solution emerging.

I do not believe in life after death so I want to use what time I have left well. Part of me wants to explore unpredictable and exciting new realms of life (though I am not sure exactly what those are). Sometimes I believe I have to conquer some inner demons—and then I can break through to wonderful joys on the other side.

Through all of this turmoil I have gained a greater appreciation of the deep—and in many ways crazy and unfathomable—attraction that men have to women. Certain women bring out in me great feelings of energy and trust, seemingly beyond all reason and good sense. In some ways I yearn for a hypnotic engagement and merging of the flesh and senses that would take my breath away and give me an ultimate experience of existence, of being alive. Am I chasing a fantasy? Perhaps, but I don't want to give up seeking it.

Andrew is highly critical of himself and feels guilty when his relationships collapse, especially when he does the collapsing. Whether he's still acting out his anger from his parents' divorce, or is driven by his romantic search for a deeper happiness, to try to feel good about himself he uses conventional benchmarks: his professional accomplishments, being conscious of other people's feelings and always being helpful, and being a good father to his three children. He's desperately looking to be loved and validated. He's most comfortable when he has peer acceptance, as in college where he was a gifted athlete, or when he finds self-discovery and solace in his art and books and therapy—and least comfortable when he's in conflict, or confused about what to do with his life. If somehow he could trust himself more, he could then trust others, set boundaries, *and* be more confident in his explorations.

In the meantime, Andrew will struggle with balancing his needs against meeting the needs of others. He should realize that his definition of "serving others" is really just an effort to get love and attention. Rather than helping, he often hurts those he loves. Instead of stewing in a perpetual identity crisis, he might try to find ways to forgive himself, and stop creating so much conflict in his life. Reaching out and making a firm commitment to Marie, for example, would clarify some of his identity issues and end much of the conflict.

11

Eddie's Story

All happy families resemble one another,
but each unhappy family is unhappy in its own way.
—Leo Tolstoy

Eddie is in his late fifties and retired from several business careers. His build is stocky, his hair thinning, and his skin has a grayish pallor. Like Jim Carrey, he can make his face into a comical mask, which is appropriate for his sophisticated wit and sometimes caustic humor. He has been married and divorced twice and has no children. By his own admission, no relationship seems to last more than four years. Either it implodes or, feeling emotionally starved or abandoned, Eddie moves on. An intellectual who is drawn to ideas and politics, he describes himself as charming, extroverted, and sensitive, but also cynical and distrusting. High-strung, he admits to being his own worst enemy at times, and looks at his childhood and adolescence to understand why. Unfortunately, he says, explanations don't equal solutions. Falling in love with women becomes more complex and difficult as he gets older, and he believes it's the same for women. He wonders if this is just the natural by-product of accumulating too much baggage, or does pop culture today raise our expectations to such a high level that everyone ends up disappointed with everyone else?

Eddie grew up in the late forties in an old, crumbling New England mill town. His family was Jewish in what was mostly a Catholic, blue-collar suburb of Boston. Eddie and his older brother Arthur were offered a blend of public schools, values that aspired to be middle-class, and conservative politics. American flags and bumper sticks urging prayer in the classroom were rampant, "just as they are today," he says. Eddie was raised mostly in the presence of women: mother, aunts, and grandmothers. "During the Jewish holiday 'bake-fests,' the house would fill with relatives both known and unknown, great aromas, and all the bakers' chattering," he says with a smile. "Those are some of my fondest memories."

Before she married my dad, my mom was a runway model at Filene's (then a fashionable Boston department store) and old photos of Dad and her from the fifties show her to be quite a dish. She was curvy and had legs that most women would die for. The day after she married Dad, she quit her job and never worked again professionally. When I was about three years old she had some sort of emotional breakdown. It was all a big mystery what the problem was; to this day I don't understand it. In general, our family had one of those quiet, secretive lifestyles. This was a period in history before some shrink came up with the term "communication." My grandmother (on my mom's side) more or less did the parenting until my mother had convalesced to the point of resuming her duties. I think she mostly recovered, but she never quite had her wheels under her again. I can't remember much from that period. I do recall the smell of my grandmother's perfume, White Shoulders. To this day it reminds me of old women. That, and her breath. She died in 1959 of a painful, wasting cancer that made a grotesquerie of her once gentle, grandmotherly face. It's her breath on her deathbed that I'll always remember.

Despite my mother's emotional frailness, our home seemed to run okay, but it was not a very cheerful place. It took me years to realize that television life as depicted by Ozzie and Harriet was fantasy. My older brother had already figured this out but he didn't clue me in. No hum in our household, no radio, no pitter-patter of little feet. Shades down, a calm, cool, flatline atmosphere. There were degrees of quiet, some decidedly cooler than others, but I can't recall an argument between my folks that ever spilled into my earshot. I couldn't figure out my folks' emotional connection, and as of today, I don't think I'll try. They were fairly social, and had occasional dinner parties with a large group of friends. They dressed well, and the women all looked like Donna Reed. I was always made to come down to the living room and say good night to the guests. The mixed aroma of cigarettes, Chanel, and aged scotch still triggers a few primal responses in me.

My dad was a handsome guy, and financially successful, but neither he nor my mother ever really went in for displays of public affection. I like to hold hands, and can think of few things more reaffirming than your girl giving you a squeeze or a "claiming hug" in public. Our whole family was on the undemonstrative side when it came to emotions. Even though as a grown-up I tried to hang with my brother Arthur from time to time, our seven-year age difference and our family's reticent temperament probably doomed us. We were never close after we grew up. In family terms, being born so "late," I believe that I was the gift that couldn't be returned. Jewish families don't really plan to have children seven years apart. Arthur's childhood antics were probably what spawned Dennis the

Menace. He took my folks screaming to the edge of the precipice once too often for them to be interested in revisiting the terror that child rearing could be. Maybe I wasn't planned at all. But once I arrived, I think, thanks to Art, I was destined for benign neglect.

Being Jewish was a rarity in our small mill town, which was predominantly Catholic. I'd like to say that the innocence of the fifties translated to love and tolerance all around, but the fact was my brother and I got beat up regularly for being kikes and the only way to deal with it was with our fists. I would have preferred to give a lecture on tolerance, but that would have presupposed a level of intelligence on the part of my listeners that was pure fantasy. Racism and bigotry are learned at the dinner table—I think they go down as smoothly as a spoonful of ice cream—and then can take a lifetime to unlearn.

Mom and Dad seemed never to have a grip on what my brother and I, or kids in general, needed to be happy. Somewhere along the way they decided the less parental involvement, the better for everyone. Or maybe they lost the parenting handle when Mom had her breakdown. Maybe my brother and I caused her breakdown! In any case, my arrival was just the marriage damper that couples dread. They acted like I'd learn whatever I needed by the time I got to wherever I was going in life. "Eddie, what would you like to be when you grow up?" "A fireman," I would answer. "Are you kidding? A fireman? You think you can just be a fireman? You have to do a lot of work for that job. You can't be lazy!" At six years of age all I wanted were hugs and kisses. Instead I got a lecture on professionalism.

To my folks, who'd endured the Depression and God knows what else, everything, down to the smallest and most simple task in life, was like walking through a minefield. Maybe it's a Jewish thing, but even a successful bowel movement seemed out of my ken. The negative reinforcement ploy as a child-rearing aid will never get a ringing endorsement from me. It's been that way with my mother (I think it's how she was raised) for most of my life. I also believe that aspect of my upbringing, that kind of negativity and doubt, helped to dampen my self-confidence to such a degree that it never completely recovered. Someone said, "Happiness comes in moments, and then it's gone until the next time. Sadness, on the other hand, settles in." That's my mother, all over.

Dad, on the other hand, was smart, athletic, and a much more positive person than Mom. A local man in his town saw him play baseball and helped get him a full scholarship to a good New England prep school. His brains and baseball skills got him into Brown, Georgetown Law, and Boston College Law. He even received two "letters of intent" from baseball scouts from the Boston Braves and the Brooklyn Dodgers. Just the things a kid would want to hold on to, wouldn't you think? My mother tossed the letters in a near-fatal housecleaning attack just after my dad died. My memories of Dad are scant but generally warm. Amazingly, he never spent a moment teaching me to throw or hit a baseball. Never a "Let's sit down and read this book together," or "Let's go watch airplanes land at Logan." Not purposely neglectful, not mean, just kind of on another planet. A terrible loss I see now, a terrible waste to a kid who needed some attention. Dad was there occasionally, to be sure. "Make the honor roll, Eddie, and I'll get you a motor to work on in the basement."

Typical of most men whose parents were raised in the Depression, Eddie learns that hard work, responsibility, and duty are valued more than displays of emotion, communication, and acting out. Life was black or white then. Conformity, patriotism, and small-town innocence were a virtue. The dark side of relationships, or "problems" like Eddie's mother's breakdown, or the racial and religious intolerance that Eddie experienced, were largely kept under wraps. Television's family shows—long before the age of backlash when *All in the Family, Married With Children,* and *The Simpsons,* replaced *Ozzie and Harriet, Leave It to Beaver,* and *My Three Sons*—provided the escape and optimism that American families like Eddie's clung to.

I can say that I always liked girls. Even in grade school they were a magnet. I liked their silliness, their spontaneous smiles, the way they whispered to one another, especially in the presence of boys, and just the way they walked down the hall. Throughout late junior high and high school I was a serial dater. I managed to stay with one girl or another for a few months at a time, and then moved on. At that age, the combination of raging hormones and tender egos makes a relationship one big treacherous lake covered with thin ice. I was always trying to be cool, but it was a learn-as-you-go environment.

I lost my virginity at fifteen in the backseat of my dad's '65 Bonneville. Paula was sixteen and a half but looked and acted like she was already in college. We had been dating for a month or two when my parents went out of town one weekend. Dad left the Bonneville keys on the entry table. I didn't even have my driver's license, but given the opportunity before me, was I going to sit home and watch TV? Paula was a somewhat experienced sixteen-year-old. I knew she'd had intercourse with several guys, and I had a sense that if I just hung in there, with a little luck I was going to join that elite group. It was raining and cold outside that night. We parked on a dark side street in a quiet, residential neighborhood. Clothes started to be peeled off, and the groping got to a heated level, when out of nowhere Paula said, "Stop!" I froze on the spot. It was as if a giant hand had entered the car from outer space and grabbed me by the collar. I stepped out of the car to take a few breaths, assuming that when I returned Paula would be all put back together, and things would be over for the night. I opened the door and to my delight Paula was naked from the waist down, sort of sprawled on the seat. Just when you think that God doesn't answer prayers. . . . I even remember the song that was playing on the radio: "All Day and All of the Night," by the Kinks. The song can't be more than two minutes and twenty-four seconds long. It gives you a fairly accurate idea of the duration of our sexual encounter that night. But it felt like an hour, thank you. Wherever you are today, Paula, thanks!

Two years later I had my first real, fall-in-love, go-mental, high-school attachment. I was a senior. Sandy, a junior, was five foot five and had a tight little body, dark green eyes, long auburn hair, and a few strategically placed freckles. I thought that she was one of the best-kept secrets in the entire school. Another outsider like me, bright and really pretty. I can't remember our first few dates, but after a while, we just clicked and quickly became inseparable. When you're young and not hung up on judgment, it's amazing how well things can go. Art, who was twenty-five by then, had an apartment that he let us use, and Sandy and I were like two minks. Her parents liked me too, and her mom took Sandy to a doctor for birth control pills. That kind of trust just never happened in my house. My mother was in my life so little at this point that I was really living at Sandy's house most of the time. My mom barely asked where I was. I left her a phone number, and she seemed just to be happy that I wasn't breaking into any 7-Elevens.

With Sandy in my life, my attitude, grades, and friendships improved dramatically—the influence of a woman on a man's self-esteem—but when I finally left that autumn for college, the relationship fizzled out. Not my choice exactly. Sandy said she was sure I would immerse myself in my new environment, making new friends, meeting new women, and anyway she wanted time to think things out for herself. I was stunned, not to mention naïve. I had thought after a few months with Sandy that our relationship would last forever. I didn't want to break up. I didn't even want to meet new women. Sandy made me happy and secure. What's the lesson I eventually learned? That women can be incredibly tidy about their emotions and self-assured about their decisions. The stereotype is that women are the emotional gender, but most of the ones in my life have been incredibly rational and direct when they want something. It's guys who are emotionally a mess. Even though I was only eighteen and the whole world was before me, I took Sandy's decision hard. I was left with the pain of loss that one can only experience the first time you lose someone you're in love with.

I think I've always been a little naïve about, and oblivious to, the idea of planning for the future. Maybe it's my existential leanings. Live for the moment and don't worry about tomorrow because it might not even be there. My brother believed that and passed down to me his personal wisdom, along with all his books on existentialism. But they didn't help me at this moment with Sandy. I was devastated by her decision, and the emotional loss I felt was only compounded by another life-changing event that happened around the same time.

Eddie is another example of a young man imbued with romantic notions about love and women that are as naïve as they are sincere. Young men make the mistake—because women don't tell them otherwise—of believing that when it comes to romance, women think like, and want the same things as, men. Clearly, Sandy has a different agenda, or a different interpretation of her relationship with Eddie. In terms of the future, as we'll learn, she sees Eddie as adrift, while she's anchored like a skyscraper. As Eddie alleges, women are very rational and tidy when assessing their emotional needs. But does Sandy have any more understanding of how men work emotionally than Eddie does of Sandy? Most of the women I talked to believed that men younger than twenty-five were more consumed with their physical needs and masculine postures than any deep emotional bond. Eddie disagrees. "It's guys who are an emotional mess," he says, with some prescience. Quite a few men I interviewed said that if they are shut down emotionally as adults, it's because they were so open—and burned for it—as teenagers.

M y dad suffered a heart attack in his early fifties and spent time in the hospital. My mom wouldn't allow my brother or me to see him. Even when he came home from the hospital, and our dining room was converted into a first-floor bedroom, Art and I were told to keep away so as not to disturb Dad's recovery. Instead, I'd get pronouncements like: "Your father says to do your homework." Or "Eddie, make sure that the walk and driveway are shoveled for guests." They got an audience and a clean front walk; I got secondhand messages from Dad that I wasn't that important to him.

A year later, things must have been going well financially because my folks decided to go to Europe. At the time we had a comfortable home, a house on Lake Winnipesaukee, a beautiful Victorian home in Maine, and a new house under construction. Then Dad went to the doctor for a checkup and was told he had to have surgery to repair an aneurysm on his aorta. It wasn't the routine procedure that it is now. Two days later, he was dead. I still have the condolence letter from the surgeon and the hospital.

Between my dad's passing and breaking up with Sandy, I was thrown for a double loop. To this day, every time I break up with a woman the loss is never a simple matter. It's always associated with other losses. Maybe that's true for everyone; their losses are entwined and hooked together like a string of paper clips, and with each new one the pain burns a little deeper.

I didn't have the guidance or personal motivation, or the balls, to seek help. I thought I'd appear weak if I told my mother "I think I need to see a shrink." She needed one far worse than I did, and if I spoke up, I thought it would just add to her stress and throw us all into a deeper tailspin.

Instead of therapy, I chose a man's path for dealing with emotional pain. I ignored it. I lost myself in the physical world. I'd saved money for two years to go motorcycling through Europe, do the Hemingway thing in Spain, and try the beaches of Ibiza. It was great fun, though there were not a few moments when I was flooded with thoughts about Sandy and my father. When I returned to Boston a year later and got to our house, I didn't have a key, so I rang the doorbell. An unfamiliar woman came to the door. "Where's Mom?" I asked, startled. The woman explained that she and her husband had purchased the house several months earlier. She didn't know where my mother lived now. I was finally able to reach my brother. Art apologized—he'd forgotten to tell me about the move too! Mom later explained that she hadn't expected me home so early, and her new apartment had a den with a sleeper sofa. She said it was mine anytime I came home from school. Somehow that didn't ease my sense of loss, or make me feel less discounted. When moving, Mom had also thrown out virtually all of my and Art's belongings without wondering what we might want to keep. That woman could really clean when she put her mind to it. Ever since, I've had trouble unpacking anywhere I've lived. I have nightmares about waking up in a room that is absolutely bare.

I kept in touch with Sandy after I started college. No other

guy was in her life for a few years after we broke up, but that
didn't make me feel better, not enough to raise my morale.
Sandy was simply determined to meet her educational and
career goals. I wasn't in the same camp. If I could only pass
this exam, or pay that bill, or climb that next hill—God, I'd
made it! I was content just to get by. I think most men, certainly
at this age, aren't as focused as women.

I had many relationships throughout my college years, but
few were more than physical. I was always looking at the next
girl, and down deep I told myself that I didn't trust any woman
to really care about me. In the back of my mind I kept thinking I
wasn't worthy. No doubt some of that distrust came from my
mom's attitude and behavior, but what I'd gone through with
Sandy didn't help matters. The truth was, I lacked confidence in
myself, and if I didn't believe in myself, I really couldn't see
anyone else volunteering for the job. A very insecure man, I
regretfully admit. I didn't feel like I had anything behind me to
prop me up. No role models, no mentor, no one to speak with
along the way.

Still in college, Eddie has already experienced enough rejection and loss to have developed significant trust issues. One moment he's on top of the world, part of a prosperous family, then
Sandy breaks up with him, his dad dies, his mother sells his
childhood home and throws out his possessions, and he can't
bring himself to ask for a therapist. As the song goes, the first
cut is the deepest, but that doesn't mean that subsequent
wounds heal any faster. With "no role models, no mentor, no
one to speak to along the way," as Eddie says, it's no surprise
that, like other men in this book, the inability to find support and
understanding among friends ultimately translates to losing love
for himself—and drifting from woman to woman. He secretly
craves a healthy, sustained relationship to make up for all his

losses. Having been failed by his mother, Eddie is another example of a man wanting to be saved by a loving, forgiving, understanding woman. But just as we'll see, just the opposite happens.

After college, I lived in Boston with a woman named Lorna
for four years. She was a buyer for a big department
store, and came home every day with a purchase from that
store. She'd watched her mother wilt under the domineering
behavior of her dad, so the moment she left home and moved
in with me she set out on a personal quest for freedom by
exercising her purchasing power every chance she got. I
worked hard to try to make her happy with what I considered to
be very civil, loving, cooperative behavior, but there was no way
that I could—unless, possibly, I bought her the entire
department store. At the time, I couldn't quite see the
destructive, obsessive, narcissistic behavior in her, nor did I
realize its impact on me. I think I chose my mother's worst
traits in the woman I was living with. That's been a pattern with
me. I seem to seek out the "difficult" cases.

Lorna became even more acquisitive in our last year
together. Tensions grew between us, and she began an affair
with her boss. I had strong feelings for Lorna, so her affair
really hurt. It's not hard to fall out of love when you've been
betrayed and become bitter. But I'm not sure which I was hurt
by more: my failure to please Lorna or the ego blow of another
relationship failure. Lorna and I have kept in touch over the
years. To this day, she exhibits the same self-destructive traits,
and hasn't been in a solid relationship for twenty years. She
still can't see that she's hurting herself more than she's
proving anything to her (now dead) father, who was forever
oblivious to his own behavior. It's not any less painful when it's
obvious that the circumstances from which we come are strong
indicators of which way we'll go in our adult lives.

More relationships followed, more disappointments, but I was still young (in my mid-thirties) and I saw the future before me, even if I couldn't define it. I began seeing my first wife-to-be, Kay, after she called one afternoon looking for my old girlfriend, Lorna. I gave Kay a brief history of our breakup, earned a little sympathy, and the next thing I knew we were having regular lunches. Kay had just graduated from law school and was determined to make a life for herself in Colorado, where she had interned the previous summer.

Kay and I spent the best part of a year getting to know one another. This one felt like the "healthy relationship" that you read about in women's magazines. I knew I was Mr. Right for Kay. Our personalities and interests meshed, the sex was fantastic, and she endlessly attracted me in her slightly distant, self-interested, and independent way. I felt like I was constantly chasing her, which was a turn-on for me. Besides making clear her strong feelings for me, and mine for her, she was forthright about leaving Massachusetts and setting up a life in the Rockies. I was torn between following her or staying in Boston, where I now had friends, a good job, and a comfortable way of life. Very reluctantly, I told Kay I wanted to stay put, at least for the moment. I don't know why I said this. Maybe I was testing her feelings for me. Maybe I wanted her to beg me to come with her. I wanted to be wanted. But she didn't really comment, except to affirm her plans to move. We didn't discuss the future of our relationship, as if somehow that would just take care of itself.

One day we packed up Kay's things in a U-Haul and had a misty final dinner. Afterwards there were more choked good-byes. As she was pulling her U-Haul out of the drive, Kay abruptly stopped and ran over to my car. She leaned into my window, pulled a ring off her finger, and asked me to marry her. I couldn't believe my ears. I was stunned. It was a genuine

Hollywood moment. This was my fantasy come true. I was wanted! We talked like crazy for a few minutes, and planned to speak the first time she stopped on the road.

Mysteriously, I didn't hear a word from Kay while she was en route. Neither did her family. This was the era before cell phones, so I couldn't call her. I grew frantic after the four days it was supposed to take her to reach Colorado. This was the woman who said she wanted to marry me—why wasn't she calling? I imagined some terrible tragedy. Finally, ten days later, I heard from Kay. She explained that after she left Massachusetts she'd picked up a "friend" to make the drive with her. She'd never mentioned him to me over the past year. During the trip she'd had a change of heart about us, she said, and "needed time to think about our relationship." Guys, when you hear that phrase, make like it's a fire drill—keep low to the floor and head for the nearest exit. Trouble is brewing. For those ten suspenseful days, despite my anxiety, I was living and dreaming of a future with the woman I loved. Suddenly, with one phone call, I'd been reduced to a state of anguished waiting.

This was a kind of warning sign about Kay's personality, I think, and if love weren't blind (as it certainly was in this case) I might have seen my future more clearly. Kay was leaving behind a core group of people, including me, who loved her! Most of us might find that exceedingly hard, but not Kay. She could cut off the past and fearlessly jump into an unknown, insecure universe as easily as falling off a log. She liked it!

For the next year I traveled back and forth between Massachusetts and Kay's new digs in Colorado. Slowly, our relationship got back on track. Kay loved her new job and I also knew what she wanted from me—a commitment not just to love her but to move to Colorado. I didn't understand the meaning of the word "control" then. Maybe the better word was simply "fickle." I was so happy to be reunited with Kay that I just signed on the bottom line.

We married a few months later, after I had completed my move to Colorado. I really did come to like the wilderness and mountains of the Rockies and the small-town ambiance. However, I was never as happy as Kay. I missed my old friends and hangouts but tried to hide my feelings. Kay grew wary whenever I became too moody or quiet (though she could be quite the mood queen herself). I got a job in antiques restoration—something I'd done successfully back east—but the money wasn't great, certainly not what it was back home, and nothing close to what Kay was bringing in. It was also insufficient for the standard of living we desired. Frustrated, I suggested to Kay that I should go back East for a few months, where a friend had promised me a large commercial job, then return with a good sum of money to take the pressure off. Kay gave her reluctant blessing. That is, she said yes, but she really meant no. I'm not sure whether this was an abandonment issue for her, or loss of control, or if she genuinely loved and missed me. Maybe she wondered why I couldn't find a decent job in our new town, as though I wasn't trying hard enough or was taking the easy way out. The net result was that the phone calls between us grew briefer and cooler while I was away, and when I did return to Colorado with a healthy chunk of money, instead of being praised and congratulated, the temperature between us grew even cooler.

I finally landed a decent job, but something inside Kay had shifted, an internal compass that now pointed in another direction. I didn't know where. She could shut down her emotions with the snap of her fingers. Kay would never win the Pulitzer for communication skills. More and more she would work late at the office. Staying away from our house one weekend, she came back on Monday to tell me there was someone new in her life and she wanted a divorce. She no longer found me attractive. We'd been married exactly four years. Before I could open my mouth (actually, my jaw was already on the floor) Kay said she didn't want to talk about it. She added that there was no way for me to change her mind. I wasn't allowed a single option but to accept her will. I couldn't remember feeling this level of hurt, abandonment, and loneliness since my dad died and Sandy left me. After a few months I pulled myself together, but felt diminished by the whole experience. When I called home and finally told my mom and brother what had happened, it didn't help my morale. No words of consolation or compassion from Mom—I might as well have been giving her the weather report—and my brother had just ended a six-year relationship, so he had little advice or solace to offer.

Kay and I didn't speak for a while, but we gradually developed a postdivorce friendship. I like to stay connected to people, even after a relationship is over, and even if I've been hurt. I don't know whether that qualifies me as a masochist, or someone, unlike Kay, who just has a hard time letting go. Maybe it's a fundamental loneliness. One day, years after our divorce, on an otherwise pleasant spring drive, Kay said to me out of the blue, "Have I ever apologized to you for ruining your life?" I bit my tongue. What I wanted to scream was, "You broke my heart into a million pieces!" But what would be the point? I had begun to internalize a lot of the blame that had been tossed my way over the years. I had begun to think automatically that if something went wrong in a relationship, it just had to be my fault. I couldn't separate personal feelings of inadequacy from actual culpability. Kay never really gave me objective reasons why she'd fallen out of love with me, or what I'd done wrong. I craved information as much as she craved her privacy. Major stalemate.

I can spend an inordinate amount of time philosophizing about my life or life in general, about the choices that are presented to us and the ones we make. I take it very hard when I make the wrong choice. I hear about women who beat themselves up because they have negative self-images, but do they know there are an equal number of men who suffer from the same unrelenting self-scrutiny? No, I take that back. I think there are more men.

The "fading of attraction" argument may be the most common rationalization for men—and in this case, Kay—who want out of a relationship. It doesn't involve a great amount of introspection, nor does it summon much emotion, and perhaps only minimal pain. "I just lost interest in my partner" or "We weren't getting along anymore" is enough of a reason for many men and some women to move on without too much guilt. Whenever analysis and communication about emotions is difficult, it's easy to resort to clichés like "Hey, it's nobody's fault, things just happen."

For Kay and Eddie, the cause of their breakup may be a mutual unwillingness to deal with anger, feelings of distrust, a minimum of childhood nurturing, and a lack of self-love. Understandably, Eddie's need for love, validation, and communication only grew stronger after each relationship setback. The fact that after the breakup Eddie once again couldn't get support or sympathy from anyone, not even his mother or brother, only greases the path for more relationship challenges in the future.

After his break with Kay, Eddie does what a lot of men do when they've experienced several relationship "failures"—they begin to internalize guilt and blame. Something is clearly wrong with *them*. They're *never* going to succeed at this game. Women also beat themselves up, but they usually have friends to rally around them, and often redirect the blame. For men, especially when there's a lack of support, it's easy to put yourself on the rack because torturing yourself, taking your punishment, may be the only thing to make you feel better.

This leads me to my second, and final (to date) marriage. Four years after the divorce from Kay, I was still in Colorado, finally adjusted to my new environment, when I met a woman thirteen years my junior. Cali had recently joined the sales company where I was now one of the top producers, and as a rookie she would come to me for advice about clients. She was divorced, and shared custody of her toddler daughter with her ex-husband, a local contractor. After a year of office socializing, one afternoon she asked me to lunch. In one of those perfect settings—the cloudscape, the outdoor café, the food, the cabernet sauvignon!—she told me she had a crush on me, and asked how I felt about her. Imagine, you're looking at a woman thirteen years younger, her eyes sparkling, her smile as beatific as a Raphael painting, and she's wearing tight jeans that showed off a pair of hips any model would covet—how would you respond? Plus she was sweet, gentle, and kind. She wasn't the uncommunicative, calculating, aloof, willful woman I usually gravitated to. Cali laid it right on the line, and her eyes backed it up—she had a crush on me! What's wrong with this picture? I'm a big, dumb male, lonely and hurt from the past, as easy a mark as they come. A little flattery at the right time from a very pretty woman and I'm on the floor, like a dog waiting for its belly to be scratched. Defenseless? You bet! That's the reason I'm here today in divorce court, Your Honor. I plead guilty to being flattered into willful submission. I was charmed. I was seduced. I don't think many men have looked at Cali and not thought about sex. My heart ached and in one magic moment she healed it. Talk about the emotional power of a woman.

Cali and I lived together for two years before deciding to get married. Getting burned in past relationships will make anyone cautious, but we were in love and told each other that over and over. I was devoted only to her, I swore, and I meant it. The afternoon of our wedding, Cali suddenly got cold feet. I had to keep our guests waiting for half an hour until I talked her out of her anxiety and fears, which she couldn't articulate, no matter how sympathetic I was. This would prove to be a sign of a troubled past that Cali hadn't yet revealed to me. That would come later. The wedding ended up a happy day, and we were now man and wife.

I was never more determined to make a relationship work. Cali's daughter, Elizabeth, now five, was a charmer, and I had been bonding well with her. It's not to say Cali and I didn't feel some stress as we set up house and planned our lives. Money was one problem. The sales market was softening, and Cali, in order to be a full-time mom, no longer wanted to work. To economize, we moved into a small house on a very pretty lot—complete with trees and a stream—that was owned by Cali's Aunt Gloria, who gave us what she called "a favorable rent."

A mistake, in retrospect. We would have been better off staying at Motel 6. Aunt Gloria just didn't like men, and she didn't hesitate to tell me about it. Whether I wasn't considered good enough or I was too old for her niece, Aunt Gloria was domineering, bigoted, racist, and mean as a rattlesnake. When I asked Cali why she put up with this woman's tyranny, I began to learn about Cali's childhood, something she had concealed from me—and for good reason. I believe she thought it would repulse me. Her parents were manipulative, selfish, and deceitful, in my opinion, and basically used Cali as bait in their divorce. At the tender age of thirteen, she had to choose which parent to live with—the abusive, alcoholic mother or the philandering, alcoholic father. In the end, she was whisked off to another town where she knew no one, and her bedroom was in a cramped basement with no windows, with no personal possessions, and no sense of belonging to anything. She was raised by an insensitive half sister, a teen bride with children and issues of her own.

Cali's upbringing was significant in how she viewed raising Elizabeth. To say that Cali was overprotective was more than an understatement. It was a living, breathing reality, and in my opinion ultimately helped undermine our relationship. Cali constantly worried about Elizabeth's happiness and well-being, and sacrificed virtually anything for her. In my opinion it was a classic case of a parent reinventing her childhood through her own kid. Initially, I thought one of my attractions to Cali was as a father figure, the good father she never had, so I naturally assumed I was to have a role in helping raise her child. I wanted a family just as much as Cali did—maybe even more than she did, after my own dysfunctional upbringing. But anytime I made a suggestion about how she might discipline Elizabeth, Cali almost always vetoed it. She would bark, "No one is going to tell me how to raise my child."

In retrospect, I can't blame her, because of her own childhood, but she had no idea how she was shutting me out of a process that was critical for my happiness, and our happiness as a couple. Combine that with our chronic money shortages and things began to fall apart. Aunt Gloria, despite all my efforts to bow and scrape, considered me barely worthy to take out the trash. How many times did I come home, tired and frazzled and in need of companionship, to "our" house and find Aunt Gloria there on the couch, like she was the one paying the rent.

After only eighteen months, despite trying to control our stress and reassure each other about the future, Cali and I ran out of energy. Maybe neither of us cared enough to keep the marriage going. Looking back, neither of us were able to deal with our own childhood issues and therefore had no way to deal with each other's. To this day, as with Kay, I am in touch with Cali. She has a long-term boyfriend, but doesn't seem eager to try marriage again. Like me, if you're burned twice, the third time fills you with more dread than you want to admit.

With Cali, despite his best intentions, Eddie strikes out again. He feels enough pain and self-loathing now to just throw in the towel rather than conduct a deep postmortem. "Despite trying to control our stress . . . maybe neither of us cared enough to keep the marriage going," he comments. Perhaps the deeper truth is that Eddie wants more attention from Cali than she's capable of giving. In Eddie's case, the fading of attraction is definitely linked to self-esteem and validation issues. Even if he seems to know her limitations, he asks for the attention anyway—he desperately needs to feel needed—then gets frustrated when the impossible doesn't happen. Do some men, especially those with abandonment issues like Eddie, set themselves up to fall out of love by setting impossible standards for their partners to live up to? Used to being abandoned, they think this is what they deserve, or that this is their fate.

Some men I spoke with said they tend to fall out of love when they feel their partners take them for granted. This was how Eddie felt much of the time with Kay. If your partner stops giving you a kiss at breakfast, forgets the errand she promised to run for you, or is repeatedly late for the dinner you fixed, resentment builds. Perhaps this is partly the fault of men who pretend that there is no problem they can't solve, that nothing—no setback, no disappointment—fazes them. They act this way in part because they think stoicism is what women expect from men. In trying to appear capable, autonomous, and self-sufficient, they give the impression they don't need special attention. But they need attention just as much as women do, maybe even more. When men tell their partners that they're no longer attracted to them, it is often code for "I'm not getting enough love."

After my divorce from Cali I moved back East. These days I content myself with what I call "the life of the mind." It grows in importance as one gets older. I like what people throughout history have thought, the bold and inventive ideas they came up with. I like sharing that with a woman. I can say with some confidence that I'm wired pretty well in the intellect department. I "get" some ponderous issues, and can converse with confidence on quite a few. I like the origin of the forces that power life, evolution, behavior, consciousness, and everything else from economics to governments. I'm interested in a universe of things and love the pursuit of knowledge. Here's a tidbit: geneticists have discovered that women are far and away the more important of the two sexes. Apparently, new analyses of the human genome have shown that women were only a few small bits of DNA away from not needing men at all in their reproductive cycle. I'm told that one tenth of one percent of all women are born with penises—no kidding! I think I know which way evolution is going. Kind of leaves us men with just the heavy lifting and trash duties, doesn't it? Maybe Aunt Gloria was right. Women are now goddesses, and children are the new gods. Stop looking for other deities. Just listen to the way people carry on about their kids today. They treat them like Baccarat crystal. I mean, talk about overprotection and creating a sense of entitlement.

Some things I know for sure. Women want to be loved and appreciated, coddled, and perhaps most importantly, listened to and understood. Funny—just like men! But they're emotionally wired in a fashion so open and yet so complex that sooner or later many men can't deal with it. I'm emotional but, like most men, my emotions would likely burn through my guts and on towards China before I'd let them be a part of casual table talk. But we never catch on to that soon enough to avoid the damaging effects. Some days I understand women pretty well; other times I'm as clueless about their logic as I am to particle physics. To me, women are unfathomable creatures dressed in human skin. I love them. I like their smell, their feel, and the way they make me feel. I like the way they dress in autumn. Cashmere and perfume were invented for women, or for the men lucky enough to feel them in it. If you can get in sync with that, it's aces for you. The killer is, we all have personalities, and as we age a few personal peculiarities throw the romance off track for just a fraction of a second. But that's enough for a total derailment. It confuses the objective, and pretty soon the cashmere starts smelling like a big wet dog and that whiff of love dies.

Of course, I'm no walk in the park either. In the late seventies I was dating a beautiful attorney. She later became a managing partner of a prestigious firm, married well, had a few troubled kids, and was big in the Republican Party. But I somehow managed to interest her for several months of blissful dating in an otherwise bleak New England winter. She was a high-maintenance princess, but the sex was great, and it was a no-stress situation. One cold Saturday morning after a rather satisfying and spirited roll, we were lying in bed just looking at one another. I knew something was boiling up in her, so I bit and asked the question. "What are you thinking?" It's a question a man should never ask a woman unless he's truly desperate, and then you have to be prepared for something akin to nuclear annihilation. I'm hoping her answer is sex-related, of course, but honestly, in your dreams! After several attempts to cajole it out of her, she dropped the bomb. "I was just thinking that if you had money, you'd be perfect!" I was stunned. Why the sudden meanness? What does money have to do with love and companionship and affection? If I'd said that to her, I'd be digging shell fragments out of my skull for a year. I thought for a moment and replied vengefully. "If I had money, I wouldn't be interested in anyone like you." We started to drift apart in about twenty seconds. That is among the worst conversations I've ever had with a woman.

I think a lot of women, even if they have successful careers and see themselves as independent, still like the company of wealthy, successful men. Part of it is the age-old attraction to power. But chasing money is also an insurance policy if the love thing goes out the window. Just ask any divorce attorney, or the exes of Steven Spielberg, Rupert Murdoch, and Michael Douglas. In retrospect, most if not all the women in my life (except Cali), whether they liked money or not, were emotionally distant, intelligent, strong willed, inflexible, and demanding. As far as I know, none have been able to maintain long-term relationships, and, my guess is they don't have a very high opinion of men. But I found these women! I found just the type of woman who is like kryptonite to me! And as damaged as they may be, I've chosen several! What does that say about me? As much as I'd like not to believe it, maybe I've chosen my mother, over and over!

Here's one you'll never find in a fortune cookie but should: "Relationships are like damaged china. Sometimes even when you work your hardest to repair it, and you feel that it's as strong as it ever was, the crack is still there." I tend to focus on the crack and question its fragility, rather than marvel at the piece's overall strength. Maybe that's why I give up on women.

Eddie's pessimism about relationships is in large part driven by his sensitivity to loss and rejection. His high standards for his partners and low threshold of tolerance also play a role. Perhaps his relationship standards are, subconsciously, his way of putting a distance between himself and his mother. He wants to be as different from her as possible. Yet choosing his mother, over and over, was not unique among the men I interviewed. As observed in other stories in this book, men often settle for the demons they know best, or there's the belief in one's power to change and make over a partner into what we wish our caregiver had been. On the positive side, keeping in touch with many of his former girlfriends and his two ex-wives indicates Eddie's desire for some kind of positive connection, warmth, and reconciliation. Despite his pessimism, and his sense of the inevitability of more abandonment, another part of him wants to keep trying to get it right.

That a lot of women rank security, and hence money, high on their "must have" list for a partner shouldn't have surprised Eddie. Maybe his need for being nurtured runs so deep that in his heart he's still a young man, naïvely thinking that women just want love, affection, and companionship. That's what *he* has to offer. Women do want love and companionship, but especially as they age, money and security mean comfort and freedom. Whether it's a female sense of entitlement or just survival, women will often lose interest in a man if he stops providing for them in a material way.

The Fading of Attraction
Conclusions

Much in our gender culture has changed in forty years. A number of men have adopted what were once perceived as strictly feminine values—empathy, sensitivity, and nurturing—while women have transitioned to male attributes of aggressiveness, competitiveness, and power. What is noteworthy to many men is that women wielding power elicit mostly praise from other women, while men in power are still regarded skeptically. They are sometimes viewed as members of a de facto old boys' club, or just insensitive to, jealous of, or competitive with women. Some professional men I interviewed said they're unlikely to date women who have "power careers," either because they know the relationship will be too competitive, or they won't have the time for the intimacy and attention that each partner presumably wants. These same men said they would rather have relationships where the roles are clearly defined, and where the man is the "leader." The inclination of men to be comforted by hierarchy and consistency, not to mention leadership, is another way for them to feel in control.

Everyone has heard about a woman's "secret garden," a special and mysterious place, an oasis of self-intimacy that is healing and empowering. Whether its meaning is sexual, spiritual, or existential, the "secret garden" is all about self-discovery and self-understanding, and hints at a core identity that has no equivalent in the lives of men. In the novel *The Da Vinci Code,* reference to "the sacred feminine" is made repeatedly, and supported by an argument that invokes not just history but the order of the cosmos. If someone were to talk about "the sacred masculine," it's unlikely there would be many believers. Yet is there not, somewhere, a hallowed place for men to affirm their uniqueness and authenticity? Most men, consciously or unconsciously, seek out, in addition to their partner, an emotional support system to help them through life. Religion, sports, male groups or clubs, or the love of their children, for example, are systems of affirmation. For health and survival, men need their own universes where they can define and develop their identities as well as get support.

Until a man finds that kind of sanctuary, or has a deep passion or personal vision to drive him through life, his emotional resources are likely to be exhaustible and finite. His relationship will remain vulnerable, and falling out of love, or emotionally giving up on his partner, not uncommon. Fading of attraction is yet another way of saying a man has no outside support system, nor perhaps any clear idea of what he is doing with his life. Andrew's existence is so full of thrashing around, making wrong turns, and general paralysis and evasion that he's lucky Marie is tolerant and understanding enough to hang around.

Eddie makes reference to a scientific study asserting that women were only a few bits of DNA away from reproductive self-sufficiency. Are women the superior gender? Because of their evolutionary role as child bearers, their gift for nurturing, the necessity of knowing how to survive if a partner dies, the ability to bond and seek help from others, women seem better equipped than men to endure pain, to socialize, to love, and to simply endure. The physiology of the brain and genetic and biological explanations of gender differences are still far from clear, but it can be argued that the integrated emotional circuitry of women allows for greater adaptability than men possess. The expression "women bend, men break" is another metaphor for a man's reluctance to venture into areas where he's not competent or comfortable, engage in battles where he fears he will lose, or to take on emotional pain that he knows he can't handle. If put under extreme stress, he breaks because he's just not flexible. No matter how starved they might be to find an exit from their rigid, toxic masculinity, men are biased toward decisive solutions and not letting go. They are inclined to keep pounding square pegs into round holes until their fingers bleed.

Tips for Avoiding This Relationship Buster

1. Ask yourself what would happen if the qualities that bond you to someone suddenly disappeared, or you no longer found those attributes attractive. Would you call it quits? What else might keep your relationship alive? Are flexibility, creativity, and not giving up part of your definition of love?

2. Accept that most men, even in healthy relationships, are hardwired to be attracted to a fresh face, a new personality, or someone who flatters them, outside of their relationship. This is not necessarily a threat so long as their partners pay ample attention to them. What you need from your partner is exactly what he needs from you.

3. Recognize that when two deeply connected people begin to slip out of sync with each other and don't understand why, the temptation is to pretend that things will fall back into alignment on their own. Don't put off dealing with the problem, because the longer you wait the more potentially serious the damage.

4. Understand that more men are latent romantics than women might realize. On his deathbed, Joe DiMaggio, still grieving over losing Marilyn Monroe, allegedly said, "Now I can finally be with Marilyn." This was not untypical of stories I heard. It's the romantic tendencies in men, not just their egos, that you might pay attention to in order to keep your relationship healthy.

5. Even in long-term relationships, being romantic is not difficult if it is interpreted as a discipline and not just an impulse. Pick a day once a week or month, then consistently do something for your partner that he or she

doesn't expect. It doesn't have to be obvious, such as buying a gift. It can just be a level of support that's not anticipated. At first your partner may not see the pattern, but ultimately it will be discovered, and its surprise is a magic that pays dividends.

The Thinking Heart

A Rational Look at Love

The cliché about men is that they are the aggressive gender, often alpha dogs with a limited range of emotions centered on power and self-preservation. Some men do chase power, authority, and domination because their egos are huge, or they are following their role models or their definitions of masculinity. But the vast majority are not power hungry; they are more like the men in this book, driven by an internal and cultural mandate to survive and succeed, meet female and family expectations, and find happiness through communication, support, and camaraderie—be it sports or hobbies, or from their partners, families, and peers. Sex is equally crucial to their happiness. There will always be some behaviors dictated by testosterone and ego, but most men, even if they're reluctant to say it, crave sex for its openness and intimacy as much as women do. Their key failure in not getting that intimacy, and a primary reason for falling out of love, is not being assertive enough about their emotions. More than one man told me he was too busy pleasing his partner and worrying about her happiness to focus on expressing and meeting his own needs.

Why are so many men insecure and inadequate communicators, and why do they often repress their needs, frustration, and anger? Is it fear of losing control? Do they want to deny they have vulnerability and dependency needs? Is it just easier "to go with the flow" and pretend that everything is okay? All of these may be accurate. Sometimes, as we've seen in the ten stories, men are intimidated or confused by a woman's mode of communicating, and they become "pleasers" or "enablers" because it's the safest and easiest way to get attention, or just to get along. To achieve the level of intimacy they really want, however, means having to master some understanding of their own and women's emotions.

The art-house movie *What the Bleep Do We Know?* is an unusual look at the origin of emotions, relying on quantum physics to explain human behavior. Because of its scientific, rational perspective, perhaps it's an analysis to which a lot of men can relate. *What the Bleep Do We Know?* asks the baffling but practical question: why do human beings do the same inexplicable things over and over, such as choosing the wrong partners, making the wrong career decisions, eating the wrong foods, getting angry at their kids, or abusing themselves in countless small but cumulative ways? The talking heads of the film suggest our brains are a complex web of neuron receptors which translate our external experiences into chemical reactions that produce what we call emotions. Attraction, abandonment, anxiety, envy, fear—all have their origins when we're very young, in a precognitive state that is made up, essentially, of neurons. That is, we feel before we think. Those emotions, negative and positive, get reinforced, over and over, by life experiences. Getting fired from your job, losing someone you love, or gaining lots of weight—

these may be different experiences but they stimulate the same neuroreceptors to produce the same emotions of pain, anxiety, loss, and frustration. Hostages to chemical reactions, we are in a state of addiction, whether we know it or not, and the only way out is a consciousness of the process, and a belief in the power of one's will to override chemical receptors. While achieving this level of consciousness requires focus and discipline, it can be a healthy way to overcome our negative emotions, and help us avoid making the same mistakes over and over.

12

The Need for a Relationship Audit

An optimist is someone who believes that this is
the best of all possible worlds. A pessimist is
someone who is afraid that this is true.

—Oscar Wilde

We are at once a culture that talks too much and doesn't talk enough. What makes us happy or unhappy in our relationships is crucial, yet most of us don't ask that question, at least with any urgency, until we're already unhappy. When a relationship becomes a crash-and-burn scenario, and we realize we *have* made the mistake of repeatedly choosing the wrong person, we suddenly question everything: Why does this hurt so much? Whom should I be mad at? Was it my fault? How do I make myself feel better? How can I stop doing this in the future? Our self-esteem is often uprooted, and we search everywhere to fix once and for all our "happiness problem."

Popular culture markets the idea that not only is happiness the closest thing to a Constitutional right, but something must be wrong with us if we can't achieve it. Had the Founding Fathers not defined one of our entitlements in the Declaration of Independence as "the pursuit of *happiness*," but instead "the pursuit of *common sense*," we would have the basis for a less neurotic culture. Instead, we are stuck, if not obsessed, with the iconic "smiley face." When your life changes dramatically, the first question a friend asks is: "What are you doing now?" The second question is, inevitably, "Are you happy?" We are a living, breathing happiness culture. Nothing means more, even if we don't always know what happiness means. Emotions are us, we think, and there is no emotion more worshipped, or sought after, than happiness.

The next mantra that popular culture sells us is that happiness equals love and commitment. Just ask the billion-dollar romance-wedding-honeymoon industry. Your soul mate is out there, and if you don't find him or her, you're not doing something right. Let Hollywood, the media, and infomercials point the way: lose some weight, look younger, buy the right car, dress the right way, have the right friends, drink the right wine, and of course make lots of money. If you follow the formula, you'll be so inescapably attractive that you're guaranteed a lasting, gratifying relationship. Just in case it's not working, don't worry: lose a little more weight, make more money, and always keep shopping. . . .

More than one sociologist has noted the correlation between fear and consumerism. In America shopping is often viewed as therapy. Consuming makes us feel good. It slakes our anxieties. It's as if it fills some vacuum—be it with food or fashion or the latest electronics—where otherwise our fears reside. When our neuroreceptors are really firing, the more we spend, the more we want to keep spending. Most of us are finally stopped by guilt or our debt load. Rather than grow neurotic with this "binge and purge" cycle, maybe it's better to admit that it's okay to be afraid, or that we're lonely at that moment, or just maybe we won't find our soul mate because soul mates aren't really "found" like a designer dress on sale at Nordstrom—they're nutured and grown over time.

Clichés about soul mates are hard to escape because they've become ingrained in popular culture. They also give us hope. It's similar to the "journey of magic" that men take when they become infatuated. They believe that romantic attraction is fate, that in a matter of days, even hours, they've found their soul mate and permanent happiness. We are a culture that wants both instant and lasting gratification. Rather than look for new ideas or perspectives on relationships, we repeatedly give ourselves the same tired messages about romance and happiness. We shop for and consume relationship clichés like any other commodity. We are inclined to believe rather than doubt what we think because, by telling ourselves the same things over and over, they must be true. We're too overwhelmed, and don't have the time, to find the separate and unique truths about what each of us needs. In our culture, one size fits all.

At some point, with maturity, or precipitated by a crisis, we come to realize that our "happiness problem" can't be fixed by popular culture or external solutions. The problem lies within. How we reach that core anxiety or discontent, analyze it, and change it, is perhaps the hardest thing any of us will ever do. The men in this book, when their relationships collapsed, finally began to question their behaviors, attitudes, and personas, and most became stronger for their explorations even if they didn't find instant answers. Changing ourselves doesn't necessarily mean keeping our relationships, or leaving them either. Anything can happen. What's crucial is that we don't necessarily need to lose weight, take a new job, or buy a sports car to feel better. We *do* have to question our behaviors and the choices we make. We have to admit mistakes. We have to go through a little pain as we dig under the surface. None of this is easy. Everyone wants to get to heaven, but no one wants to die to get there.

The lessons from this book notwithstanding, for most men it's far easier to hide in the traditional masculine shelters of work, achievement, anger, and denial than to take on the hard, sweaty work of self-exploration. Traditional interpretations of masculinity, we rationalize, were good enough for our fathers, uncles, and brothers, why shouldn't they work for us? The answer is that the world has changed, women have changed, and men need to change as well—if they want more fulfilling lives, and to pass on to their children a more sustainable definition of masculinity. Just as in the sixties and seventies there were many women unhappy with their lives and their relationships—until they were galvanized by self-realization and peer support to do something about it—there are many men today who need to take a fresh look at their grinding reality and how to change it.

It's often assumed that being objective about your own relationship is almost impossible. Not only are you too close, but relationships, by their very definition, are about emotion and therefore highly subjective, volatile, and unpredictable. If relationships were rational, the argument goes, there would be obvious solutions, templates, and cures for specific issues, and we wouldn't have a fifty percent divorce rate. But for many couples, nothing is obvious until a crisis hits them over the head. Then they seek out a psychologist or therapist to lead them down the path of understanding and corrective action.

Therapists and counselors have a definite value, but for a lot of couples, getting professional help is a step often taken after considerable, even irreparable, damage has been done to their relationships. A preemptive strike in the name of love may not be a bad idea. No one is claiming that relationships are purely rational, but examining them not through an emotional prism, but by using a compass of cool-headed rationality gives you a different and helpful perspective. Western culture since the Renaissance has been biased toward defining intimate relationships in emotional and romantic terms, but other cultures are different. While I couldn't find statistics, several East Indian friends told me that in their country the divorce rate for couples who were introduced in "arranged marriages" was far less than those who had fallen in love and married. Obviously, arranged marriages can be repressive and unhappy as well, but falling in love doesn't necessarily correlate to lasting bliss.

A relationship "audit" is as daunting an idea as it is healthy and premonitory. Daunting because it takes time and thought and can seem like the antithesis of romance. It can also be threatening by turning over rocks that have never even been nudged, and because it should be done every year or so, as dreaded a prospect as filing a tax return. But in fact, its very practicality can preserve romance and trust, spell out what you need from your partner, and eliminate the numerous gray areas that, often unspoken, work to undermine relationships. Audits are also a way to force men to finally deal with and define their feelings. It's a way of applying rationality to emotions, of connecting head and heart, just as women have always done.

The Relationship Audit

On a weekend afternoon with no distractions, sit down with your partner and two legal pads. Start by asking yourselves, separately, if you're aware of any of the following warning signs. As a highlighted list they may seem obvious, but with the stress and responsibilities of daily life they easily go unnoticed.

1. Your partner has lost interest in you physically, no matter what his or her excuse.

2. Over the last year, your partner's general behavior and habits have changed, either slowly or abruptly, in small ways or large.

3. Your partner picks arguments, or finds fault with you, for no perceived reason.

4. Your partner communicates with you less and less on significant issues, or refuses to discuss subjects that you think are important.

5. Your partner suddenly changes his or her schedule, comes home late from work, or decides to spend his or her free time away from you.

6. Whereas you once made decisions together about money, vacations, and child rearing, your partner suddenly defers everything to you, or insists that he or she make all the decisions.

7. Your partner shows a lack of self-confidence, gets depressed, or grows angry without apparent provocation.

8. Your partner complains that no one respects him or her, or they're being taken advantage of, or they're overworked, or not feeling well.

9. Your partner spends an unusual amount of time at work, or talks continually about the importance of his or her career, or has some other interest that takes the place of you and the family.

10. Your partner expounds about life before he or she met you, or an old flame, or the times when he or she "was really happy."

When you're finished, get together and compare answers. If you've both been honest, and your notes are radically different, you have some exploration ahead of you. If your answers are fundamentally the same but negative, you have even more digging. Any of the behaviors cited above could mean, for example, that your partner has become infatuated with another person or is vulnerable to doing so; is angry with you or disappointed in your relationship; is coming to grips with some personal trauma, past or present; or is perhaps slipping into some form of depression. If he or she becomes too talkative or too silent, drops old friends, has bouts of insomnia, or frequently stresses out, your partner is disengaging from you for a specific reason, even if he or she doesn't know what it is. Maybe they're putting up walls because you're not giving them the same attention they're used to. Are you giving it to something or someone else? Maybe you're suddenly assuming more power and control in the relationship. Or you've become too judgmental, inflexible, or intolerant—too much of a perfectionist, perhaps. Maybe your partner had a falling-out with a best friend, or changed jobs, or lost a loved one. Traumas, major and minor, that happen outside of your relationship are often the ones that affect it the most.

Even if the ten warning signs largely turn out *not* to be applicable to you, your audit should include questions specific to your relationship. It can refer to pattern issues that never seem to have a solution, anxieties about future decisions that keep getting postponed, and emotional wounds that have not healed. Just caring enough to be aware is a big relationship plus. As we've seen in the ten stories, certain subjects—money, children, work, sex, responsibility, and time alone—should always be in an audit because they're the trip wires for deeper issues. Also, identify what new concerns are bothering you. How much do you think you and your partner have changed? Is that a positive or a negative? Do you still have chemistry? Are you suddenly moving in the same or different directions? Are the new directions purposeful and healthy? If not, what's pushing you?

Of those I interviewed, most said they were too busy to do an audit. A few thought it was a great idea, but admitted they found it hard to ask tough questions. Maybe they would get to it later, when their lives had calmed down. When I pointed out that passivity, inertia, and denial are major causes of relationship crises, they all said they knew that. But I wondered. One man said he would conduct an audit privately and see how it turned out before he approached his partner. I thought that was far better than doing nothing.

An audit should also stress the positive. What do you like best about your partner? Has that changed over time and in what way? Write down the positives, both for you and your partner. Identify the strongest glue that keeps you together, assess why, and discuss whether you think it will always be an irreplaceable bond.

End your audit with a "needs" list that is frank and personal. While there should always be an element of mystery in romance, being up-front about what makes you happy, what you expect from your partner, and what he or she expects from you eliminates a lot of gray areas and guesswork. A list, studied objectively, tells you if what you want is reasonable, and how compatible you and your partner are. There's a major difference between filling out a personality questionnaire for an online dating service, for example, and an in-the-trenches reality check. One is written in the glow of anticipation, just before you get to the party, and the other is composed the morning after.

If an honest poll were taken, perhaps we would find that the world is evenly divided between optimists and pessimists. A healthy intimate relationship usually requires at least one optimist, certainly on the subject of love and commitment. Besides Oscar Wilde's quote at the top of the chapter, it helps to remember what, according to Plato, Socrates told his students over two thousand years ago: the life which is unexamined is not worth living.

13

Hope for Every Couple

It takes a lot of courage to release the familiar and completely
secure, to embrace the new. But there is no real
security in what is no longer meaningful.
—Alan Cohen

I t is often adversity that sets us on our inward journey. Without
our relationship failures, without stepping back and taking a
fresh look at ourselves, we wouldn't arrive at the truths that are
worth holding on to. Ideally, we get a better idea of who we are,
we learn from our mistakes, and we have more successful relationships in the future. The dilemma of someone who senses
something wrong in his or her relationship is whether to speak
up or to wait it out, under the theory that all couples have their
ups and downs. Sometimes waiting *is* effective if the tension is
tied to a temporary problem—like an end-of-the-month money
crunch, or someone is ill and incapacitated for a period. However, it's a very blurry line between giving a problem time to resolve itself, and denial that something is serious enough to
require special attention such as a relationship audit. Virtually

everybody in this book was presented with this dilemma, and most fell into rationalization and denial rather than confront their problems head-on. For many of us, how hard it is to let go.

Of the relationships that crashed in this book, could any have been saved? If not all, then several, I think—if the partners had been more aware of their issues and been better communicators. Almost everybody—men and women—were too defensive, unsure about their needs or how to express them, and unwilling to explore and learn with their partners. For anyone reading these stories and facing a similar crisis, what is critical is that at least one person be intuitive enough to recognize the storm clouds and have the courage—and be enough of an optimist—to speak up.

The problem is compounded by men who may not understand the reasons behind their unhappiness and will never speak up. For other men (and women), the pain of dealing with emotional trauma is simply too high a price for saving a relationship. For some, it's easiest to let go. If we were all realists, perhaps the vow "Till death do us part" would be replaced by "I'm in this relationship until one or both of us feels otherwise." Popular culture tells us that if things don't work out with one person, take solace: around the corner is someone new, someone better, to meet your needs.

But around the corner, first and foremost, is the same old you. The inescapability of ourselves is dramatized effectively in a film like Noah Baumbach's *The Squid and the Whale*. The story takes place in the eighties in the middle-class Brooklyn neighborhood where Baumbach grew up. In a rapidly deteriorating marriage, the husband is a college professor and fading novelist, while his wife is a stay-at-home mom but an up-and-coming writer. They have two sons, around sixteen and eleven, who struggle with their own identities. The story is a wrenching look not just at middle age and the ego collisions that come with divorce, but the even bigger struggle of moving on. The bitter, narcissistic father finds that "around the corner" is not just his old insecure self, but a new persona with even more flaws, one he barely recognizes. He's more helpless and destructive than he thought, and his search to find something authentic or redeeming in himself, not unlike some of the men in this book, seems at times hopeless. It's obvious to the audience what his problems are—he's too dependent on the approval of others, and trying to live up to some impossible definition of success—but like a lot of men, all he can see is the effect of his problems, not the cause. He is filled with self-pity, anger, arrogance, and pain. Because he can't handle living alone, he tries to seduce a student, as well as reconcile with his wife, only to be rebuffed by both and experience more rage. His self-destruction and failed masculinity soon become transparent to his ex-wife, friends, children, and the whole world. Eventually he has a heart attack, but rather than win sympathy from his family, he loses the allegiance of his older son, who through most of the story had been his sole ally. In the end, the father is a god in ruins.

The tragedy is not his fall from grace, but that he learns nothing from his suffering. Refusing to examine the reasons for his misery, he misses the opportunity to forgive himself and rebuild his life. Like a lot of men, he avoids redemption because he thinks it's some kind of trap, or an admission that he's failed miserably with his life. He is an easy character to dislike or pity, but underneath his confusion there is the glimmer of what might have been. If he'd had some support from friends, and a few key insights about himself, been open and vulnerable, his life could have taken a different and healthy direction. Instead, filled with shame, he is constantly erupting like a volcano, leaving in his wake the debris of a life that's now in a myriad of smoldering pieces.

The imperative for someone who loves his or her partner is

not to wait for the explosion of the volcano, or to endure its endless smoldering. After you conduct and review your audit, if you feel your relationship is in jeopardy, here are ten suggestions for putting it back on track. Not only can you repair it, you can make it better.

1. Be aware of how your partner's emotions work—the triggers, the difference between canned responses and honest emotion, and the best time of day, and place, to talk. After the audit, the gloves are off in the most positive sense. You need to be open and candid on every subject, without being confrontational. If you want to save your relationship, let your partner know your bias for working things out. Recognize that the person you fell in love with may not be the same person you are talking to, or end up sharing your life with. His or her real self, slowly revealed, may be one hundred eighty degrees different. So might yours. Be prepared for change. If change and flexibility are difficult for you, work with a therapist.

2. Be conscious of the impact on your partner of your own image, power, and lifestyle as your relationship has evolved. While they are not likely to admit it, most men feel at an inherent disadvantage in discussing relationships mostly because, in the end, relationships are about emotions. Until they learn to be more assertive, men need acknowledgment that their feelings count too. If you want intimacy and attention from your partner, be prepared to give it back to him or her in equal measure. In addition, while you might be madly in love with each other, for a man to commit long-term to a woman who has, for example, more friends than he, is better educated, or more successful professionally, he has to be very confident. Don't be reluctant to ask him his definition of masculinity.

3. Understand the differences in how each gender processes information. In the company I used to run, a man would come into my office and explain, for example, the facts of a dispute with a client, in a straight, direct manner, leaving nothing out but taking as little time as possible in his rendition—then ask for my opinion. A woman with a similar issue would first inquire how I was doing, how my family was, and if the company was doing well. Then she would explain the problem to me, starting somewhere in the middle, jumping ahead to the end, and slide back to the beginning. She would repeat parts of her analysis, and offer a point of view other than her own—usually someone else she had talked to—then go off on several more tangents that might seem to me irrelevant to the solution process. Altogether it took her twice as long as her male colleague to complete her story. It took me years to grasp that, in general, when women give information, it is a process that involves both emotion and reason; it is circular and not linear; it is often built on consensus; and in repeating themselves it's not to make sure *I* understand her point so much as *they* understand all the facts and angles. At the same time that they are giving information, women are processing and reprocessing—problem solving as they speak—coming up with their own solutions. It is the same for relationships. While women can multitask mentally as they give information, men usually cannot. Most men need to give and receive information in a linear fashion. Emotional reasoning from a woman is as subtle as it is complex, and subtlety is sometimes misunderstood or just ignored by men. "Why can't she just get to the point?" is as common a response from men as "How many ways do I have to explain it before he gets the point?" is from women. From a man's perspective, by not getting to the

point a woman is being evasive, trying to take control, or not giving him a chance to give his input. From a woman's view, a man, by being obtuse, is not paying attention, doesn't care what she thinks, or has already made up his mind. Be conscious of how each gender processes information and take the necessary steps to accommodate those differences. Be very explicit in making your point, specifically about emotions, your needs, and the direction you think your relationship is heading or should head.

4. While it may be difficult, be supportive of your partner when he or she is drifting away from you. Be sympathetic to whatever he or she is going through. When you tap into your courage, the emotional satisfaction you get is more powerful than the fear that comes from not dealing with the problem, or that you might lose your partner. Show that you're concerned about him or her as well as yourself. If you become defensive and accusatory, the breach between you only widens.

5. If your partner is in crisis, or just turning away from you, urge him or her to let you in on the problem. While there is no stigma in seeing a therapist, many men will deny there *is* a problem, at least one that they can't solve. By taking the lead, you might explain what you would do if this were your problem. Also, urge him to talk to friends he trusts. Discuss ways for him to heal by getting away from judging himself. If he gains confidence in you, he not only has a better chance of getting through his problem, but of building a deeper relationship with you.

6. If you work through your partner's issues together, honesty and openness are much easier in the future, but they should never be taken for granted. There are always new challenges, distractions, and temptations. Still, you need to

grant your partner a certain amount of independence and freedom to keep growing. Boundaries should be drawn (for example, no infidelity), but for any relationship to work it has to breathe. A trusting relationship might be defined as one where each partner is not afraid to tell everything to the other, but neither finds it necessary to do so.

7. In working through your problems, start by figuring out when things first went wrong. Try to remember the last time each of you felt happy, carefree, and truly in love. Then write down how and why you think all that slipped away. Usually the disengagement process is gradual, precipitated by the arrival of children, a change in employment or financial status, or a myriad of unanticipated responsibilities, traumas, and stress that comes along. One scarcely notices anything is amiss until, one day, it's impossible not to see everything. Like many men and women in this book, sometimes the crisis comes from a reconnection to issues from the past, a need to move in a different direction, or acts of self-destruction. Whatever the issues, identify them and allow yourself plenty of time to work through them. Your relationship, in being uprooted, may begin to feel unfamiliar, as if it belongs to somebody else, but it's still your responsibility. Be supportive, patient, and nonthreatening.

8. To argue for a moment with Tolstoy, perhaps all happy couples do not resemble one another. A successful relationship is built on many things, one of which is understanding what makes your partnership unique. In addition to affection and understanding, it's crucial to identify the common denominator that leads to the greatest happiness: a deep friendship; religious, ethical, or

family values; a shared passion; a work ethic; a type of intelligence; a tolerance and respect for the other's space; or an understanding of how to balance time together and time apart. What's important is knowing what works and why. When your relationship breaks down, connecting to your areas of strength is the first objective.

9. Relationships can't be a successful "us" until they are first a healthy "you" and "me." Relationship rebuilding may require many things, but if the major stumbling block is low self-worth, here is an obvious but helpful insight. In *The Squid and the Whale,* the father was so dependent on the approval of others—his family, students, peers, and his publisher—that when the approbation vanished, he couldn't get beyond that loss as a definition of failure. Emotionally he fell into a black hole, and didn't know how to climb out because he had no underlying identity, no sense of himself beyond what he was *supposed to be.* Likewise, people sometimes jump into relationships with the vague hope that their partner will flesh out their identity, giving them new respect for themselves and from others. Just because you *want* to be someone else doesn't mean you'll make it. If this is the center of your crisis, work with a therapist and be prepared for a difficult but rewarding journey if you stick it out.

10. If you have a smart heart, a thinking heart, you know that forgiving and loving yourself is an intellectual as well as an emotional enterprise. It's an act of acceptance and will as much as wallowing and rehashing. Being purely emotional about emotions pays few dividends. One of the ironies of men is that they believe they are supposed to run their lives by logic and rationality, yet in a relationship crisis, when logic and rationality don't hold up, they often come apart emotionally. On the other hand, women hold the fort,

perhaps because they are better problem solvers than men. They seem to better understand nuance, ambiguity, and the multiplicity of approaches and choices. This is what relationships are all about—openness, flexibility, and multidimensionality. Men should listen to healthy women, and no matter what season of his life, it's never too late to connect head with heart.

For all the differences between men and women, in the end it's the values we teach our children—compassion, tolerance, honesty, forgiveness, and trust—that we may need to reteach ourselves. Besides these basic virtues, I hope this book illustrates not just the traps of popular culture, masculinity, intimacy, validation, and perfectionism, but the need for continual self-awareness and reevaluating who we are. Opportunity is everywhere, starting in our relationships. The writer and philosopher Charles DuBois said it succinctly: "The important thing is this: to sacrifice at any moment what we are for what we could become."

Bibliography

In a Time of Fallen Heroes: The Re-Creation of Manhood. William R. Betcher. (Atheneum)

Sex on the Brain: The Biological Differences Between Men and Women. Deborah Blum. (Viking)

Strong Mothers, Strong Sons: Raising the Next Generation of Men. Ann F. Caron. (Perennial)

Masculinities. R. W. Connell. (Berkeley: University of California Press)

The Men and the Boys. R. W. Connell. (Berkeley: University of California Press)

Stiffed. Susan Faludi. (HarperCollins)

The Myth of Male Power. Warren Farrell. (Simon & Schuster)

The Liberated Man. Warren Farrell. (Random House)

The Seasons of a Man's Life. Daniel J. Levinson. (Ballantine Books)

The Tender Bar. J. R. Moehringer. (Hyperion)

A Choice of Heroes: The Changing Faces of American Manhood.
Mark Gerzon. (Houghton Mifflin)

Manhood in the Making: Cultural Concepts of Masculinity.
David D. Gilmore. (Yale University Press)

Fathering. Will Glennon. (Yale University Press)

The Hazards of Being Male: Surviving the Myth of Masculine Privilege. Herb Goldberg. (Penguin Books)

The New Male: From Self-Destruction to Self-Care. Herb Goldberg. (SelfHelpBooks.com)

The Wonder of Boys. Michael Gurian. (Penguin Books)

Manhood in America: A Cultural History. Michael Kimmel (Free Press)

Brain Sex: The Real Difference Between Men and Women. Anne Moir and David Jesse. (Dell)

The Men They Will Become: The Nature and Nurture of Male Character. Eli H. Newberger. (Perseus Books)

Man Enough: Fathers, Sons, and the Search for Masculinity. Frank Pittman. (Perigee Books)

Finding Our Fathers. Samuel Osherson. (McGraw-Hill)

Real Boys: Rescuing Our Sons from Myths of Boyhood. William Pollack and Mary Pipher. (Random House)

I Don't Want to Talk About It: Overcoming the Secret Legacy of Male Depression. Terrence Real. (Fireside)

Standup Guy: Manhood After Feminism. Michael Segell. (Villard)

The War Against Boys: How Misguided Feminism Is Harming Our Young Men. Christina Hoff Sommers. (Simon & Schuster)

Raising Cain: Protecting the Emotional Life of Boys. Dan Kindlon and Michael Thompson. (Ballantine Books)

MICHAEL FRENCH is a businessman and author who divides his time between Santa Barbara, California, and Santa Fe, New Mexico. He is an avid high-altitude mountain trekker, as well as a collector of first editions of twentieth-century fiction.

He has published twenty books, including fiction, young adult fiction, biographies, and art criticism. His novel, *Abingdon's,* was a best seller and a Literary Guild Alternate Selection. His young adult novel, *Pursuit,* was awarded the California Young Reader Medal.

Why Men Fall Out of Love: What Every Woman Needs to Understand is his most recent book.

About the Type

This book was set in Sabon, a typeface designed by the well-known German typographer Jan Tschichold (1902–74). Sabon's design is based upon the original letter forms of Claude Garamond and was created specifically to be used for three sources: foundry type for hand composition, Linotype, and Monotype. Tschichold named his typeface for the famous Frankfurt typefounder Jacques Sabon, who died in 1580.